CAPITAL PUNISHMENT

CRUEL AND UNUSUAL?

Kim Masters Evans

INFORMATION PLUS® REFERENCE SERIES
Formerly Published by Information Plus, Wylie, Texas

GALE
CENGAGE Learning™

Detroit • New York • San Francisco • New Haven, Conn • Waterville, Maine • London

GALE
CENGAGE Learning™

Capital Punishment: Cruel and Unusual?

Kim Masters Evans

Kepos Media, Inc.: Paula Kepos and Janice Jorgensen, Series Editors

Project Editors: Elizabeth Manar, Kathleen J. Edgar

Rights Acquisition and Management: Jacqueline Flowers, Kelly Quin, Robyn Young

Composition: Evi Abou-El-Seoud, Mary Beth Trimper

Manufacturing: Cynde Lentz

For product information and technology assistance, contact us at **Gale Customer Support, 1-800-877-4253.** For permission to use material from this text or product, submit all requests online at **www.cengage.com/permissions.** Further permissions questions can be e-mailed to **permissionrequest@cengage.com**

Cover photograph: Image copyright Kim Seidl, 2009. Used under license from Shutterstock.com.

While every effort has been made to ensure the reliability of the information presented in this publication, Gale, a part of Cengage Learning, does not guarantee the accuracy of the data contained herein. Gale accepts no payment for listing; and inclusion in the publication of any organization, agency, institution, publication, service, or individual does not imply endorsement of the editors or publisher. Errors brought to the attention of the publisher and verified to the satisfaction of the publisher will be corrected in future editions.

Gale
27500 Drake Rd.
Farmington Hills, MI 48331-3535

ISBN-13: 978-0-7876-5103-9 (set)
ISBN-13: 978-1-4144-4115-3

ISBN-10: 0-7876-5103-6 (set)
ISBN-10: 1-4144-4115-0

ISSN 1538-6678

This title is also available as an e-book.
ISBN-13: 978-1-4144-7002-3 (set)
ISBN-10: 1-4144-7002-9 (set)
Contact your Gale sales representative for ordering information.

Printed in the United States of America
1 2 3 4 5 6 7 14 13 12 11 10

CAPITAL PUNISHMENT

CRUEL AND UNUSUAL?

TABLE OF CONTENTS

supporting or opposing the death penalty, rate of imposition, fairness of the death penalty, the death penalty as a deterrent, and the likelihood that an innocent person has been convicted of murder or executed.

CHAPTER 10

This chapter offers an international consideration of the death penalty. Information includes United Nations resolutions regarding capital punishment, statistics on countries that have retained capital punishment and those that have abolished it, rulings on U.S. death penalty cases by the International Court of Justice, and international public opinion polls on the death penalty.

CHAPTER 11

This chapter contains statements that have been made in support of capital punishment by William J. Bratton (police chief of Los Angeles, California), Justice Antonin Scalia of the U.S. Supreme Court, members of the Maryland Commission on Capital Punishment, John McAdams (a professor of political science), and Ann Scott (the mother of a murder victim).

CHAPTER 12

This chapter contains statements that have been made in support of capital punishment by the late Senator Edward Kennedy, Justice John Paul Stevens of the U.S. Supreme Court, Bryan A. Stevenson (a professor of law), Hilary O. Shelton (National Association for the Advancement of Colored People), and Vicki A. Schieber (the mother of a murder victim).

PREFACE

Capital Punishment: Cruel and Unusual? is part of the *Information Plus Reference Series*. The purpose of each volume of the series is to present the latest facts on a topic of pressing concern in modern American life. These topics include today's most controversial and most studied social issues: abortion, care for senior citizens, crime, education, the environment, health care, immigration, minorities, national security, social welfare, sports, women, youth, and many more. Although written especially for the high school and undergraduate student, this series is an excellent resource for anyone in need of factual information on current affairs.

By presenting the facts, it is the intention of Gale, Cengage Learning to provide its readers with everything they need to reach an informed opinion on current issues. To that end, there is a particular emphasis in this series on the presentation of scientific studies, surveys, and statistics. These data are generally presented in the form of tables, charts, and other graphics placed within the text of each book. Every graphic is directly referred to and carefully explained in the text. The source of each graphic is presented within the graphic itself. The data used in these graphics are drawn from the most reputable and reliable sources, in particular from the various branches of the U.S. government and from major independent polling organizations. Every effort has been made to secure the most recent information available. The reader should bear in mind that many major studies take years to conduct, and that additional years often pass before the data from these studies are made available to the public. Therefore, in many cases the most recent information available in 2010 is dated from 2007 or 2008. Older statistics are sometimes presented as well if they are of particular interest and no more-recent information exists.

Although statistics are a major focus of the *Information Plus Reference Series*, they are by no means its only content. Each book also presents the widely held positions and important ideas that shape how the book's subject is discussed in the United States. These positions are explained in detail and, where possible, in the words of their proponents. Some of the other material to be found in these books includes: historical background; descriptions of major events related to the subject; relevant laws and court cases; and examples of how these issues play out in American life. Some books also feature primary documents or have pro and con debate sections giving the words and opinions of prominent Americans on both sides of a controversial topic. All material is presented in an even-handed and unbiased manner; the reader will never be encouraged to accept one view of an issue over another.

HOW TO USE THIS BOOK

Few topics are as controversial as capital punishment. Capital punishment has been debated in America since the colonial period and is currently a worldwide issue. This book includes the history of capital punishment plus discussions of numerous court cases, legal decisions, and historical statistics. Also included is information about execution methods, minors and the death penalty, public attitudes, and capital punishment around the world.

Capital Punishment: Cruel and Unusual? consists of 12 chapters and 3 appendixes. Each of the chapters is devoted to a particular aspect of capital punishment. For a summary of the information covered in each chapter, please see the synopses provided in the Table of Contents at the front of the book. Chapters generally begin with an overview of the basic facts and background information on the chapter's topic, then proceed to examine subtopics of particular interest. For example, Chapter 5: Death Penalty Laws: State, Federal, and U.S. Military defines the crimes that are considered capital offenses and describes the appeals process that is available to condemned inmates. The chapter also describes the methods of executions that are used by different jurisdictions with capital punishment. Readers can find their way through a chapter by looking for the section and subsection headings, which are clearly set off from the text. Or, they can refer to the book's extensive index if they already know what they are looking for.

Statistical Information

The tables and figures featured throughout *Capital Punishment: Cruel and Unusual?* will be of particular use to the reader in learning about this issue. The tables and figures represent an extensive collection of the most recent and important statistics on capital punishment and related issues—for example, graphics in the book cover jurisdictions with and without the death penalty; public opinion concerning capital punishment; capital offenses by state; federal laws that provide for the death penalty; demographic characteristics of prisoners under sentence of death; and number of executions and methods used by state. Gale, Cengage Learning believes that making this information available to the reader is the most important way in which we fulfill the goal of this book: to help readers understand the issues and controversies surrounding capital punishment in the United States and reach their own conclusions about them.

Each table or figure has a unique identifier appearing above it for ease of identification and reference. Titles for the tables and figures explain their purpose. At the end of each table or figure, the original source of the data is provided.

In order to help readers understand these often complicated statistics, all tables and figures are explained in the text. References in the text direct the reader to the relevant statistics. Furthermore, the contents of all tables and figures are fully indexed. Please see the opening section of the index at the back of this volume for a description of how to find tables and figures within it.

Appendixes

In addition to the main body text and images, *Capital Punishment: Cruel and Unusual?* has three appendixes. The first is the Important Names and Addresses directory. Here the reader will find contact information for a number of government and private organizations that can provide further information on aspects of capital punishment. The second appendix is the Resources section, which can also assist readers in conducting their own research. In this section the author and editors of *Capital Punishment: Cruel and Unusual?* describe some of the sources that were most useful during the compilation of this book. The final appendix is the index, making it even easier to find specific topics in this book.

ADVISORY BOARD CONTRIBUTIONS

The staff of Information Plus would like to extend its heartfelt appreciation to the Information Plus Advisory Board. This dedicated group of media professionals provides feedback on the series on an ongoing basis. Their comments allow the editorial staff who work on the project to continually make the series better and more user-friendly. Our top priorities are to produce the highest-quality and most useful books possible, and the Advisory Board's contributions to this process are invaluable.

The members of the Information Plus Advisory Board are:

- Kathleen R. Bonn, Librarian, Newbury Park High School, Newbury Park, California
- Madelyn Garner, Librarian, San Jacinto College, North Campus, Houston, Texas
- Anne Oxenrider, Media Specialist, Dundee High School, Dundee, Michigan
- Charles R. Rodgers, Director of Libraries, Pasco-Hernando Community College, Dade City, Florida
- James N. Zitzelsberger, Library Media Department Chairman, Oshkosh West High School, Oshkosh, Wisconsin

COMMENTS AND SUGGESTIONS

The editors of the *Information Plus Reference Series* welcome your feedback on *Capital Punishment: Cruel and Unusual?* Please direct all correspondence to:

Editors
Information Plus Reference Series
27500 Drake Rd.
Farmington Hills, MI 48331-3535

CHAPTER 1
A CONTINUING CONFLICT: A HISTORY OF CAPITAL PUNISHMENT IN THE UNITED STATES

Capital punishment is the ultimate punishment—death—administered by the government for the commission of serious crimes. The word *capital* comes from the Latin word *capitalis*, meaning "of the head." Throughout history societies have considered some crimes so appalling that the death penalty has been prescribed for them. Over time, changing moral values and ideas about government power have limited the number and types of offenses deemed worthy of death. Many countries have eliminated capital punishment completely, dismissing it as an inhumane response to criminal behavior. The United States is one of only a handful of modern societies that still administers the death penalty. This distinction from this nation's peers is not easily explainable. It arises from a complicated mix of social, legal, and political factors that shape American ideas about justice and the role of government in matters of law and order.

Capital punishment enjoys popular support in the United States. Figure 1.1 shows the results of a poll conducted in October 2008 by the Gallup Organization. Nearly two-thirds (64%) of respondents at that time favored the death penalty for a person convicted of murder, compared with 30% who opposed it. In spite of the overwhelming support, the topic is rife with controversy. Proponents and opponents of the death penalty are passionate in their beliefs. People on both sides of the debate often use philosophical, moral, and religious reasoning to justify their positions. This makes capital punishment a highly charged issue in which emotional opinions can outweigh all other arguments.

The U.S. system of governance is based on the separation of federal and state powers. This means that individual states decide for themselves if they want to practice capital punishment. As of September 2009 the death penalty was approved by the statutes of the federal government (including the U.S. military) and 35 states. (See Table 1.1.) The other 15 states that do not have the death penalty are listed in Table 1.2. The legality of capital punishment has historically hinged on the interpretation of the short, but monumental, statement that composes the Eighth Amendment to the U.S. Constitution: "Excessive bail shall not be required, nor excessive fines imposed, nor cruel and unusual punishments inflicted." Is capital punishment cruel and unusual or not? American society has struggled with this question since the founding of the nation and continues to do so in the 21st century.

THE COLONIAL PERIOD

Since the first European settlers arrived in North America, the death penalty has been accepted as just punishment for a variety of offenses. In fact, the earliest recorded execution occurred in 1608, only a year after the English constructed their first settlement in Jamestown, Virginia. Captain George Kendall, one of the original leaders of the Virginia colony, was convicted of mutiny by a jury of his peers and sentenced to death by shooting in Jamestown. In 1632 Jane Champion, a slave, became the first woman to be put to death in the new colonies. She was hanged in James City, Virginia, for the murders of her master's children.

According to *Society's Final Solution: A History and Discussion of the Death Penalty* (Laura E. Randa, ed., 1997, http://www.pbs.org/wgbh/pages/frontline/shows/execution/readings/history.html#fn8), capital law in the early colonies was based on British law, which prescribed the death penalty for hundreds of crimes by the 1700s. Actual practice, however, varied from colony to colony. The Quakers, who settled in the mid-Atlantic region, initially adopted much milder laws than those who settled in the Massachusetts, New York, and Virginia colonies.

The methods of execution in the fledgling North American colonies could be especially brutal. M. Watt Espy and John Ortiz Smykla note in *Executions in the United States, 1608–2002: The ESPY File* (2005) that even though hanging was the preferred method, some criminals were burned alive

FIGURE 1.1

Public opinion poll on the death penalty, October 2008

ARE YOU IN FAVOR OF THE DEATH PENALTY FOR A PERSON CONVICTED OF MURDER?

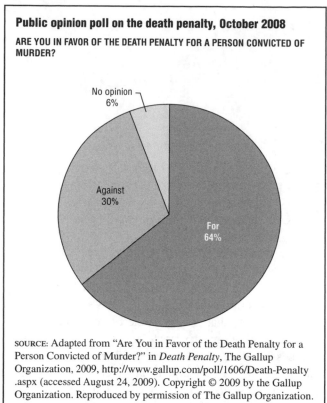

- No opinion 6%
- Against 30%
- For 64%

SOURCE: Adapted from "Are You in Favor of the Death Penalty for a Person Convicted of Murder?" in *Death Penalty*, The Gallup Organization, 2009, http://www.gallup.com/poll/1606/Death-Penalty .aspx (accessed August 24, 2009). Copyright © 2009 by the Gallup Organization. Reproduced by permission of The Gallup Organization.

TABLE 1.1

States with the death penalty, August 2009

Alabama	Nebraska
Arizona	Nevada
Arkansas	New Hampshire*
California	North Carolina
Colorado	Ohio
Connecticut	Oklahoma
Delaware	Oregon
Florida	Pennsylvania
Georgia	South Carolina
Idaho	South Dakota
Illinois	Tennessee
Indiana	Texas
Kansas*	Utah
Kentucky	Virginia
Louisiana	Washington
Maryland	Wyoming
Mississippi	- plus
Missouri	U.S. Gov't
Montana	U.S. Military*

*Jurisdictions with no executions since 1976.

SOURCE: "States with the Death Penalty," in *Facts about the Death Penalty*, Death Penalty Information Center, August 14, 2009, http://www .deathpenaltyinfo.org/documents/FactSheet.pdf (accessed August 24, 2009)

TABLE 1.2

States without the death penalty, August 2009

Alaska	New York
Hawaii	North Dakota
Iowa	Rhode Island
Maine	Vermont
Massachusetts	West Virginia
Michigan	Wisconsin
Minnesota	- plus
New Jersey	District of Columbia
New Mexico*	

*Two inmates remain on death row in New Mexico.

SOURCE: "States without the Death Penalty," in *Facts about the Death Penalty*, Death Penalty Information Center, August 14, 2009, http://www .deathpenaltyinfo.org/documents/FactSheet.pdf (accessed August 24, 2009)

the spokes of a large wheel like meaty ribbons. The prisoner would then be left outside to die of blood loss and exposure.

These executions were held in public as a warning to others, and often a festival atmosphere prevailed. Crowds of onlookers gathered near the gallows, and merchants sold souvenirs. Some spectators got drunk, turning unruly and sometimes violent. After the execution, the body of the convict was sometimes left hanging above the square in a metal cage.

David G. Chardavoyne describes a typical 19th-century execution scene in *A Hanging in Detroit: Stephen Gifford Simmons and the Last Execution under Michigan Law* (2003). One of only two executions in Michigan before the death penalty was outlawed there in 1846, Simmons was hanged in September 1830 for murdering his pregnant wife. Chardavoyne explains that at the time, "public executions owed much of their continuing legitimacy to the use of ritual." The associated rituals could last for hours and included parading the condemned prisoner through the crowd with a coffin by his side and a noose around his neck, speeches by public officials and religious leaders denouncing the crime, and in some cases a repentance speech by the prisoner.

Over time, the colonies phased out the crueler methods of execution, and almost all death sentences were carried out by hanging. The colonies also rewrote their death penalty statutes to cover only serious crimes involving willful acts of violence or thievery. By the late 1700s typical death penalty crimes included arson, piracy, treason, murder, and horse stealing. Southern colonies executed people for slave stealing or aiding in a slave revolt. After the American Revolution (1775–1783), some states went further by adopting death penalty statutes similar to those of Pennsylvania, which in 1682 had limited its death penalty to treason and murder. New York built its first penitentiary in 1796. With a place to house burglars and nonviolent criminals, the state reduced its capital offenses from 13 to 2. Other states followed suit by constructing large

or pressed to death by heavy stones. Probably the cruelest punishment was known as "breaking at the wheel," wherein the executioner would snap all the offender's arm and leg joints with a chisel and then weave the extremities through

jails and cutting their capital offenses to just a few of the worst crimes.

THE DEATH PENALTY ABOLITION MOVEMENT

Even though the founders of the United States generally accepted the death penalty, many early Americans did oppose capital punishment. In the late 18th century Benjamin Rush (1746–1813), a physician who helped establish the slavery abolition movement, decried capital punishment. He attracted the support of Benjamin Franklin (1706–1790), and it was at Franklin's home in Philadelphia that Rush became one of the first Americans to propose a "House of Reform," a prison where criminals could be detained until they changed their antisocial behavior. Consequently, in 1790 the Walnut Street Jail, the primitive seed from which the U.S. penal system grew, was built in Philadelphia.

Rush published many pamphlets, the most notable of which was *Considerations on the Justice and Policy of Punishing Murder by Death* (1792). He argued that the biblical support given to capital punishment was questionable and that the threat of hanging did not deter crime. Influenced by the philosophy of the Enlightenment (an intellectual movement in the 17th and 18th centuries), Rush believed the state exceeded its granted powers when it executed a citizen. Besides Franklin, Rush attracted many other Pennsylvanians to his cause, including William Bradford (1755–1795), the attorney general of Pennsylvania. Bradford suggested the idea of different degrees of murder, some of which did not warrant the death penalty. As a result, in 1794 Pennsylvania repealed the death penalty for all crimes except first-degree murder, which was defined as "willful, deliberate, and premeditated killing or murder committed during arson, rape, robbery, or burglary."

The 19th Century

Rush's proposals attracted many followers, and petitions aiming to abolish all capital punishment were presented in New Jersey, New York, Massachusetts, and Ohio. No state reversed its laws, but the number of crimes punishable by death was often reduced.

The second quarter of the 19th century was a time of reform in the United States. Capital punishment opponents rode the tide of righteousness and indignation created by antisaloon and antislavery advocates. Abolitionist societies (organizations against the death penalty) sprang up, especially along the East Coast. In 1845 the American Society for the Abolition of Capital Punishment was founded.

PUBLIC EXECUTIONS ARE PHASED OUT. Prior to the 1830s, executions were mostly public (and festive) events that attracted large and sometimes unruly crowds. Maine outlawed public executions and in 1835 put into effect a temporary moratorium (suspension) of executions after one public execution brought in 10,000 people, many of whom became violent after the execution and had to be restrained by the police. Other states followed suit. According to *Society's Final Solution: A History and Discussion of the Death Penalty*, many capital punishment abolitionists were opposed to these measures. They believed that executions conducted in public would eventually arouse the revulsion of American society against capital punishment.

In the late 1840s Horace Greeley (1811–1872), the founder and editor of the *New York Tribune* and a leading advocate of most abolitionist causes, led the crusade against the death penalty. In 1846 Michigan became the first state to abolish the death penalty for all crimes except treason (until 1963), making it the first English-speaking jurisdiction in the world to abolish the death penalty for common crimes. Common crimes, also called ordinary crimes, are crimes committed during peacetime. Ordinary crimes that could lead to the death penalty include murder, rape, and, in some countries, robbery or embezzlement of large sums of money. In comparison, exceptional crimes are military crimes committed during exceptional times, mainly wartime. Examples are treason, spying, or desertion (leaving the armed services without permission). The Michigan law took effect on March 1, 1847. In 1852 and 1853 Rhode Island and Wisconsin, respectively, became the first two states to outlaw the death penalty for all crimes. Most states began limiting the number of capital crimes. Outside the South, murder and treason became the only acts punishable by death.

As the Civil War (1861–1865) neared, concern about the death penalty was lost amid the growing antislavery movement. It was not until after the Civil War that Maine and Iowa abolished the death penalty. Almost immediately, however, their legislatures reversed themselves and reinstated the death penalty. In 1887 Maine again reversed itself and abolished capital punishment. It has remained an abolitionist state ever since. Colorado abolished capital punishment in 1897, a decision apparently against the will of many of its citizens. In 1901 the state restored the death penalty. Meanwhile, the federal government, following considerable debate in Congress, reduced the number of federal crimes punishable by death to treason, murder, and rape.

INTRODUCTION OF ELECTROCUTION AS A METHOD OF EXECUTION. Around the end of the 19th century, the use of electricity came into favor as a new means of execution. According to *Society's Final Solution: A History and Discussion of the Death Penalty*, the Edison Company electrocuted animals in public demonstrations. In 1888 New York became the first state to tear down its gallows and erect an electric chair. Two years later the chair was first used on a convict named William Kemmler. Even though the electrocution is described as "clumsy, at best," other states quickly embraced the electric chair for carrying out capital punishment.

THE ANTI–DEATH PENALTY MOVEMENT

At the start of the 20th century, death penalty abolitionists again benefited from American reformism as the Progressives (liberal reformers) worked to correct perceived problems in the U.S. legal system. *Society's Final Solution: A History and Discussion of the Death Penalty* reports that by 1917 capital punishment had been abolished or limited to a handful of very serious crimes in nine states. However, many of these states reversed their decisions in the following decades. The Prohibition Era (1920–1933), characterized by frequent disdain for law and order, almost destroyed the abolitionist movement, as many Americans began to believe that the death penalty was the only proper punishment for gangsters who committed murder.

The movement's complete collapse was prevented by the determined efforts of the famed Clarence Darrow (1857–1938), the "attorney for the damned"; Lewis E. Lawes (1883–1947), the abolitionist warden of Sing Sing Prison in New York; and the American League to Abolish Capital Punishment (founded in 1927). Nonetheless, between 1917 and 1957 no state abolished the death penalty.

Society's Final Solution: A History and Discussion of the Death Penalty reports that the abolitionist movement made a mild comeback in the mid-1950s. In 1957 the U.S. territories of Alaska and Hawaii abolished the death penalty. In the states, however, the movement's singular success in Delaware (1958) was reversed three years later (1961), a major disappointment for death penalty opponents. In 1963 Michigan, which in 1847 had abolished capital punishment for all crimes except treason, finally outlawed the death penalty for that crime as well. Oregon (1964), Iowa (1965), New York (1965), Vermont (1965), West Virginia (1965), and New Mexico (1969) all abolished capital punishment, whereas many other states sharply reduced the number of crimes punishable by death.

RESOLVING THE CONSTITUTIONAL ISSUES

Until the mid-20th century there was legally no question that the death penalty was acceptable under the U.S. Constitution. In 1958, however, the U.S. Supreme Court opened up the death penalty for reinterpretation when it ruled in *Trop v. Dulles* (356 U.S. 86) that the language of the Eighth Amendment (which states that criminals cannot be subjected to a cruel and unusual punishment) held the "evolving standards of decency that mark the progress of a maturing society." Opponents of capital punishment believed the death penalty should be declared unconstitutional in light of the *Trop* decision (which did not specifically address capital punishment). The abolitionists claimed that society had evolved to a point where the death penalty was cruel and unusual by the established "standards of decency." As such, the death penalty violated the Eighth Amendment of the Constitution.

In 1963 Justice Arthur J. Goldberg (1908–1990), joined by Justices William O. Douglas (1898–1980) and William J. Brennan (1906–1997), dissenting from a rape case in which the defendant had been sentenced to death (*Rudolph v. Alabama*, 375 U.S. 889), raised the question of the legality of the death penalty. The filing of many lawsuits in the late 1960s led to an implied moratorium on executions until the court could decide whether the death penalty was constitutional.

In 1972 the high court finally handed down a landmark decision in *Furman v. Georgia* (408 U.S. 238), when it ruled that the death penalty violated the Eighth and Fourteenth Amendments (the right to due process) because of the arbitrary nature with which the death penalty was administered across the United States. The court also laid down some guidelines for states to follow, declaring that a punishment was cruel and unusual if it was too severe, arbitrary, or offended society's sense of justice.

Before the late 1960s U.S. death penalty laws varied considerably from state to state and from region to region. Few national standards existed on how a murder trial should be conducted or which types of crimes deserved the death penalty. Specifically, *Furman* brought into question the laws of Georgia and a number of other states that allowed juries complete discretion in delivering a sentence. Critics feared the punishments such juries meted out were arbitrary and discriminatory against minorities.

CREATING A UNIFORM DEATH PENALTY SYSTEM ACROSS THE UNITED STATES

Within a year of the Supreme Court's ruling in *Furman*, most states had updated their laws regarding the death penalty. Many of these new statutes were brought before the high court in the mid-1970s. By issuing rulings on the constitutionality of these state statutes, the court created a uniform death penalty system for the United States. Table 1.3 provides a summary of the major cases decided by the court dealing with the death penalty since 1972.

States amended their laws once again after the Supreme Court issued the new rulings. Every state switched to a bifurcated (two-part) trial system, where the first trial is used to determine a defendant's guilt, and the second trial determines the sentence of a guilty defendant. Generally, only those convicted of first-degree murder were eligible for the death penalty. Most states also required the jury or judge in the sentencing phase of the trial to identify one or more aggravating factors (circumstances that may increase responsibility for a crime) beyond a reasonable doubt before they could sentence a person to death. State legislatures drafted lists of aggravating factors that could result in a penalty of death. Typical aggravating factors included murders committed during robberies, the murder of a pregnant woman, murder committed after a rape, and the murder of

TABLE 1.3

Major U.S. Supreme Court decisions involving the death penalty, selected years 1972–2008

Case	Year decided	Decision	Major effect
Furman v. Georgia	1972	5 to 4	The death penalty as administered by states at the time was deemed cruel and unusual punishment in violation of the Eighth and Fourteenth Amendments.
Gregg v. Georgia Proffit v. Florida Jurek v. Texas	1976	7 to 2	New death penalty statutes in Georgia, Florida, and Texas ruled constitutional.
Woodson v. North Carolina	1976	5 to 4	Mandatory death sentences ruled unconstitutional.
Coker v. Georgia	1977	5 to 4	The death penalty may not be imposed for raping an adult woman if the victim does not die.
Godfrey v. Georgia	1980	6 to 3	State statutes must clearly define the circumstances that qualify a crime as a capital crime.
Spaziano v. Florida	1984	5 to 3	Upheld as constitutional a judge's decision to impose a death sentence despite jury's recommendation of life in prison.
Ford v. Wainwright	1986	5 to 4	Inflicting the death penalty upon the insane ruled unconstitutional.
Murray v. Giarratamo	1989	5 to 4	Defendants under sentence of death do not have a constitutional right to counsel during postconviction proceedings.
Ring v. Arizona	2002	7 to 2	Only juries, not judges, can determine the presence of aggravating circumstances that warrant a death sentence.
Atkins v. Virginia	2002	6 to 3	Inflicting the death penalty upon the mentally retarded ruled unconstitutional.
Roper v. Simmons	2005	5 to 4	Death sentences imposed against minors (i.e., those less than 18 years of age when crime committed) ruled unconstitutional.
Baze and Bowling v. Rees	2008	7 to 2	Found that Kentucky's lethal injection "cocktail" (which was widely used in other death penalty states) did not violate the Eighth Amendment.
Kennedy v. Louisiana	2008	5 to 4	The death penalty may not be imposed for raping a child if the crime was not intended to cause, nor resulted in, the child's death.

SOURCE: Created by Kim Masters Evans for Gale, 2009

an on-duty firefighter or police officer. In the mid-1970s the long appeals process for capital cases was also established.

THE END OF THE NATIONWIDE MORATORIUM

With the Supreme Court–approved laws in place, the states resumed executions. In January 1977 the nationwide moratorium ended when the state of Utah executed Gary Gilmore (1940–1977). Gilmore had been convicted of killing Ben Bushnell, a motel manager in Provo, Utah, on July 20, 1976. Authorities had also charged him with the July 19 murder of Max Jensen, a gas station attendant, in Orem, Utah. Gilmore received the death penalty for the Bushnell murder. He refused to appeal his case, demanding that his sentence be carried out swiftly. Gilmore requested the state supreme court to grant his wish because he did not want to spend his life on death row. The court granted his wish, but interventions by Gilmore's mother, as well as by anti–death penalty organizations, resulted in several stays (postponement) of execution. These organizations were concerned that the defendant's refusal to appeal his case and the court's agreement to carry out his wish might establish a precedent that would hurt the causes of other inmates. After several suicide attempts, Gilmore was finally executed by firing squad on January 17, 1977.

Several other states reinstated the death penalty after the Supreme Court declared it constitutional. Oregon brought back the death penalty in 1978. In 1995 New York became the 38th state to reinstate the death penalty, ending its 18-year ban on capital punishment.

After the nationwide moratorium ended in 1977, the number of executions began to rise. (See Figure 1.2.) As shown in Table 1.4 executions hit the double digits in 1984, when 21 people were put to death in the United States, and peaked in 1999, when 98 inmates were executed. The number of criminals put to death then dipped to 37 in 2008—the lowest level in about a decade and a half. Overall, between 1977 and 2008, 1,136 people were put to death. Of course, these numbers were much smaller than the number of executions that occurred in the early part of the 20th century. In 1938 alone, for instance, 190 people were executed.

As shown in Figure 1.3, more than 400 people were on death row in 1977. The number climbed dramatically over the following decades, peaking at just over 3,600 in 2000. It then began a downward trend, dropping to 3,220 in 2007. During 2008 the number increased slightly to 3,297. Figure 1.3 clearly shows the rarity with which executions are carried out in the United States, compared with the large

FIGURE 1.2

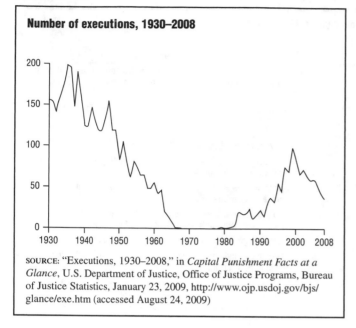

Number of executions, 1930–2008

SOURCE: "Executions, 1930–2008," in *Capital Punishment Facts at a Glance*, U.S. Department of Justice, Office of Justice Programs, Bureau of Justice Statistics, January 23, 2009, http://www.ojp.usdoj.gov/bjs/glance/exe.htm (accessed August 24, 2009)

TABLE 1.4

Number of persons executed, 1977–2008

Year	Number executed
1977	1
1979	2
1981	1
1982	2
1983	5
1984	21
1985	18
1986	18
1987	25
1988	11
1989	16
1990	23
1991	14
1992	31
1993	38
1994	31
1995	56
1996	45
1997	74
1998	68
1999	98
2000	85
2001	66
2002	71
2003	65
2004	59
2005	60
2006	53
2007	42
2008	37
Total:	**1136**

SOURCE: Adapted from Tracy L. Snell, "Table 15. Number of Persons Executed, 1977–2007," in *Capital Punishment, 2007—Statistical Tables*, U.S. Department of Justice, Office of Justice Programs, Bureau of Justice Statistics, December 23, 2008, http://www.ojp.usdoj.gov/bjs/pub/html/cp/2007/cp07st.pdf (accessed August 24, 2009)

nearly 3,381 per year. This constitutes an execution rate of less than 2% per year.

THE HOMICIDE RATE CONNECTION

Figure 1.4 compares the homicide (murder) rate and the number of executions conducted each year between 1960 and 2008. The increasing usage of capital punishment during the 1980s and early 1990s was a response to rising homicide rates in the country. According to data from the U.S. Department of Justice's Bureau of Justice Statistics (http://www.ojp.usdoj.gov/bjs/homicide/tables/totalstab.htm), between 1960 and 1980 the homicide rate doubled from 5.1 cases per 100,000 population to 10.2 cases per 100,000 population. After falling slightly in the early 1980s, it surged again, reaching its penultimate (second-highest) level in 1991, when 9.8 homicides occurred for every 100,000 people. Since that time the rate has generally declined. By 2000 it was 5.5 per 100,000 population. It remained around that level through 2008.

The country also experienced a surge of homicides in the early 1930s, during the Prohibition Era. As mentioned earlier, this was a time when support for the death penalty strengthened around the country. As shown in Figure 1.2, the execution rate was historically high at that time.

NEW RULES IN THE MODERN DEATH PENALTY ERA

U.S. Supreme Court decisions continued to redefine state death penalty laws well after the *Furman* opinion. In particular, the court has ruled the death penalty to be unconstitutional for three groups of defendants—the insane, the mentally retarded, and juveniles.

Executing the Insane

In *Ford v. Wainwright* (477 U.S. 399, 1986), the U.S. Supreme Court ruled that executing an insane person constituted a cruel and unusual punishment and was thus in violation of the Eighth Amendment. Because a precedent did not exist in U.S. legal history about executing the insane, the justices looked to English common law to make this ruling. English law expressly forbade the execution of insane people. The English jurist Sir Edward Coke (1552–1634) observed that even though the execution of a criminal was to serve as an example, the execution of a madman was considered "of extreme inhumanity and cruelty, and can be no example to others."

Executing Mentally Retarded People

In 1989 the Supreme Court held, in *Penry v. Lynaugh* (492 U.S. 302), that it was not unconstitutional to execute a mentally retarded person found guilty of a capital crime. According to the court, there was no emerging national consensus against such execution. Just two death penalty states—Georgia and Maryland—banned putting mentally

number of people under the sentence of death. Between 2000 and 2008, the United States executed an average of 60 people per year, whereas the number on death row averaged

FIGURE 1.3

Number of prisoners under sentence of death and number of executions, 1953–2008

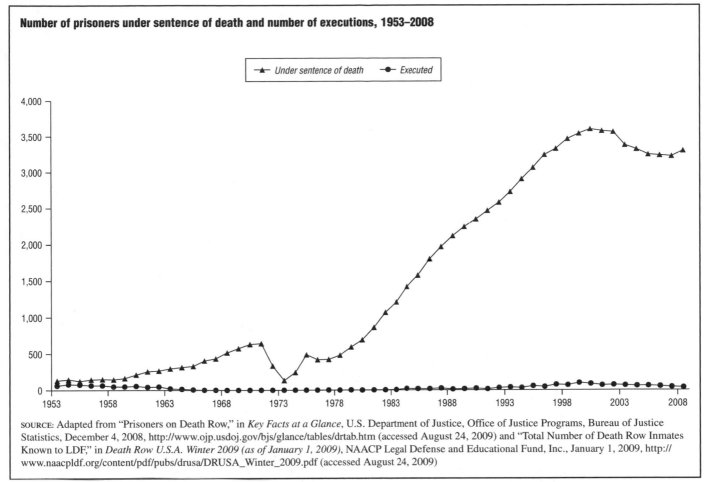

SOURCE: Adapted from "Prisoners on Death Row," in *Key Facts at a Glance*, U.S. Department of Justice, Office of Justice Programs, Bureau of Justice Statistics, December 4, 2008, http://www.ojp.usdoj.gov/bjs/glance/tables/drtab.htm (accessed August 24, 2009) and "Total Number of Death Row Inmates Known to LDF," in *Death Row U.S.A. Winter 2009 (as of January 1, 2009)*, NAACP Legal Defense and Educational Fund, Inc., January 1, 2009, http://www.naacpldf.org/content/pdf/pubs/drusa/DRUSA_Winter_2009.pdf (accessed August 24, 2009)

retarded people to death. In 1988 Georgia became the first state to prohibit the execution of murderers found "guilty but mentally retarded." The legislation resulted from the 1986 execution of Jerome Bowden, who had an intelligence quotient (IQ) of 65. It is generally accepted that an IQ below 70 is evidence of mental retardation. (Normal IQ is considered 90 and above.) In 1988 Maryland passed similar legislation, which took effect in July 1989.

Between 1989 and 2001, 18 states outlawed the execution of offenders with mental retardation. The federal government also forbids the execution of mentally retarded inmates. In the Anti-Drug Abuse Act of 1988, the government permits the death penalty for any person working "in furtherance of a continuing criminal enterprise or any person engaging in a drug-related felony offense, who intentionally kills or counsels, commands, or causes the intentional killing of an individual," but forbids the imposition of the death penalty against anyone who is mentally retarded who commits such a crime. In 1994, when Congress enacted the Federal Death Penalty Act, adding more than 50 crimes punishable by death, it also exempted people with mental retardation from the death sentence.

Even though the Supreme Court had agreed to review the case of the North Carolina death row inmate Ernest McCarver in 2001 to consider whether it is unconstitutional to execute inmates with mental retardation, the case was rendered moot when a state bill was passed that banned such executions. On June 20, 2002, the Supreme Court finally ruled on a case involving the execution of mentally retarded convicts. In *Atkins v. Virginia* (536 U.S. 304), the court ruled 6–3 that executing the mentally retarded violates the Eighth Amendment ban against a cruel and unusual punishment. The court did not say what mental retardation consists of, leaving it to the states to set their own definitions.

Juveniles

Under state laws, the term *juvenile* refers to people below the age of 18. Literature on the death penalty typically considers "juvenile offenders" as people younger than 18 at the time of their crimes. According to Victor L. Streib of Ohio Northern University, in *The Juvenile Death Penalty Today: Death Sentences and Executions for Juvenile Crimes, January 1, 1973–December 31, 2004* (2005), the first execution of a juvenile in the United States took place in Plymouth Colony, Massachusetts, in 1642. Through 2004 an estimated 366 inmates who were juveniles during the commission of their crimes had been executed in the United

FIGURE 1.4

Homicide rate and number of executions, 1960–2008

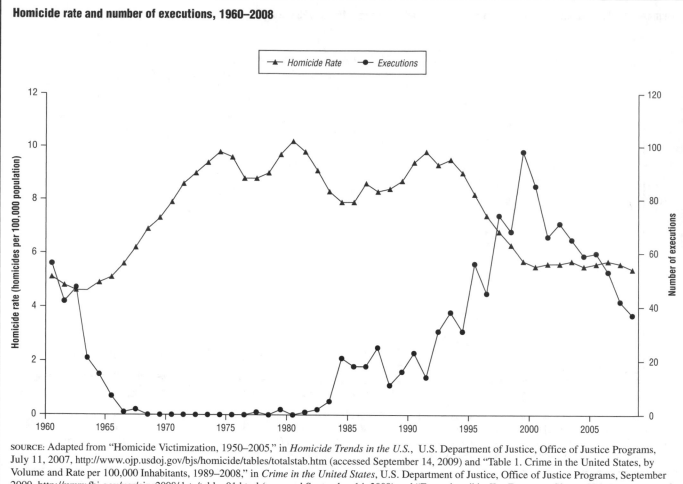

SOURCE: Adapted from "Homicide Victimization, 1950–2005," in *Homicide Trends in the U.S.*, U.S. Department of Justice, Office of Justice Programs, July 11, 2007, http://www.ojp.usdoj.gov/bjs/homicide/tables/totalstab.htm (accessed September 14, 2009) and "Table 1. Crime in the United States, by Volume and Rate per 100,000 Inhabitants, 1989–2008," in *Crime in the United States*, U.S. Department of Justice, Office of Justice Programs, September 2009, http://www.fbi.gov/ucr/cius2008/data/table_01.html (accessed September 14, 2009) and "Executions," in *Key Facts at a Glance*, U.S. Department of Justice, Office of Justice Programs, Bureau of Justice Statistics, January 23, 2009, http://www.ojp.usdoj.gov/bjs/glance/tables/exetab.htm (accessed September 14, 2009)

States. Inmates spent from 6 years to more than 20 years on death row before execution.

Before 1999, the last execution of a person who was 16 at the time of his crime occurred on April 10, 1959, when Maryland executed Leonard Shockley. After a 40-year respite in the United States, in February 1999 Oklahoma executed Sean Sellers, who was 16 years old when he committed his crime and 29 years old at the time of execution. He had been convicted for the murders of his mother, stepfather, and a convenience-store clerk. His supporters claimed Sellers suffered from multiple personality disorder, which was diagnosed after his conviction.

According to the Death Penalty Information Center (DPIC), 22 inmates who were juveniles at the time of their crimes have been executed since 1973. (See Table 1.5.) The last execution occurred in 2003. Texas implemented the death penalty of 13 juvenile offenders, followed by Virginia (3) and Oklahoma (2). Florida, Georgia, Missouri, and South Carolina each executed one juvenile offender.

In *Roper v. Simmons* (543 U.S. 633, 2005), the court decided that executing Donald Roper was cruel and unusual based on the fact that Roper was younger than 18 when he committed murder. The majority reasoned that adolescents do not have the emotional maturity or understanding of lasting consequences that adults have and therefore should not be held to an adult standard or punished with a sentence of death.

DNA TAKES THE STAND

In the 1980s and 1990s deoxyribonucleic acid (DNA) testing procedures advanced to the point where such evidence could be used in criminal cases. Across the United States, police suddenly had the ability to identify a suspect and place him or her squarely at the scene of a crime with a small sample of hair, blood, or other biological material. Because of the accuracy of DNA testing, DNA evidence could hold as much sway in a courtroom as an eyewitness or camera footage. States started collecting biological sam-

TABLE 1.5

Juveniles executed in the United States in the modern era since January 1, 1973

Name	Date of execution	Place of execution	Race	Age at crime	Age at execution
Charles Rumbaugh	9/11/85	Texas	White	17	28
J. Terry Roach	1/10/86	South Carolina	White	17	25
Jay Pinkerton	5/15/86	Texas	White	17	24
Dalton Prejean	5/18/90	Louisiana	Black	17	30
Johnny Garrett	2/11/92	Texas	White	17	28
Curtis Harris	7/1/93	Texas	Black	17	31
Frederick Lashley	7/28/93	Missouri	Black	17	29
Ruben Cantu	8/24/93	Texas	Latino	17	26
Chris Burger	12/7/93	Georgia	White	17	33
Joseph Cannon	4/22/98	Texas	White	17	38
Robert Carter	5/18/98	Texas	Black	17	34
Dwayne Allen Wright	10/14/98	Virginia	Black	17	24
Sean Sellers	2/4/99	Oklahoma	White	16	29
Douglas Christopher Thomas	1/10/00	Virginia	White	17	26
Steven Roach	1/13/00	Virginia	White	17	23
Glen McGinnis	1/25/00	Texas	Black	17	27
Shaka Sankofa (Gary Graham)	6/22/00	Texas	Black	17	36
Gerald Mitchell	10/22/01	Texas	Black	17	33
Napoleon Beazley	5/28/02	Texas	Black	17	25
T.J. Jones	8/8/02	Texas	Black	17	25
Toronto Patterson	8/28/02	Texas	Black	17	24
Scott Allen Hain	4/3/03	Oklahoma	White	17	32

Note: No juveniles were executed between January 1, 1973 and September 10, 1985.

SOURCE: "Juveniles Executed in the United States in the Modern Era (since January 1, 1973)," in *Execution of Juveniles in the U.S. and Other Countries*, Death Penalty Information Center, 2005, http://www.deathpenaltyinfo.org/execution-juveniles-us-and-other-countries (accessed August 24, 2009)

ples, such as blood and saliva, from criminal offenders and storing these DNA profiles in databases.

In 1994 Virginia became the first state to execute a person who was convicted as a result of DNA evidence. The defendant, Timothy Spencer, was convicted in 1988 for several rapes and murders he committed starting in 1984. Virginia also became the first state to execute someone based on a DNA "cold hit" when it executed James Earl Patterson in March 2002. (A cold hit is when DNA evidence collected at a crime scene matches a DNA sample already in a database.) In 1999 Patterson was in prison on a rape conviction when DNA from the 1987 rape and murder of Joyce Aldridge was found to match his DNA in the database. He confessed to the Aldridge crime in 2000 and was sentenced to death. Patterson waived his appeals to let his execution proceed as scheduled.

First Death Row Inmate Is Freed by DNA Testing

Not only has DNA evidence been useful in convicting felons but also it has been crucial in proving the innocence of falsely convicted criminals. Kirk Bloodsworth of Maryland was the nation's first death row inmate to be exonerated based on postconviction DNA testing. Bloodsworth was convicted for the rape and murder of a nine-year-old girl in 1984. He was sentenced to death in 1985. On retrial, Bloodsworth received two life terms. DNA testing in 1992 excluded him from the crime. In 1993 Bloodsworth was released from prison. In 1999 the state paid Bloodsworth

$300,000 for wrongful conviction and imprisonment, including time on death row.

State and Federal Legislatures Enact Laws to Expand DNA Testing

The Innocence Protection Act of 2004 became law on October 30, 2004. The law laid down the conditions with which a federal prisoner who pleaded not guilty could receive postconviction DNA testing. If a trial defendant faced conviction, the act called for the preservation of the defendant's biological evidence. A five-year, $25 million grant program was also established to help eligible states pay for postconviction testing.

Many state legislatures have passed similar DNA testing legislation. The American Society of Law, Medicine, and Ethics (2009, http://www.aslme.org/DNA_ELSI_Grant#databases) maintains databases that list the relevant statutes and testing protocols on a state-by-state basis.

CAPITAL PUNISHMENT RECONSIDERED

During the 1980s and early 1990s public opinion polls showed strong support for capital punishment. According to the Gallup Organization (2009, http://www.gallup.com/poll/1606/Death-Penalty.aspx), this support reached its highest level in 1994 when 80% of Americans favored use of the death penalty for murderers.

During the mid-1990s support for capital punishment began to wane for a variety of reasons. The advent of DNA testing resulted in highly publicized cases of inmates being released from prison, and even from death row. Abolitionists seized on these opportunities as proof that the U.S. capital punishment system was flawed. In addition, studies were released indicating that racial biases were occurring in death penalty cases and raising questions about the fairness of the system. By the turn of the 21st century capital punishment had been abolished in Canada and nearly all of Europe, leading to intense criticism in the international press of the United States' reliance on the death penalty. Pope John Paul II (1920–2005) also condemned capital punishment. Two popular movies—*Dead Man Walking* (1995) and *The Green Mile* (1999)—raised questions about the morality of the death penalty.

Two particular death penalty cases also aroused passion about the morality of capital punishment. Karla Faye Tucker became a born-again Christian while on death row in Texas for the brutal 1984 slayings of two people. In the months leading up to her execution in 1998, she received widespread media attention and garnered support nationally and internationally for commutation of her sentence to life in prison. Her supporters included some unlikely allies: a handful of conservative-minded religious and political figures who believed that Tucker's religious conversion merited clemency (an act of leniency by a convening authority to reduce a sentence). Nevertheless, the Texas governor, George W. Bush (1946–), signed her death warrant.

In 2005 the execution of Stanley "Tookie" Williams also garnered considerable public attention. Williams received a death sentence for killing three people in 1981. At the time, he was a leading figure in the notorious and violent Crips gang in Los Angeles. During his decades on death row Williams became an outspoken critic of gangs and wrote books encouraging children to avoid gangs and violence. For his work he received nominations for the Nobel Peace Prize. His supporters included Hollywood celebrities who lobbied California Governor Arnold Schwarzenegger (1947–) for clemency, arguing that Williams had redeemed himself while in prison. The governor refused, noting that Williams had never expressed remorse for his crimes.

The onset of America's economic recession in 2007 and 2008 spurred some states to reconsider the financial costs associated with administering the death penalty. In general, capital cases are more costly than non-capital homicide cases, because capital cases take much longer to proceed through the court system. Legal safeguards, such as automatic appeals, mean that judges, prosecutors, and defense attorneys spend more time on capital cases. These litigation costs are largely paid through tax dollars. In addition, there are extra expenses associated with housing death row inmates, because they are kept in specially designed facilities and receive much more intense supervision than non–death row inmates.

According to the Associated Press in "To Execute or Not: A Question of Cost?" (March 7, 2009, http://www.msnbc.msn.com/id/29552692/print/1/displaymode/1098), budget shortfalls in some death penalty states have motivated legislators to reconsider the high costs associated with capital punishment. The article notes that "time and money" were primary factors in New Jersey's decision to ban executions in 2007. Legislation has been introduced in at least eight other states to follow suit. Richard Dieter, the director of the DPIC, is quoted as saying, "This is the first time in which cost has been the prevalent issue in discussing the death penalty." The DPIC is opposed to capital punishment. It and other abolitionist groups hope that the high financial costs associated with the death penalty will help turn American sentiment against capital punishment in a way that moral arguments have failed to do.

In October 2009, the DPIC issued the report *Smart on Crime: Reconsidering the Death Penalty in a Time of Economic Crisis* (http://www.deathpenaltyinfo.org/documents/CostsRptFinal.pdf). Noting that police chiefs in the United States generally believe the death penalty is ineffective in reducing the number of murders, Dieter provides examples of some of the high costs involved in such programs. He observes: "California is spending an estimated $137 million per year on the death penalty and has not had an execution in three and a half years. Florida is spending approximately $51 million per year on the death penalty, amounting to a cost of $24 million for each execution it carries out. A recent study in Maryland found that the bill for the death penalty over a twenty-year period that produced five executions will be $186 million. Other states like New York and New Jersey spent well over $100 million on a system that produced no executions. Both recently abandoned the practice. This kind of wasteful expenditure makes little sense."

However, death penalty proponents argue that the system just needs reforms to streamline the process and lower expenses. Some believe that the benefits of capital punishment to society outweigh the costs. In "Budget Concerns Force States to Reconsider the Death Penalty" (CNN, March 2, 2009, http://www.cnn.com/2009/CRIME/03/02/economy.death.penalty/index.html), Emanuella Grinberg quotes District Attorney Pat Lykos of Texas—a state that strongly supports capital punishment—as saying, "We will spare no expense. We will go after them. Justice has no price tag."

WORLDWIDE TREND

The de facto moratorium on the death penalty in the United States from 1967 to 1976 paralleled a general worldwide movement, especially among Western nations, toward the abolition of capital punishment. Even though the United States resumed executions in 1977, most of the Western world either formally or informally abolished capital punishment.

As of 2009, among the Western democratic nations (with which the United States traditionally compares itself), only the United States imposed the death penalty. There are technical exceptions: for example, Israel maintains the death penalty in its statute books for "crimes against mankind" but has executed only Adolf Eichmann (1906–1962). As a Schutzstaffel (SS) officer, Eichmann was responsible for the murder of millions of Jews in Nazi-occupied Europe during the Holocaust and World War II. Some countries still maintain the death penalty for treason—although no Western democracy has actually imposed it. One of the first acts of the parliaments of many of the east European countries after the fall of communism was to abolish capital punishment.

According to Amnesty International (AI), in "Abolitionist and Retentionist Countries" (2009, http://www.amnesty .org/en/death-penalty/abolitionist-and-retentionist-countries# allcrimes), 58 countries and territories around the world continued to maintain and use the death penalty for ordinary crimes (crimes committed during peacetime). However, some of these countries had not actually implemented a death sentence for many years. The AI reports that there were at least 2,390 executions carried out in 25 countries in 2008 (2009, http://www.amnesty.org/en/death-penalty/death-sente nces-and-executions-in-2008). The vast majority (1,838) were in Asia. The five countries with the highest number of executions in 2008 were China, Iran, Saudi Arabia, Pakistan, and the United States.

CHAPTER 2

SUPREME COURT RULINGS I: CONSTITUTIONALITY OF THE DEATH PENALTY, GUIDELINES FOR JUDGES AND JURIES, JURY SELECTION, AND SENTENCING PROCEDURES

In 1967 a coalition of anti–death penalty groups sued Florida and California, the states with the most inmates on death row at that time, challenging the constitutionality of state capital punishment laws. An unofficial moratorium (temporary suspension) of executions resulted, pending U.S. Supreme Court decisions on several cases on appeal. The defendants in these cases claimed that the death penalty is a cruel and unusual punishment in violation of the Eighth Amendment to the U.S. Constitution. Moreover, they alleged that the death penalty also violates the Fourteenth Amendment, which prevents states from denying anyone equal protection of the laws. This moratorium lasted until January 17, 1977, when convicted murderer Gary Gilmore (1940–1977) was executed by the state of Utah.

IS THE DEATH PENALTY CONSTITUTIONAL?

On June 29, 1972, a split 5–4 Supreme Court reached a landmark decision in *Furman v. Georgia* (408 U.S. 238, which included *Jackson v. Georgia* and *Branch v. Texas*), holding that "as the statutes before us are now administered.... [The] imposition and carrying out of death penalty in these cases held to constitute a cruel and unusual punishment in violation of Eighth and Fourteenth Amendments." In other words, the justices did not address whether capital punishment as a whole is unconstitutional. Rather, they considered capital punishment in the context of its application in state statutes (laws created by state legislatures). The justices, whether they were of the majority opinion or of the dissenting opinion, could not agree on the arguments explaining why they opposed or supported the death penalty. As a result, the decision consisted of nine separate opinions, the lengthiest ruling in court history to date.

Majority Opinions in *Furman*

Justice William O. Douglas (1898–1980), in his concurring majority opinion, quoted the observation of former U.S. attorney general Ramsey Clark (1927–) in his book *Crime in America: Observations on Its Nature, Causes,*

Prevention, and Control (1970): "It is the poor, the sick, the ignorant, the powerless, and the hated who are executed." Douglas added, "We deal with a system of law and of justice that leaves to the uncontrolled discretion of judges or juries the determination whether defendants committing these crimes should die or be imprisoned. Under these laws no standards govern the selection of the penalty. People live or die, dependent on the whim of one man or of 12.... Thus, these discretionary statutes are unconstitutional in their operation. They are pregnant with discrimination and discrimination is an ingredient not compatible with the idea of equal protection of the laws that is implicit in the ban on 'cruel and unusual' punishments."

Justice William J. Brennan (1906–1997) stated, "At bottom, then, the Cruel and Unusual Punishments Clause prohibits the infliction of uncivilized and inhuman punishments. The State, even as it punishes, must treat its members with respect for their intrinsic worth as human beings. A punishment is 'cruel and unusual,' therefore, if it does not comport with human dignity."

Justice Potter J. Stewart (1915–1985) stressed another point, saying, "These death sentences are cruel and unusual in the same way that being struck by lightning is cruel and unusual. For, of all the people convicted of rapes and murders in 1967 and 1968, many just as reprehensible as these, the petitioners are among a capriciously selected random handful upon whom the sentence of death has in fact been imposed."

This did not mean that Justice Stewart would rule out the death penalty. He believed that the death penalty was justified, but he wanted to see a more equitable system of determining who should be executed. He explained, "I cannot agree that retribution is a constitutionally impermissible ingredient in the imposition of punishment. The instinct for retribution is part of the nature of man, and channeling that instinct in the administration of criminal justice serves an important purpose in promoting the stability of a society governed by law. When people begin to believe that organized society is unwilling or unable to impose upon criminal offenders the punishment they 'deserve,' then there are sown the seeds of anarchy—of self-help, vigilante justice, and lynch law."

Justice Byron R. White (1917–2002), believing that the death penalty was so seldom imposed that executions were ineffective deterrents to crime, chose instead to address the role of juries and judges in imposing the death penalty. He concluded that the cases before the courts violated the Eighth Amendment because the state legislatures, having authorized the application of the death penalty, left it to the discretion of juries and judges whether or not to impose the punishment.

Justice Thurgood Marshall (1908–1993) thought that "the death penalty is an excessive and unnecessary punishment that violates the Eighth Amendment." He added that "even if capital punishment is not excessive, it nonetheless violates the Eighth Amendment because it is morally unacceptable to the people of the United States at this time in their history." Justice Marshall also noted that the death penalty was applied with discrimination against certain classes of people (the poor, the uneducated, and members of minority groups) and that innocent people had been executed before they could prove their innocence. He also believed that it hindered the reform of the treatment of criminals and that it promoted sensationalism during trials.

Dissenting Opinions

Chief Justice Warren Burger (1907–1995), disagreeing with the majority, observed that "the constitutional prohibition against 'cruel and unusual punishments' cannot be construed to bar the imposition of the punishment of death." Justice Harry A. Blackmun (1908–1999) was disturbed by Justices Stewart's and White's remarks that as long as capital punishment was mandated for specific crimes, it could not be considered unconstitutional. He feared "that statutes struck down today will be re-enacted by state legislatures to prescribe the death penalty for specified crimes without any alternative for the imposition of a lesser punishment in the discretion of the judge or jury, as the case may be."

Justice Lewis F. Powell Jr. (1907–1998) declared, "I find no support—in the language of the Constitution, in its history, or in the cases arising under it—for the view that this Court may invalidate a category of penalties because we deem less severe penalties adequate to serve the ends of penology.... This Court has long held that legislative decisions in this area, which lie within the special competency of that branch, are entitled to a presumption of validity."

In other words, the court would not question the validity of a government entity properly doing its job unless its actions were way out of line.

Justice William H. Rehnquist (1924–2005) agreed with Justice Powell, adding, "How can government by the elected representatives of the people co-exist with the power of the federal judiciary, whose members are constitutionally insulated from responsiveness to the popular will, to declare invalid laws duly enacted by the popular branches of government?"

Summary of Court Decision

Only Justices Brennan and Marshall concluded that the Eighth Amendment prohibited the death penalty for all crimes and under all circumstances. Justice Douglas, while ruling that the death penalty statutes reviewed by the high court were unconstitutional, did not necessarily require the final abolition of the death penalty. Justices Stewart and White also did not rule on the validity of the death penalty, noting instead that, because of the capricious imposition of the sentence, the death penalty violated the Eighth Amendment. However, Justices Rehnquist, Burger, Powell, and Blackmun concluded that the Constitution allows capital punishment.

Consequently, most state legislatures went to work to revise their capital punishment laws. They strove to make these laws more equitable to swing the votes of Stewart and White (and later that of John Paul Stevens [1920–], who replaced the retired Justice Douglas).

PROPER IMPOSITION OF THE DEATH PENALTY

Four years later, on July 2, 1976, the Supreme Court ruled decisively on a series of cases. In *Gregg v. Georgia* (428 U.S. 153), perhaps the most significant of these cases, the justices concluded 7–2 that the death penalty was, indeed, constitutional as presented in some new state laws. With Justices Brennan and Marshall dissenting, the court stressed (just in case *Furman* had been misunderstood) that "the death penalty is not a form of punishment that may never be imposed, regardless of the circumstances of the offense, regardless of the character of the offender, and regardless of the procedure followed in reaching the decision to impose it." Furthermore, "the infliction of death as a punishment for murder is not without justification and thus is not unconstitutionally severe."

The court upheld death penalty statutes in Georgia (*Gregg v. Georgia*), Florida (*Proffitt v. Florida*, 428 U.S. 242, 1976), and Texas (*Jurek v. Texas*, 428 U.S. 262, 1976), but struck down laws in North Carolina (*Woodson v. North Carolina*, 428 U.S. 280, 1976) and Louisiana (*Roberts v. Louisiana*, 428 U.S. 40, 1976). It ruled that laws in the latter two states were too rigid in imposing mandatory death sentences for certain types of murder.

Citing the new Georgia laws in *Gregg*, Justice Stewart supported the bifurcated (two-part) trial system, in which the accused is first tried to determine his or her guilt. Then, in a separate trial, the jury considers whether the convicted person deserves the death penalty or whether mitigating factors (circumstances that may lessen or increase responsibility for a crime) warrant a lesser sentence, usually life imprisonment. This system meets the requirements demanded by *Furman*. Noting how the Georgia statutes fulfilled these demands, Justice Stewart observed:

> These procedures require the jury to consider the circumstances of the crime and the criminal before it recommends sentence. No longer can a Georgia jury do as Furman's jury did: reach a finding of the defendant's guilt and then, without guidance or direction, decide whether he should live or die. Instead, the jury's attention is directed to the specific circumstances of the crime: Was it committed in the course of another capital felony? Was it committed for money? Was it committed upon a peace officer or judicial officer? Was it committed in a particularly heinous way or in a manner that endangered the lives of many persons? In addition, the jury's attention is focused on the characteristics of the person who committed the crime: Does he have a record of prior convictions for capital offenses? Are there any special facts about this defendant that mitigate against imposing capital punishment (e.g., his youth, the extent of his cooperation with the police, his emotional state at the time of the crime). As a result, while some jury discretion still exists, "the discretion to be exercised is controlled by clear and objective standards so as to produce non-discriminatory application."

In addition, the Georgia law required that all death sentences be automatically appealed to the state supreme court, an "important additional safeguard against arbitrariness and caprice." The bifurcated trial system has since been adopted in the trials of all capital murder cases.

In *Proffitt v. Florida*, the high court upheld Florida's death penalty laws that had a bifurcated trial system similar to Georgia's. In Florida, however, the sentence was determined by the trial judge rather than by the jury, who assumed an advisory role during the sentencing phase. (This is often referred to as a trifurcated trial system, because there are three levels of decision-making involved.) The court found Florida's sentencing guidelines adequate in preventing unfair imposition of the death sentence.

Predictability of Future Criminal Activity

In *Jurek v. Texas*, the issue centered on whether a jury can satisfactorily determine the future actions of a convicted murderer. The Texas statute required that during the sentencing phase of a trial, after the defendant had been found guilty, the jury would determine whether it is probable the defendant would commit future criminal acts of violence that would threaten society. Even though agreeing with Jurek's attorneys that predicting future behavior is not easy, Justice Stewart noted:

The fact that such a determination is difficult, however, does not mean that it cannot be made. Indeed, prediction of future criminal conduct is an essential element in many of the decisions rendered throughout our criminal justice system. The decision whether to admit a defendant to bail, for instance, must often turn on a judge's prediction of the defendant's future conduct. And any sentencing authority must predict a convicted person's probable future conduct when it engages in the process of determining what punishment to impose. For those sentenced to prison, these same predictions must be made by parole authorities. The task that a Texas jury must perform in answering the statutory question in issue is thus basically no different from the task performed countless times each day throughout the American system of criminal justice.

Flexible Guidelines for Judges and Jurors Are Required

In *Woodson v. North Carolina*, the Supreme Court addressed for the first time the question of whether the jury's handing down of a death sentence under North Carolina's mandatory death penalty for all first-degree murders constituted a cruel and unusual punishment within the meaning of the Eighth and Fourteenth Amendments. If a person was convicted of first-degree murder in North Carolina, he or she was automatically sentenced to death. The justices held that as a whole the American public rejected the idea of mandatory death sentences long ago. In addition, North Carolina's new statute provided "no standards to guide the jury in its inevitable exercise of the power to determine which first-degree murderers shall live and which shall die." Furthermore, the North Carolina law did not let the jury consider the convicted defendant's character, criminal record, or the circumstances of the crime before the imposition of the death sentence.

The Louisiana mandatory death sentence for first-degree murder suffered from similar inadequacies. It did, however, permit the jury to consider lesser offenses such as second-degree murder. In *Roberts v. Louisiana*, the Supreme Court rejected the Louisiana law because it forced the jury to find the defendant guilty of a lesser crime to avoid imposing the death penalty. In other words, if the crime was not heinous enough to warrant the death penalty, then the jury was forced to convict the defendant of second-degree murder or a lesser charge. The jury did not have the option of first determining if the accused was indeed guilty of first-degree murder for the crime he or she had actually committed and then recommending a lesser sentence if there were mitigating circumstances to support it.

As a result of either *Furman* or *Gregg* or both, virtually every state's capital punishment statute had to be rewritten. These statutes would provide flexible guidelines for judges and juries so that they might fairly decide capital cases and consider, then impose, if necessary, the death penalty.

JURY MAY CONSIDER A LESSER CHARGE

In 1977 Gilbert Beck was convicted of robbing and murdering 80-year-old Roy Malone. According to Beck, he and an accomplice entered Malone's home and were tying up the victim to rob him when Beck's accomplice unexpectedly struck and killed Malone. Beck admitted to the robbery but claimed the murder was not part of the plan. Beck was tried under an Alabama statute for "robbery or attempts thereof when the victim is intentionally killed by the defendant."

Under Alabama law the judge was specifically prohibited from giving the jury the option of convicting the defendant of a lesser, included offense. Instead, the jury was given the choice of either convicting the defendant of the capital crime, in which case he possibly faced the death penalty, or acquitting him, thus allowing him to escape all penalties for his alleged participation in the crime. The judge could not have offered the jury the lesser alternative of felony murder, which did not deal with the accused's intentions at the time of the crime.

Beck appealed, claiming this law created a situation in which the jury was more likely to convict. The Supreme Court, in *Beck v. Alabama* (447 U.S. 625, 1980), agreed and reversed the lower court's ruling, thus vacating (annulling) his death sentence. The high court observed that, while not a matter of due process, it was virtually universally accepted in lesser offenses that a third alternative be offered. The court noted, "That safeguard would seem to be especially important in a case such as this. For when the evidence unquestionably establishes that the defendant is guilty of a serious, violent offense—but leaves some doubt with respect to an element that would justify conviction of a capital offense—the failure to give the jury the 'third option' of convicting on a lesser included offense would seem inevitably to enhance the risk of an unwarranted conviction."

According to the ruling, such a risk could not be tolerated in a case where the defendant's life was at stake. *Beck*, however, did not require a jury to consider a lesser charge in every case, but only where the consideration would be justified.

EXCLUSION FROM JURIES OF THOSE AGAINST CAPITAL PUNISHMENT

In *Witherspoon v. Illinois* (391 U.S. 510, 1968), the Supreme Court held that a death sentence cannot be carried out if the jury that imposed or recommended such punishment was selected by excluding prospective jurors simply because they have qualms against the death penalty or reservations against its infliction. The court found that the prosecution excluded those who opposed the death penalty without determining whether their beliefs would compel them to reject capital punishment out of hand. The defendant argued that this selective process had resulted in a jury that was not representative of the community.

The justices could not definitively conclude that the exclusion of jurors opposed to the death penalty results in an unrepresentative jury. However, they believed that a person who opposes the death penalty can still abide by his or her duty as a juror and consider the facts presented at trial before making his or her decision about the defendant's punishment. The court observed, "If the State had excluded only those prospective jurors who stated in advance of trial that they would not even consider returning a verdict of death, it could argue that the resulting jury was simply 'neutral' with respect to penalty. But when it swept from the jury all who expressed conscientious or religious scruples against capital punishment and all who opposed it in principle, the State crossed the line of neutrality. In its quest for a jury capable of imposing the death penalty, the State produced a jury uncommonly willing to condemn a man to die."

The court specifically noted that its findings in *Witherspoon* did not prevent the infliction of the death sentence when the prospective jurors excluded had made it "unmistakably clear" that they would automatically vote against the death sentence without considering the evidence presented during the trial or that their attitudes toward capital punishment would keep them from making a fair decision about the defendant's guilt. Consequently, based on *Witherspoon*, it has become the practice in most states to exclude prospective jurors who indicate that they could not possibly in good conscience return a death penalty.

This ruling was reinforced in *Lockett v. Ohio* (438 U.S. 586, 1978). The defendant in Lockett contended, among several things, that the exclusion of four prospective jurors violated her Sixth Amendment right to trial by an impartial jury and Fourteenth Amendment rights under the principles established in *Witherspoon*. The Supreme Court upheld *Witherspoon* in this case because the prospective jurors told the prosecutor that they were so against the death penalty they could not be impartial about the case. They had also admitted that they would not take an oath saying they would consider the evidence before making a judgment of innocence or guilt.

A Special Selection Process Is Not Required When Selecting Jurors in Capital Cases

In *Wainwright v. Witt* (469 U.S. 412, 1985), a 7–2 Supreme Court decision eased the strict requirements of *Witherspoon*. Writing for the majority, Justice Rehnquist declared that the new capital punishment procedures left less discretion to jurors. Rehnquist indicated that potential jurors in capital cases should be excluded from jury duty in a manner similar to how they were excluded in noncapital cases. (In a noncapital case, the prospective jurors typically go through a selection process in which the prosecution and the defense question them about their attitudes toward the crime and the people and issues related to it to determine if they are too biased to be fair.)

No longer would a juror's "automatic" bias against imposing the death penalty have to be proved with "unmistakable clarity." A prosecutor could not be expected to ask all the questions necessary to determine if a juror would automatically rule against the death penalty or fail to convict a defendant if he or she were likely to face execution. Fundamentally, the question of exclusion from a jury should be determined by the interplay of the prosecutor and the defense lawyer and by the decision of the judge based on his or her initial observations of the prospective juror. Judges can see firsthand whether prospective jurors' beliefs would bias their ability to impose the death penalty.

In his dissent, Justice Brennan claimed that making it easier to eliminate those who opposed capital punishment from the jury created a jury not only more likely to impose the death sentence but also more likely to convict. He also attacked the majority interpretation that now treated exclusion from a capital case as being similar to exclusion from any other case.

It Does Not Matter if "Death-Qualified" Juries Are More Likely to Convict

In *Lockhart v. McCree* (476 U.S. 162, 1986), the Supreme Court firmly resolved the issue presented in *Witherspoon* regarding a fair trial with a death-qualified jury. (A death-qualified jury is another name for a jury that is willing to sentence a person to death after hearing the evidence of the case.)

Ardia McCree was convicted of murdering Evelyn Boughton while robbing her gift shop and service station in Camden, Arkansas, in February 1978. In accordance with Arkansas law, the trial judge removed eight prospective jurors because they indicated they could not, under any circumstances, vote for the imposition of the death sentence. The resulting jury then convicted McCree and, even though the state sought the death penalty, sentenced the defendant to life imprisonment without parole.

McCree appealed, claiming that the removal of the so-called *Witherspoon* excludables violated his right to a fair trial under the Sixth and Fourteenth Amendments. These amendments guaranteed that his innocence or guilt would be determined by an impartial jury selected from a representative cross-section of the community, which would include people strongly opposed to the death penalty. McCree cited several studies, revealing that death-qualified juries were more likely to convict. Both the federal district court and the federal court of appeals agreed with McCree, but in a 6–3 decision, the Supreme Court disagreed.

The high court majority did not accept the validity of the studies. Speaking for the majority, Justice Rehnquist argued that, even if the justices did accept the validity of these studies, "the Constitution does not prohibit the States from 'death qualifying' juries in capital cases." Justice Rehnquist further observed:

> The exclusion from jury service of large groups of individuals not on the basis of their inability to serve as jurors, but on the basis of some immutable characteristic such as race, gender, or ethnic background, undeniably gave rise to an "appearance of unfairness."

> [Nevertheless], unlike blacks, women, and Mexican-Americans, "*Witherspoon*-excludables" are singled out for exclusion in capital cases on the basis of an attribute that is within the individual's control. It is important to remember that not all who oppose the death penalty are subject to removal for cause in capital cases; those who firmly believe that the death penalty is unjust may nevertheless serve as jurors in capital cases so long as they state clearly that they are willing to temporarily set aside their own beliefs in deference to the rule of law. Because the group of "*Witherspoon*-excludables" includes only those who cannot and will not conscientiously obey the law with respect to one of the issues in a capital case, "death qualification" hardly can be said to create an "appearance of unfairness."

Writing in dissent, Justice Marshall observed that if the high court thought in *Witherspoon* that excluding those who opposed the death penalty meant that a convicted murderer would not get a fair hearing during the sentencing part of the trial, it would also logically mean that he or she would not get a fair hearing during the initial trial part. The court minority generally accepted the studies showing "that 'death qualification' in fact produces juries somewhat more 'conviction-prone' than 'non-death-qualified' juries."

DOES THE BUCK STOP WITH THE JURY?

During the course of a robbery Bobby Caldwell shot and killed the owner of a Mississippi grocery store in October 1980. He was tried and found guilty. During the sentencing phase of the trial Caldwell's attorney pleaded for mercy, concluding his summation by emphasizing to the jury, "I implore you to think deeply about this matter.... You are the judges and you will have to decide his fate. It is an awesome responsibility, I know—an awesome responsibility."

Responding to the defense attorney's plea, the prosecutor played down the responsibility of the jury, stressing that a life sentence would be reviewed by a higher court: "[The defense] would have you believe that you're going to kill this man and they know—they know that your decision is not the final decision.... Your job is reviewable.... They know, as I know, and as Judge Baker has told you, that the decision you render is automatically reviewable by the Supreme Court."

The jury sentenced Caldwell to death, and the case was automatically appealed. The Mississippi Supreme Court upheld the conviction, but split 4–4 on the validity of the death sentence, thereby upholding the death sentence by an equally divided court. Caldwell appealed to the Supreme Court.

In a 5–3 decision (Justice Powell took no part in the decision), the Supreme Court, in *Caldwell v. Mississippi* (472 U.S. 320, 1985), vacated (annulled) the death sentence. Writing for the majority, Justice Marshall noted, "It is constitutionally impermissible to rest a death sentence on a determination made by a sentencer who has been led to believe, as the jury was in this case, that the responsibility for determining the appropriateness of the defendant's death rests elsewhere.... [This Court] has taken as a given that capital sentencers would view their task as the serious one of determining whether a specific human being should die at the hands of the State."

Furthermore, the high court pointed out that the appeals court was not the place to make this life-or-death decision. Most appellate courts would presume that the sentencing was correctly done, which would leave the defendant at a distinct disadvantage. The jurors, expecting to be reversed by an appeals court, might choose to "send a message" of extreme disapproval of the defendant's acts and sentence him or her to death to show they will not tolerate such actions. Should the appeals court fail to reverse the decision, the defendant might be executed when the jury only intended to "send a message."

The three dissenting judges believed "the Court has overstated the seriousness of the prosecutor's comments" and that it was "highly unlikely that the jury's sense of responsibility was diminished."

KEEPING PAROLE INFORMATION FROM THE JURY

In 1990 Jonathan Dale Simmons beat an elderly woman to death in her home in Columbia, South Carolina. The week before his capital murder trial began, he pleaded guilty to first-degree burglary and two counts of criminal sexual conduct in connection with two prior assaults on elderly women. These guilty pleas resulted in convictions for violent offenses, which made him ineligible for parole if convicted of any other violent crime.

At the capital murder trial, over the defense counsel's objection, the court did not allow the defense to ask prospective jurors if they understood the meaning of a "life" sentence as it applied to the defendant. Under South Carolina law a defendant who was deemed a future threat to society and receiving a life sentence was ineligible for parole. The prosecution also asked the judge not to mention parole.

During deliberation, the jurors asked the judge if the imposition of a life sentence carried with it the possibility of parole. The judge told the jury, "You are instructed not to consider parole or parole eligibility in reaching your verdict.... The terms life imprisonment and death sentence are to be understood in their plan [*sic*] and ordinary meaning."

The jury convicted Simmons of murder, sentencing him to death. On appeal the South Carolina Supreme Court upheld the sentence. The case was brought before the U.S. Supreme Court. In *Simmons v. South Carolina* (512 U.S. 154, 1994), the high court overruled the South Carolina Supreme Court in a 6–2 decision, concluding:

> Where a defendant's future dangerousness is at issue, and state law prohibits his release on parole, due process requires that the sentencing jury be informed that the defendant is parole ineligible. An individual cannot be executed on the basis of information which he had no opportunity to deny or explain. Petitioner's jury reasonably may have believed that he could be released on parole if he were not executed. To the extent that this misunderstanding pervaded its deliberations, it had the effect of creating a false choice between sentencing him to death and sentencing him to a limited period of incarceration. The trial court's refusal to apprise the jury of information so crucial to its determination, particularly when the State alluded to the defendant's future dangerousness in its argument, cannot be reconciled with this Court's well established precedents interpreting the Due Process Clause.

JUDGE SENTENCING
Florida

Under Florida's trifurcated trial system for capital cases, the jury decides the innocence or guilt of the accused. If the jury finds the defendant guilty, it recommends an advisory sentence of either life imprisonment or death. The trial judge considers mitigating and aggravating circumstances, weighs them against the jury recommendation, and then sentences the convicted murderer to either life or death. (Mitigating circumstances may lessen the responsibility for a crime, whereas aggravating circumstances may increase the responsibility for a crime.)

In 1975 a Florida jury convicted Joseph Spaziano of torturing and murdering two women. The jury recommended that Spaziano be sentenced to life imprisonment, but the trial judge, after considering the mitigating and aggravating circumstances, sentenced the defendant to death. In his appeal, Spaziano claimed the judge's overriding of the jury's recommendation of life imprisonment violated the Eighth Amendment's prohibition against a cruel and unusual punishment. The Supreme Court, in a 5–3 decision in *Spaziano v. Florida* (468 U.S. 447, 1984), did not agree.

Spaziano's lawyers claimed juries, not judges, were better equipped to make reliable capital-sentencing decisions and that a jury's decision of life imprisonment should not be superseded. They reasoned that the death penalty was unlike any other sentence and required that the jury have the ultimate word. This belief had been upheld, Spaziano claimed, because 30 out of 37 states with capital punishment had the jury decide the prisoner's fate. Furthermore, the primary justification for the death penalty was retribution and an expression of community outrage. The jury served as the voice of the community and knew best whether a particular crime was so terrible that the community's response must be the death sentence.

The high court indicated that even though Spaziano's argument had some appeal, it contained two fundamental flaws. First, retribution played a role in all sentences, not just death sentences. Second, a jury was not the only source of community input: "The community's voice is heard at least as clearly in the legislature when the death penalty is authorized and the particular circumstances in which death is appropriate are defined." That trial judges imposed sentences was a normal part of the judicial system. The Supreme Court continued, "In light of the facts that the Sixth Amendment does not require jury sentencing, that the demands of fairness and reliability in capital cases do not require it, and that neither the nature of, nor the purpose behind, the death penalty requires jury sentencing, we cannot conclude that placing responsibility on the trial judge to impose the sentence in a capital case is unconstitutional."

The court added that just because 30 out of 37 states let the jury make the sentencing decision did not mean states that let a judge decide were wrong. The court pointed out that there is no one right way for a state to establish its method of capital sentencing.

Writing for the dissenters, Justice Stevens indicated, "Because of its severity and irrevocability, the death penalty is qualitatively different from any other punishment, and hence must be accompanied by unique safeguards to ensure that it is a justified response to a given offense. . . . I am convinced that the danger of an excessive response can only be avoided if the decision to impose the death penalty is made by a jury rather than by a single governmental official [because a jury] is best able to 'express the conscience of the community on the ultimate question of life or death.'"

Justice Stevens also gave weight to the fact that 30 out of 37 states had the jury make the decision, attesting to the "high level of consensus" that communities strongly believe life-or-death decisions should remain with the people—as represented by the jury—rather than relegated to a single government official.

Alabama

In March 1988 Louise Harris asked a coworker, Lorenzo McCarter, with whom she was having an affair, to find someone to kill her husband. McCarter paid two accomplices $100, with a promise of more money after they killed the husband. McCarter testified against Harris in exchange for the prosecutor's promise that he would not seek the death penalty against McCarter. McCarter testified that Harris had asked him to kill her husband so they could share in his death benefits. An Alabama jury convicted Harris of capital murder. At the sentencing hearing, witnesses testified to her good background and strong character. She was rearing seven children, held three jobs simultaneously, and was active in her church.

Alabama law gives capital sentencing authority to the trial judge but requires the judge to "consider" an advisory jury verdict. The jury voted 7–5 to give Harris life imprisonment without parole. The trial judge then considered her sentence. He found one aggravating circumstance (the murder was committed for monetary gain), one statutory mitigating circumstance (Harris had no prior criminal record), and one nonstatutory mitigating circumstance (Harris was a hardworking, respected member of her church).

Noting that she had planned the crime, financed it, and stood to benefit from the murder, the judge felt that the aggravating circumstance outweighed the other mitigating circumstances and sentenced her to death. On appeal, the Alabama Supreme Court affirmed the conviction and sentence. It rejected Harris's arguments that the procedure was unconstitutional because Alabama state law did "not specify the weight the judge must give to the jury's recommendation and thus permits the arbitrary imposition of the death penalty."

On appeal, the U.S. Supreme Court upheld the Alabama court's decision (*Harris v. Alabama* [513 U.S. 504], 1995). Alabama's capital-sentencing process is similar to Florida's. Both require jury participation during sentencing but give the trial judge the ultimate sentencing authority. Nevertheless, even though the Florida statute requires that a trial judge must give "great weight" to the jury recommendation, the Alabama statute requires only that the judge "consider" the jury's recommendation.

As in the *Spaziano* case, the high court ruled that the Eighth Amendment does not require the state "to define the weight the sentencing judge must give to an advisory jury verdict." The court stated, "Because the Constitution permits the trial judge, acting alone, to impose a capital sentence . . . it is not offended when a State further requires the judge to consider a jury recommendation and trusts the judge to give it the proper weight."

JURY SENTENCING

In 2002 the Supreme Court decided a case concerning death sentencing in Arizona involving the Sixth Amendment right to an impartial jury (as opposed to the Eighth Amendment, which bars a cruel and unusual punishment). Timothy Stuart Ring was convicted of murder in the armed robbery of an armored-car driver in 1994. According to

Arizona law, Ring's offense was punishable by life imprisonment or death. He would only be eligible for the death penalty if the trial judge held a separate hearing and found that aggravating factors warranted the death penalty.

One of Ring's accomplices, who negotiated a plea bargain in return for a second-degree murder charge, testified against him at a separate sentencing hearing without a jury present. The same judge who had presided at Ring's trial concluded that Ring committed the murder and that the crime was committed "in an especially heinous, cruel or depraved manner." Weighing the two aggravating circumstances against the mitigating evidence of Ring's minimal criminal record, the judge sentenced Ring to death.

Ring appealed to the Arizona Supreme Court, claiming that the state's capital sentencing law violated his Sixth and Fourteenth Amendment rights because it allowed a judge, rather than a jury, to make the factual findings that made him eligible for a death sentence. The court put aside Ring's argument against Arizona's judge-sentencing system in light of the U.S. Supreme Court's ruling in *Walton v. Arizona* (497 U.S. 639, 1990). The court held in *Walton* that Arizona's sentencing procedure was constitutional because "the additional facts found by the judge qualified as sentencing considerations, not as 'elements of the offense of capital murder.'" Next, the Arizona Supreme Court threw out the trial judge's finding of the heinous nature of the crime but concluded that Ring's minimal criminal record was not enough to outweigh the aggravating evidence of "planned, ruthless robbery and killing." The court affirmed the death sentence.

Ring took his case to the U.S. Supreme Court. On June 24, 2002, by a 7–2 vote, the court ruled in *Ring v. Arizona* (536 U.S. 584) that only juries and not judges can determine the presence of aggravating circumstances that warrant the death sentence. This case differs from the *Harris* and *Spaziano* cases in which the court ruled simply that a judge could sentence a person to death after hearing a jury's recommendation. In the *Ring* opinion the court included a discussion of *Apprendi v. New Jersey* (530 U.S. 466, 2000), in which it held that "the Sixth Amendment does not permit a defendant to be 'exposed . . . to a penalty exceeding the maximum he would receive if punished according to the facts reflected in the jury verdict alone.'" *Apprendi* involved a defendant in a noncapital case who received a prison term beyond the maximum sentence. This occurred because New Jersey law allowed sentencing judges to increase the penalty if they found that a crime was racially motivated. In *Apprendi*, the court held that any fact other than a prior conviction that increases the punishment for a crime beyond the maximum allowed by law must be found by a jury beyond a reasonable doubt. The court found *Walton* and *Apprendi* irreconcilable. The court overruled *Walton* "to the extent that it allows a sentencing judge, sitting without a jury, to find an aggra-

vating circumstance necessary for imposition of the death penalty." Justice Ruth Bader Ginsburg (1933–), who delivered the opinion of the court, wrote, "The right to trial by jury guaranteed by the Sixth Amendment would be senselessly diminished if it encompassed the factfinding necessary to increase a defendant's sentence by two years [referring to *Apprendi*], but not the factfinding necessary to put him to death. We hold that the Sixth Amendment applies to both."

However, Justice Antonin Scalia (1936–), joined by Justice Clarence Thomas (1948–), pointed out in a separate concurring opinion that under *Ring*, states that let judges impose the death sentence may continue to do so by requiring the finding of aggravating factors necessary to the imposition of the death penalty during the trial phase.

Justice Sandra Day O'Connor (1930–), in her dissenting opinion, joined by Chief Justice Rehnquist, claimed that just as the *Apprendi* decision has overburdened the appeals courts, the *Ring* decision will cause more federal appeals. O'Connor observed that *Ring v. Arizona* also invalidates the capital sentencing procedure of four other states. These included Idaho and Montana, where a judge had the sole sentencing authority, as well as Colorado and Nebraska, where a three-judge panel made the sentencing decisions. The court ruling also potentially affected Alabama, Delaware, Florida, and Indiana, where the jury rendered an advisory verdict, but the judge had the ultimate sentencing authority.

Impact of the *Ring* Decision

As a result of the *Ring* decision, Arizona, Colorado, Delaware, Idaho, Nebraska, Indiana, and Montana passed legislation providing for jury sentencing. Some legal scholars suggested at the time that states where judges previously made the life-or-death decisions would see fewer death sentences under the jury system, because judges are elected public officials who may be driven by political ambitions to issue death sentences.

However, in "Jurors Dish Out Death in Arizona; Sentencing Rate Up since Judges Lost Say" (*Arizona Republic*, November 13, 2003), Jim Walsh calculates that after the state sentencing laws were revised per *Ring*, juries in that state handed down death sentences at a higher rate than judges had done under the previous system. According to Walsh, within a one-year period (November 2002 to November 2003), jurors in Maricopa County sentenced seven out of eight (87.5%) defendants to death. Statewide, jurors imposed a total of 10 death sentences out of 15 cases heard (66.7%). In comparison, between 1995 and 1999 Maricopa County judges imposed death sentences in 11 out of 75 (14.7%) cases. Statewide, within that four-year period, judges sentenced 29 out of 143 (20.3%) defendants to death.

As of 2009 Florida and Alabama still allowed judges to override jury sentencing recommendations. The Alabama override is particularly controversial, because state law imposes no restrictions on the judge's decision-making process. In other words, the judge has full discretion to override a jury. By contrast, Florida law imposes restrictions on an override. According to the American Bar Association in *Evaluating Fairness and Accuracy in State Death Penalty Systems: The Florida Death Penalty Assessment Report* (September 2006, http://www.abanet.org/moratori um/assessmentproject/florida/FloridaReportEmbargoed 9.13.doc), Florida judges in capital cases must give "great weight" to the jury's recommended sentence. If a judge imposes a death sentence after the jury has recommended a life sentence, Florida law requires that "the facts suggesting a death sentence must be so clear and convincing that no reasonable person could differ as to the appropriate sentence."

The Equal Justice Institute (EJI) is a private, nonprofit organization based in Alabama that provides legal representation to indigent (poor) defendants. In a March 2008 report, "Judicial Override in Alabama" (http://www.eji.org/eji/files/ 03.19.08%20Judicial%20Override%20Fact%20Sheet_0.pdf), the EJI notes that 30% of new death sentences imposed during 2006 were the result of judicial overrides. The report complains, "Judges in Alabama's hotly contested partisan elections compete to appear 'tough on crime' and campaign on their willingness to get tough by imposing the death penalty." The EJI states that one fifth of the inmates then on death row "were condemned to death by a judge who threw out the jury's decision that death was not the appropriate punishment."

The *Ring* Decision Does Not Retroactively Apply to Those Already Sentenced to Murder

The Arizona death row inmate Warren Summerlin was convicted of brutally crushing the skull of bill collector Brenna Bailey and then sexually assaulting her. Summerlin was convicted by a jury, and an Arizona trial judge sentenced him to death in 1982. After the *Ring* decision was handed down, the U.S. Court of Appeals for the Ninth Circuit ruled 8–3 in *Summerlin v. Stewart* (309 F.3d 1193 [9th Cir., 2003]) that in light of *Ring v. Arizona*, Summerlin's death sentence should be vacated. The appellate court held that the Supreme Court's ruling should apply retroactively, even to those inmates who have exhausted their appeals. The prosecution brought the case to the U.S. Supreme Court.

In *Schriro v. Summerlin* (No. 03-526, 2004), the Supreme Court reversed the appellate court's decision in a 5–4 vote. The nation's highest court concluded that the *Ring* ruling only changed the procedures involved in a sentencing trial for capital punishment cases and did not alter those fundamental legal guidelines judges and juries follow when sentencing a person to death. As such, the *Ring* ruling does not call into question the accuracy of past convictions and should not be retroactive. Speaking for the majority, Justice Scalia wrote, "[We] give retroactive effect to only a small set of 'watershed rules of criminal procedure' implicating the fundamental fairness and accuracy of the criminal proceeding. That a new procedural rule is 'fundamental' in some abstract sense is not enough; the rule must be one 'without which the likelihood of an accurate conviction is seriously diminished.'"

DOUBLE JEOPARDY

In 1991 David Sattazahn was convicted for the 1987 murder of a restaurant manager in Berks County, Pennsylvania. Sattazahn and an accomplice killed the manager in the process of robbing him of the day's receipts. The state sought the death sentence and included an aggravating circumstance—the commission of murder while perpetrating a felony. During the sentencing phase the jury could not reach a verdict as to life or death. The trial judge considered the jury as hung and imposed an automatic sentence of life imprisonment as mandated by state law.

On appeal to the Pennsylvania Superior Court, Sattazahn was granted a new trial. The court held that the trial judge had erred in jury instructions relating to his offenses and reversed his murder conviction. During the second trial the state again sought the death penalty, this time adding a second aggravating factor: the defendant's history of felony convictions involving using or threatening violence to the victim. The jury convicted Sattazahn of first-degree murder and sentenced him to death.

Next, the Pennsylvania Supreme Court heard Sattazahn's case. The death row inmate claimed, among other things, that the Pennsylvania Constitution prohibits the imposition of the death penalty in his case because it guarantees protection from double jeopardy. The Double Jeopardy Clause of the Fifth Amendment states that "no person shall . . . be subject for the same offense to be twice put in jeopardy of life or limb." In other words, no person can be tried or punished twice for the same crime.

Relying on its ruling in *Commonwealth v. Martorano* (634 A.2d 1063,1071 [Pa. 1993]), the Pennsylvania Supreme Court affirmed both Sattazahn's conviction and death sentence. In *Martorano*, the court noted that the jury, as in Sattazahn's first trial, was deadlocked. The hung jury did not "acquit" the defendant of the death sentence. Therefore, there was no double jeopardy prohibition against the death penalty during the second trial.

In *Sattazahn v. Pennsylvania* (537 U.S. 101, 2003), the U.S. Supreme Court, by a 5–4 vote, agreed with the ruling of the Pennsylvania Supreme Court. Justice Scalia, writing the majority opinion, concluded that double jeopardy did not exist in this case. According to the court, "The touchstone for double-jeopardy protection in capital-sentencing proceedings is whether there has been an 'acquittal.' Petitioner here cannot establish that the jury or the court 'acquitted' him during his first capital-sentencing proceeding. As to the jury: The verdict form returned by the foreman stated that the jury deadlocked 9-to-3 on whether to impose the death penalty; it made no findings with respect to the alleged aggravating circumstance. That result—or more appropriately, that non-result—cannot fairly be called an acquittal."

The court added that the imposition of a life sentence by the judge did not "acquit" the defendant of the death penalty either because the judge was just following the state law. "A default judgment does not trigger a double jeopardy bar to the death penalty upon retrial."

Justice Ginsburg, writing for the dissent, was joined by Justices Stevens, David H. Souter (1939–), and Stephen G. Breyer (1938–). The dissenters argued that jeopardy terminated after the judge imposed a final judgment of life imprisonment when the jury was deadlocked. Therefore, he was "acquitted" of the death penalty the first time, which means that the state could not seek the death penalty the second time. Justice Ginsburg also pointed out that "the Court's holding confronts defendants with a perilous choice.... Under the court's decision, if a defendant sentenced to life after a jury deadlock chooses to appeal her underlying conviction, she faces the possibility of death if she is successful on appeal but convicted on retrial. If, on the other hand, the defendant loses her appeal, or chooses to forgo an appeal, the final judgment for life stands. In other words, a defendant in Sattazahn's position must relinquish either her right to file a potentially meritorious appeal, or her state-granted entitlement to avoid the death penalty."

SENTENCING PROCEDURES
Comparative Proportionality Review: Comparing Similar Crimes and Sentences

On July 5, 1978, in Mira Mesa, California, Robert Harris and his brother decided to steal a car they would need for a getaway in a planned bank robbery. Harris approached two teenage boys eating hamburgers in a car. He forced them at gunpoint to drive to a nearby wooded area. The teenagers offered to delay telling the police of the car robbery and even to give the authorities misleading descriptions of the two robbers. When one of the boys appeared to be fleeing, Harris shot both of them. Harris and his brother later committed the robbery, were soon caught, and confessed to the robbery and murders.

Harris was found guilty. In California, a convicted murderer could be sentenced to death or life imprisonment without parole only if "special circumstances" existed and the murder had been "willful, deliberate, premeditated, and committed during the commission of kidnapping and

robbery." This had to be proven during a separate sentencing hearing.

The state showed that Harris was convicted of manslaughter in 1975; he was found in possession of a makeshift knife and garrote (an instrument used for strangulation) while in prison; he and other inmates sodomized another inmate; and he threatened that inmate's life. Harris testified that he had an unhappy childhood, had little education, and his father had sexually molested his sisters. The jury sentenced Harris to death, and the judge concurred.

Harris claimed the U.S. Constitution, as interpreted in previous capital punishment rulings, required the state of California to give his case comparative proportionality review to determine if his death sentence was not out of line with that of others convicted of similar crimes. In comparative proportionality review, a court considers the seriousness of the offense, the severity of the penalty, the sentences imposed for other crimes, and the sentencing in other jurisdictions for the same crime. Courts have occasionally struck down punishments inherently disproportionate and, therefore, cruel and unusual. Georgia, by law, and Florida, by practice, had incorporated such reviews in their procedures. Other states, such as Texas and California, had not.

When the case reached the U.S. Ninth Circuit Court of Appeals, the court agreed with Harris and ordered California to establish proportionality or lift the death sentence. In *Pulley v. Harris* (465 U.S. 37, 1984), the U.S. Supreme Court, in a 7–2 decision, did not agree. The court noted that the California procedure contained enough safeguards to guarantee a defendant a fair trial and those convicted, a fair sentence. The high court added, "That some [state statutes] providing proportionality review are constitutional does not mean that such review is indispensable.... To endorse the statute as a whole is not to say that anything different is unacceptable.... Examination of our 1976 cases makes clear that they do not establish proportionality review as a constitutional requirement."

Justice Brennan, joined by Justice Marshall, dissented. He noted that the Supreme Court had thrown out the existing death penalty procedures during the 1970s because they were deemed arbitrary and capricious. He believed they still were, but the introduction of proportionality might "eliminate some, if only a small part, of the irrationality that currently surrounds the imposition of the death penalty."

Due Process and Advance Notice of Imposing the Death Penalty

Robert Bravence and Cheryl Bravence were beaten to death at their campsite near Santiam Creek, Idaho, in 1983. Two brothers, Bryan Lankford and Mark Lankford, were charged with two counts of first-degree murder. At the arraignment (a summoning before a court to hear and answer charges), the trial judge advised Bryan Lankford that, if convicted of either of the two charges (he was charged with both murders), the maximum punishment he might receive was either life imprisonment or death.

After the arraignment, Bryan Lankford's attorney made a deal with the prosecutor. Bryan Lankford entered a plea bargain in which he agreed to take two lie-detector tests in exchange for a lesser sentence. Even though the results were somewhat unclear, they convinced the prosecutor that Lankford's older brother, Mark, was primarily responsible for the crimes and was the actual killer of both victims. Bryan Lankford's attorney and the prosecutor agreed on an indeterminate sentence with a 10-year minimum in exchange for a guilty plea, subject to commitment from the trial judge that he would impose that sentence. The judge refused to make such a commitment, and the case went to trial.

The judge also refused to instruct the jury that a specific intent to kill was required to support a conviction of first-degree murder. The jury found Bryan Lankford guilty on both counts. The sentencing hearing was postponed until after Mark Lankford's trial. He was also charged with both murders.

Before the sentencing trial, at Bryan Lankford's request, the trial judge ordered the prosecutor to notify the court and Lankford whether it would seek the death penalty and, if so, to file a statement of the aggravating circumstance on which the death penalty would be based. The prosecutor notified the judge that the state would not recommend the death penalty. Several proceedings followed, including Lankford's request for a new attorney, a motion for a new trial, and a motion for continuance of the sentencing hearing. At none of the proceedings was there any mention that Lankford might receive the death penalty.

At the sentencing hearing, the prosecutor recommended a life sentence, with a minimum ranging between 10 and 20 years. The trial judge indicated that he considered Lankford's testimony unbelievable and that the seriousness of the crime warranted more severe punishment than recommended by the state. He sentenced Lankford to death.

Lankford appealed, asserting that the trial judge violated the U.S. Constitution by failing to give notice that he intended to impose the death penalty in spite of the state's earlier notice that it would not seek the death penalty. The judge maintained that the Idaho Code provided Lankford with sufficient notice. The judge added that the fact the prosecutor said he would not seek the death penalty had "no bearing on the adequacy of notice to petitioner that the death penalty might be imposed." The Idaho Supreme Court agreed with the judge's decision.

In *Lankford v. Idaho* (500 U.S. 110, 1991), the U.S. Supreme Court reversed the state supreme court ruling and remanded the case for a new trial. Writing for the majority, Justice Stevens stated that the due process clause of the Fourteenth Amendment was violated. Stevens noted, "If defense counsel had been notified that the trial judge was contemplating a death sentence based on five specific aggravating circumstances, presumably she would have advanced arguments that addressed these circumstances; however, she did not make these arguments, because they were entirely inappropriate in a discussion about the length of petitioner's possible incarceration."

Stevens further indicated that the trial judge's silence, in effect, hid from Lankford and his attorney, as well as from the prosecutor, the principal issues to be decided.

In a dissenting opinion, Justice Scalia wrote that Lankford's due process rights were not violated because he knew that he had been convicted of first-degree murder, and the Idaho Code clearly states that "every person guilty of murder of the first degree shall be punished by death or by imprisonment for life." At the arraignment the trial judge told Lankford that he could receive either punishment. Scalia further noted that, in Idaho, the death penalty statute places full responsibility for determining the sentence on the judge.

CHAPTER 3

SUPREME COURT RULINGS II: CIRCUMSTANCES THAT DO AND DO NOT WARRANT THE DEATH PENALTY, RIGHT TO EFFECTIVE COUNSEL, APPEALS BASED ON NEW EVIDENCE, AND CONSTITUTIONALITY OF EXECUTION METHODS

CIRCUMSTANCES FOUND NOT TO WARRANT THE DEATH PENALTY

Rape of Adult Women and Kidnapping

On June 29, 1977, a 5–4 divided U.S. Supreme Court ruled in *Coker v. Georgia* (433 U.S. 584) and in *Eberheart v. Georgia* (433 U.S. 917) that the death penalty may not be imposed for the crime of raping an adult woman that does not result in death. The court stated:

> Rape is without doubt deserving of serious punishment; but in terms of moral depravity and of the injury to the person and to the public, it does not compare with murder, which does involve the unjustified taking of human life. Although it may be accompanied by another crime, rape by definition does not include the death of or even the serious injury to another person. The murderer kills; the rapist, if no more than that, does not. Life is over for the victim of the murderer; for the rape victim, life may not be nearly so happy as it was, but it is not over and normally is not beyond repair. We have the abiding conviction that the death penalty, which "is unique in its severity and irrevocability," is an excessive penalty for the rapist who, as such, does not take human life.

Chief Justice Warren Burger (1907–1995), joined by Justice William H. Rehnquist (1924–2005), dissented. The justices stated:

> A rapist not only violates a victim's privacy and personal integrity, but inevitably causes serious psychological as well as physical harm in the process.... Rape is not a mere physical attack—it is destructive of the human personality. The remainder of the victim's life may be gravely affected, and this in turn may have a serious detrimental effect upon her husband and any children she may have.... Victims may recover from the physical damage of knife or bullet wounds, or a beating with fists or a club, but recovery from such a gross assault on the human personality is not healed by medicine or surgery. To speak blandly, as the plurality does, of rape victims who are "unharmed," or to classify the human outrage of rape, as does Mr. Justice Powell, in terms of "excessively

brutal," versus "moderately brutal," takes too little account of the profound suffering the crime imposes upon the victims and their loved ones.

The court also held that kidnapping did not warrant the death penalty. Even though the victims usually suffered tremendously, they had not lost their lives. (If the kidnapped victim was killed, then the kidnapper could be tried for murder.)

Child Rape

The Supreme Court's rulings in *Coker v. Georgia* (433 U.S. 584) and *Eberheart v. Georgia* (433 U.S. 917) were interpreted to apply only to the rape of adult women. The constitutionality of applying the death penalty for child rape remained untested. In 2008 the issue was resolved when the court ruled in *Kennedy v. Louisiana* (554 U.S. ___) that a statute in Louisiana proscribing the death penalty for child rape violated the Eighth Amendment of the U.S. Constitution. The Eighth Amendment bars "cruel and unusual punishments."

In 2003 Patrick Kennedy was convicted of raping his eight-year-old stepdaughter in 1998. The girl was severely injured by the intercourse and required emergency surgery to stem excessive bleeding and repair severe internal injuries. At that time, Louisiana law allowed the death penalty for aggravated rape of a child under the age of 12 years. In 2007 the state's Supreme Court upheld the sentence, noting that four other states—Oklahoma, South Carolina, Montana, and Georgia—had similar laws and that "children are a class that need special protection." However, Louisiana's chief Supreme Court Justice Pascal Calogero (1931–) dissented with the ruling, arguing that the U.S. Supreme Court had "set out a bright-line and easily administered rule" that forbids capital punishment for crimes in which the victim survives.

In June 2008 the U.S. Supreme Court overturned the death sentence in a narrow 5–4 decision. Supreme Court Justice Anthony Kennedy (1936–) acknowledged the heinous nature of the crime, determining: "Petitioner's crime was one that cannot be recounted in these pages in a way sufficient to capture in full the hurt and horror inflicted on his victim or to convey the revulsion society, and the jury that represents it, sought to express by sentencing petitioner to death." Nevertheless, the majority of the justices held that there was no national consensus on the imposition of capital punishment for child rape. Only a handful of states had or were attempting to pass similar laws. In addition, Louisiana was the only state at the time with persons on death row for child rape. (Another man, Richard Davis, had been sentenced to die for raping a five-year-old girl in 2006.)

The court's decision was extremely controversial and received harsh criticism from Louisiana Governor Bobby Jindal (1971–) and then–presidential candidates Senator John McCain (1936–) and Senator Barack Obama (1961–). In October 2008 Louisiana asked the court to reconsider its ruling after it came to light that the military penal code also allowed the death penalty for child rape—a fact not mentioned or apparently considered by the court in its original deliberations over the existence of a "national consensus" on the issue. The court refused to reopen the case. It did issue a modified opinion (October 2008, http://www.scotusblog.com/wp/wp-content/uploads/2008/10/07-343.pdf), which stated, "We find that the military penalty does not affect our reasoning or conclusions."

An Unconstitutionally Vague Statute

During a heated dispute with his wife of 28 years, Robert Godfrey threatened her with a knife. Mrs. Godfrey, saying she was leaving her husband, went to stay with relatives. That same day she went to court to file for aggravated assault. Several days later she initiated divorce proceedings and moved in with her mother. During subsequent telephone conversations, the couple argued over the wife's determination to leave Godfrey permanently.

About two weeks later Godfrey killed his wife and mother-in-law. Godfrey told police that his wife phoned him, telling him she expected all the money from the planned sale of their home. She also told Godfrey she was never reconciling with him. Godfrey confessed that he went to his mother-in-law's nearby trailer and shot his wife through a window, killing her instantly. He then entered the trailer, struck his fleeing 11-year-old daughter on the head with the gun, and shot his mother-in-law in the head, killing her. Godfrey believed his mother-in-law was responsible for his wife's reluctance to reconcile with him.

Godfrey was convicted of killing his wife and mother-in-law and of the aggravated assault of his daughter. The Georgia Code permits the imposition of the death penalty in the case of a murder that "was outrageously or wantonly vile, horrible, or inhuman in that it involved torture, depravity of mind, or an aggravated brutality to the victim." Aware of this law, the jury sentenced Godfrey to die. He appealed, claiming that the statute was unconstitutionally vague. After the Georgia Supreme Court upheld the lower court decision, the case was appealed to the U.S. Supreme Court.

The Supreme Court, in *Godfrey v. Georgia* (446 U.S. 420, 1980), noted that the victims were killed instantly (i.e., there was no torture), the victims had been "causing [Godfrey] extreme emotional trauma," and he acknowledged his responsibility. The high court concluded that, in this case, the Georgia law was unconstitutionally vague. Moreover, the Georgia Supreme Court did not attempt to narrow the definition of "outrageously and wantonly vile." In a concurring opinion, Justice Thurgood Marshall (1908–1993), joined by Justice William J. Brennan (1906–1997), found this an example of the inherently arbitrary (subject to individual judgment) and capricious (unpredictable) nature of capital punishment, because even the prosecutor in Godfrey's case observed many times that there was no torture or abuse involved.

CRIMINAL INTENT

On April 1, 1975, Sampson Armstrong and Jeanette Armstrong, on the pretext of requesting water for their overheated car, tried to rob Thomas Kersey at home. Earl Enmund waited in the getaway car. Kersey called for his wife, who tried to shoot Jeanette Armstrong. The Armstrongs killed the Kerseys. Enmund was tried for aiding and abetting in the robbery-murder and sentenced to death.

In *Enmund v. Florida* (458 U.S. 782, 1982), the Supreme Court ruled 5–4 that, in this case, the death penalty violated the Eighth and Fourteenth Amendments to the U.S. Constitution. The majority noted that only 9 of the 36 states with capital punishment permitted its use on a criminal who was not actually present at the scene of the crime. The exception was the case where someone paid a hit man to murder the victim.

Furthermore, over the years juries had tended not to sentence to death criminals who had not actually been at the scene of the crime. Certainly, Enmund was guilty of planning and participating in a robbery, but murder had not been part of the plan. Statistically, because someone is killed in 1 out of 200 robberies, Enmund could not have expected that the Kerseys would be murdered during the robbery attempt. The court concluded that, because Enmund did not kill or plan to kill, he should be tried only for his participation in the robbery. The court observed:

> We have no doubt that robbery is a serious crime deserving serious punishment. It is not, however, a crime "so grievous an affront to humanity that the only adequate response may be the penalty of death" [from *Gregg v. Georgia*, 428 U.S. 153, 1976]. It does not compare with

murder, which does involve the unjustified taking of human life.... The murderer kills; the [robber], if no more than that, does not. Life is over for the victim of the murderer; for the [robbery] victim, life . . . is not over and normally is not beyond repair.

Writing for the minority, Justice Sandra Day O'Connor (1930–) concluded that intent is a complex issue. It should be left to the judge and jury trying the accused to decide intent, not a federal court far removed from the actual trial.

Enmund Revisited

However, just because a person had no intent to kill does not mean that he or she cannot be sentenced to death. In the early morning of September 22, 1978, Crawford Bullock and his friend Ricky Tucker had been drinking at a bar in Jackson, Mississippi, and were offered a ride home by Mark Dickson, an acquaintance.

During the drive an argument ensued over money that Dickson owed Tucker, and Dickson stopped the car. The argument escalated into a fistfight, and, outside the car, Bullock held Dickson while Tucker punched Dickson and hit him in the face with a whiskey bottle. When Dickson fell, Tucker smashed his head with a concrete block, killing him. Tucker and Bullock disposed of the body. The next day police spotted Bullock driving the victim's car. After his arrest Bullock confessed.

Under Mississippi law a person involved in a robbery that results in murder may be convicted of capital murder regardless of "the defendant's own lack of intent that any killing take place." The jury was never asked to consider whether Bullock in fact killed, attempted to kill, or intended to kill. He was convicted and sentenced to death as an accomplice to the crime. During the appeals process the Mississippi Supreme Court confirmed that Bullock was indeed a participant in the murder.

In January 1986 a divided U.S. Supreme Court modified the *Enmund* decision with a 5–4 ruling in *Cabana v. Bullock* (474 U.S. 376). The court indicated that even though *Enmund* had to be considered at some point during the judicial process, the initial jury trying the accused did not necessarily have to consider the *Enmund* ruling. The high court ruled that even though the jury had not been made aware of the issue of intent, the Mississippi Supreme Court had considered this question. Because *Enmund* did not require that intent be presented at the initial jury trial, only that it be considered at some time during the judicial process, the state of Mississippi had met that requirement.

The four dissenting justices claimed that it was difficult for any appeals court to determine intent from reading a typed transcript of a trial. Seeing the accused and others involved was important in helping determine who was telling the truth and who was not. This was why *Enmund* must be raised to the jury so it could consider the question of intent in light of what it had seen and heard directly.

"Reckless Indifference to the Value of Human Life"

Gary Tison was a convicted criminal who had been sentenced to life imprisonment for murdering a prison guard during an escape from the Arizona State Prison in Florence, Arizona. Tison's three sons, his wife, his brother, and other relatives planned a prison escape involving Tison and a fellow prisoner, Randy Greenawalt, also a convicted murderer.

On the day of the planned escape in July 1978, Tison's sons smuggled guns into the prison's visitation area. After locking up the guards and visitors, the five men fled in a car. They later transferred to another car and waited in an abandoned house for a plane to take them to Mexico. When the plane did not come, the men got back on the road. The car soon had flat tires. One son flagged down a passing car. The motorist who stopped to help was driving with his wife, their 2-year-old son, and a 15-year-old niece.

Gary Tison then told his sons to go get some water from the motorists' car, presumably to be left with the family they planned to abandon in the desert. While the sons were gone, Gary Tison and Randy Greenawalt shot and killed the family. Several days later two of Tison's sons and Greenawalt were captured. The third son was killed, and Tison escaped into the desert, where he later died of exposure.

The surviving Tisons and Greenawalt were found guilty and sentenced to death. The sons, citing *Enmund*, appealed, claiming that they had neither pulled the triggers nor intended the deaths of the family who had stopped to help them. In *Tison v. Arizona* (481 U.S. 137, 1987), the Supreme Court ruled 5–4 to uphold the death sentence, indicating that the Tison sons had shown a "reckless indifference to the value of human life [which] may be every bit as shocking to the moral sense as an 'intent to kill.'"

The Tisons may not have pulled the triggers (and the court fully accepted the premise that they did not do the shootings or directly intend them to happen), but they released and then assisted two convicted murderers. They should have realized that freeing two killers and giving them guns could very well put innocent people in great danger. Moreover, they continued to help the escapees even after the family was killed.

"These facts," concluded Justice O'Connor for the majority, "not only indicate that the Tison brothers' participation in the crime was anything but minor; they also would clearly support a finding that they both subjectively appreciated that their acts were likely to result in the taking of innocent life." Unlike the situation in the *Enmund* case, they were not sitting in a car far from the murder scene. They were direct participants in the whole event. The death sentence would stand.

Writing for the minority, Justice Brennan observed that had a prison guard been murdered (Gary Tison had murdered a prison guard in a previous escape attempt), then the court's argument would have made sense. The murder of the family, however, made no sense and was not even necessary for the escape. The Tison sons were away from the murder scene getting water for the victims and could have done nothing to save them. Even though they were guilty of planning and carrying out an escape, the murder of the family who stopped to help them was an unexpected outcome of the escape.

Furthermore, the father had promised his sons that he would not kill during the escape, a promise he had kept despite several opportunities to kill during the actual prison escape. Therefore, it was not unreasonable for the sons to believe that their father would not kill in a situation that did not appear to warrant it. Justice Brennan concluded that "like Enmund, the Tisons neither killed nor attempted or intended to kill anyone. Like Enmund, the Tisons have been sentenced to death for the intentional acts of others which the Tisons did not expect, which were not essential to the felony, and over which they had no control."

In 1992 the Arizona Supreme Court overturned the death penalty sentences for the Tison sons. They were subsequently sentenced to life in prison.

RIGHT TO EFFECTIVE COUNSEL

In 1989 Kevin Eugene Wiggins received a death sentence for the 1988 drowning of an elderly Maryland woman in her home. The Maryland Court of Appeals affirmed his sentence in 1991. With the help of new counsel, Wiggins sought postconviction relief, challenging the quality of his initial lawyers. Wiggins claimed his lawyers failed to investigate and present mitigating evidence (evidence that may lessen responsibility for a crime) of his horrendous physical and sexual abuse as a child. The sentencing jury never heard that he was starved, that his mother punished him by burning his hand on the stove, and that after the state put him in foster care at age six, he suffered more physical and sexual abuse.

In 2001 a federal district court concluded that Wiggins's first lawyers should have conducted a more thorough investigation into his childhood abuse, which would have kept the jury from imposing a death sentence. However, the U.S. Court of Appeals for the Fourth Circuit reversed the district court decision, ruling that the original attorneys had made a "reasonable strategic decision" to concentrate their defense on raising doubts about Wiggins's guilt instead.

On June 26, 2003, the U.S. Supreme Court threw out the death sentence. In *Wiggins v. Smith* (No. 02-311), the court ruled 7–2 that Wiggins's lawyers violated his Sixth Amendment right to effective assistance of counsel. The court noted, "Counsel's investigation into Wiggins' background did not reflect reasonable professional judgment....Given the nature and extent of the abuse, there is a reasonable probability that a competent attorney, aware of this history, would have introduced it at sentencing, and that a jury confronted with such mitigating evidence would have returned with a different sentence."

When Does the Right to Counsel End?

Joseph Giarratano was a Virginia death row prisoner. He received full counsel for his trial and for his initial appeal. Afterward, Virginia would no longer provide him with his own lawyer. He went to court, complaining that because he was poor the state of Virginia should provide him with counsel to help prepare postconviction appeals. Virginia permitted the condemned prisoner the right to use the prison libraries to prepare an appeal, but it did not provide the condemned with his own personal attorney.

Virginia had unit attorneys, who were assigned to help prisoners with prison-related legal matters. A unit attorney could give guidance to death row inmates but could not act as the personal attorney for any one particular inmate. This case became a class action in which the federal district court certified a class made up of "all current and future Virginia inmates awaiting execution who do not have and cannot afford counsel to pursue postconviction proceedings."

The federal district court and the federal court of appeals agreed with Giarratano, but the Supreme Court, in *Murray v. Giarratano* (492 U.S. 1, 1989), disagreed. Writing for the majority, Chief Justice Rehnquist concluded that even though the Sixth and Fourteenth Amendments to the Constitution ensure an impoverished defendant the right to counsel at the trial stage of a criminal proceeding, they do not provide for counsel for postconviction proceedings, as the court ruled in *Pennsylvania v. Finley* (481 U.S. 551, 1987). Because *Finley* had not specifically considered prisoners on death row, but all prisoners in general, the majority did not believe the decision needed to be reconsidered just because death row prisoners had more at stake.

Chief Justice Rehnquist agreed that those facing the death penalty have a right to counsel for the trial and during the initial appeal. During these periods the defendant needs a heightened measure of protection because the death penalty is involved. Later appeals, however, involve more procedural matters that "serve a different and more limited purpose than either the trial or appeal."

In dissent, Justice John Paul Stevens (1920–), who was joined by Justices Brennan, Marshall, and Harry A. Blackmun (1908–1999), indicated that he thought condemned prisoners in Virginia faced three critical differences from those considered in *Finley*. First, the Virginia prisoners had been sentenced to death, which made their condition different from a sentence of life imprisonment. Second, Virginia's particular judicial decision forbids certain issues to be raised during the direct review or appeal process and forces them to be considered only during later postconviction appeals. This means that important issues may be considered without the benefit of counsel. Finally, "unlike the ordinary inmate, who presumably has ample time to use and reuse the prison library and to seek guidance from other prisoners experienced in preparing... petitions... a grim deadline imposes a finite limit on the condemned person's capacity for useful research."

He continued, quoting from the district court's decision on the matter, an "inmate preparing himself and his family for impending death is incapable of performing the mental functions necessary to adequately pursue his claims."

Federal Judges Can Delay Executions to Allow Habeus Corpus Reviews

In 1988 Congress passed the Anti-Drug Abuse Act, which guaranteed qualified legal representation for poor death row defendants wanting to file for habeas corpus (a prisoner's petition to be heard in federal court) so that the counsel could assist in the preparation of the appeal. In 1994 this law was brought to question before the Supreme Court by the death row inmate Frank McFarland.

In November 1989 a Texas jury found McFarland guilty of stabbing to death a woman he had met in a bar. The state appellate court upheld his conviction, and two lower federal courts refused his request for a stay (postponement) of execution. The federal courts ruled that they did not have jurisdiction to stop the execution until McFarland filed a habeas corpus. The inmate argued that without the stay, he would be executed before he could obtain a lawyer to prepare the petition.

The Supreme Court granted a stay of execution. In *McFarland v. Scott* (512 U.S. 849, 1994), the court ruled 5–4 to uphold the 1988 federal law. Once a defendant requested counsel, the federal court could postpone execution so the lawyer would have time to prepare an appeal. Justice Blackmun stated that "by providing indigent [poor] capital defendants with a mandatory right to qualified legal counsel in these proceedings, Congress has recognized that Federal habeas corpus has a particularly important role to play in promoting fundamental fairness in the imposition of the death penalty."

Does the Right to Counsel Extend to Crimes That Have Not Been Charged?

In 1994 Raymond Levi Cobb confessed to burglarizing the home of Lindsey Owings the previous year. He claimed no knowledge, however, of the disappearances of Owings's wife and infant at the time of the burglary. The court subsequently assigned Cobb a lawyer to represent him in the burglary offense. With the permission of Cobb's lawyer, investigators twice questioned Cobb regarding the disappearance of the Owings family. Both times Cobb denied any knowledge of the missing pair.

In 1995, while free on bond for the burglary and living with his father, Cobb told his father that he killed Margaret Owing and buried her baby, while still alive, with her. The father reported his son's confession to the police. When brought in, Cobb confessed to the police and waived his Miranda rights, which include the right to counsel. Cobb was convicted of the murders and sentenced to death. On appeal, Cobb claimed that his confession, obtained in violation of his Sixth Amendment right to counsel, should have been suppressed. He argued that his right to counsel attached (went into full effect) when he was reported for the burglary case, and despite his open confession to the police, he never officially gave up this right to counsel.

The Texas Court of Criminal Appeals reversed Cobb's conviction, ordering a new trial. The court considered Cobb's confession to the murders inadmissible, holding that "once the right to counsel attaches to the offense charged [burglary], it also attaches to any other offense [in this case, murder] that is very closely related factually to the offense charged."

The state appealed to the U.S. Supreme Court. In *Texas v. Cobb* (532 U.S. 162, 2001), the court, in a 5–4 decision, stated, "The Sixth Amendment right [to counsel] is... offense specific. It cannot be invoked once for all future prosecutions, for it does not attach until a prosecution is commenced, that is, at or after the initiation of adversary judicial criminal proceedings—whether by way of formal charge, preliminary hearing, indictment, information, or arraignment" (citing *McNeil v. Wisconsin*, 501 U.S. 171, 1991).

This means that Cobb's right to counsel did not extend to crimes with which he had not been charged. Because this right did not prohibit investigators from questioning him about the murders without first notifying his lawyer, Cobb's confession was admissible.

CASES INVOLVING ERROR BY THE PROSECUTION

Coerced Confessions

Oreste C. Fulminante called the Mesa, Arizona, police to report the disappearance of his 11-year-old stepdaughter, Jeneane Michelle Hunt. Fulminante was caring for the child while his wife, Jeneane's mother, was in the hospital. Several days later Jeneane's body was found in the desert east of Mesa with two shots to the head, fired at close range by a large-caliber weapon. There was a ligature (a cord used in tying or binding) around her neck. Because of the decomposed state of her body, it was not possible to determine whether she had been sexually assaulted.

Fulminante's statements about the child's disappearance and his relationship to her included inconsistencies that made him a suspect in her death. He was not, however, charged with the murder. Fulminante left Arizona for

New Jersey, where he was eventually convicted on federal charges of unlawful possession of a firearm by a felon.

Even though incarcerated, he became friendly with Anthony Sarivola, a former police officer. Sarivola had been involved in loan-sharking for organized crime but then became a paid informant for the Federal Bureau of Investigation (FBI). In prison he masqueraded as an organized crime figure. When Fulminante was getting some tough treatment from the other inmates, Sarivola offered him protection, but only on the condition that Fulminante tell him everything.

Fulminante was later indicted in Arizona for the first-degree murder of Jeneane. In a hearing before the trial, Fulminante moved to suppress the statement he had made to Sarivola in prison and then later to Sarivola's wife, Donna, following his release from prison. He maintained that the confession to Sarivola was coerced and that the second confession was the "fruit" of the first one.

The trial court denied the motion to remove the statements from the record, finding that, based on the specified facts, the confessions were voluntary. Fulminante was convicted of Jeneane's murder and subsequently sentenced to death.

In his appeal Fulminante argued, among other things, that his confession to Sarivola was coerced and that its use at the trial violated his rights of due process under the Fifth and Fourteenth Amendments to the Constitution. The Arizona Supreme Court ruled that the confession was coerced but initially determined that the admission of the confession at the trial was a harmless error because of the overpowering evidence against Fulminante. In legal terms, harmless error refers to an error committed during the trial that has no bearing on the outcome of the trial, and as such, is not harmful enough to reverse the outcome of the trial on appeal.

After Fulminante motioned for reconsideration, however, the Arizona Supreme Court ruled that the U.S. Supreme Court had set a precedent that prevented the use of harmless error in the case of a coerced confession. The harmless-error standard, as stated in *Chapman v. California* (386 U.S. 18, 1967), held that an error is harmless if it appears "beyond a reasonable doubt that the error complained of did not contribute to the verdict obtained." The Arizona Supreme Court reversed the conviction and ordered that Fulminante be retried without the use of his confession to Sarivola. Because of differences in the state and federal courts over the admission of a coerced confession with regard to harmless-error analysis, the U.S. Supreme Court agreed to hear the case.

In *Arizona v. Fulminante* (499 U.S. 279, 1991), Justice Byron R. White (1917–2002), writing for the majority, stated that even though the question was a close one, the Arizona Supreme Court was right in concluding that Fulminante's confession had been coerced. He further noted,

"The Arizona Supreme Court found a credible threat of physical violence unless Fulminante confessed. Our cases have made clear that a finding of coercion need not depend upon actual violence by a government agent; a credible threat is sufficient. As we have said, 'coercion can be mental as well as physical, and…the blood of the accused is not the only hallmark of an unconstitutional inquisition.'"

Justice White further argued that the state of Arizona had failed to meet its burden of establishing, beyond a reasonable doubt, that the admission of Fulminante's confession to Sarivola was harmless. He added, "A confession is like no other evidence. Indeed, 'the defendant's own confession is probably the most probative [providing evidence] that can be admitted against him.… The admissions of a defendant come from the actor himself, the most knowledgeable and unimpeachable source of information about his past conduct. Certainly, confessions have profound impact on the jury, so much so that we may justifiably doubt its ability to put them out of mind even if told to do so'" (from *Bruton v. United States*, 391 U.S. 123, 1968).

Presumption of Malice

Dale Robert Yates and Henry Davis planned to rob a country store in Greenville County, South Carolina, in February 1981. When they entered the store, only the owner, Willie Wood, was present. Yates and Davis showed their weapons and ordered Wood to give them money from the cash register. Davis handed Yates $3,000 and ordered Wood to lie across the counter. Wood, who had a pistol beneath his jacket, refused.

Meanwhile, Yates was backing out of the store with his gun pointed at the owner. After being told to do so by Davis, Yates fired two shots. The first bullet wounded Wood; the second missed. Yates then jumped into the car and waited for Davis. When Davis did not appear, Yates drove off. Inside the store, although wounded, Wood pursued Davis. As the two struggled, Wood's mother, Helen, came in and ran to help her son. During the struggle Helen Wood was stabbed once in the chest and died at the scene. Wood then shot Davis five times, killing him.

After Yates was arrested and charged with murder, his primary defense was that Helen Wood's death was not the probable natural consequence of the robbery he had planned with Davis. He claimed that he had brought the weapon only to induce the owner to give him the cash and that neither he nor Davis intended to kill anyone during the robbery.

The prosecutor's case for murder hinged on the agreement between Yates and Davis to commit an armed robbery. He argued that they planned to kill any witness, thereby making homicide a probable or natural result of the robbery. The prosecutor concluded, "It makes no difference who actually struck the fatal blow, the hand of one is the hand of all."

The judge told the jury that under South Carolina law, murder is defined as "the unlawful killing of any human being with malice aforethought either express or implied." In his instructions to the jury, the judge said, "Malice is implied or presumed by the law from the willful, deliberate, and intentional doing of an unlawful act without any just cause or excuse. In its general signification, malice means the doing of a wrongful act, intentionally, without justification or excuse.... I tell you, also, that malice is implied or presumed from the use of a deadly weapon."

The judge continued to instruct the jury on the theory of accomplice liability. The jury returned guilty verdicts on the murder charge and on all other counts in the indictment. Yates was sentenced to death.

Yates petitioned the South Carolina Supreme Court, asserting that the jury charge that "malice is implied or presumed from the use of a deadly weapon" was an unconstitutional burden-shifting instruction. The case was twice reviewed by the South Carolina Supreme Court, which agreed that the jury instructions were unconstitutional, but that allowing the jury to presume malice was a harmless error, one that had no bearing on the outcome of the trial. The South Carolina court found that the jury did not have to rely on presumptions of malice because Davis's "lunging" at Helen Wood and stabbing her were acts of malice.

The U.S. Supreme Court, in *Yates v. Evatt* (500 U.S. 391, 1991), reversed the decisions of the South Carolina Supreme Court and remanded the case (sent it back to the lower court for further proceedings). Justice David H. Souter (1939–), writing for the high court, ruled that the state supreme court failed to apply the proper harmless-error standard as stated in *Chapman*. "The issue under *Chapman* is whether the jury actually rested its verdict on evidence establishing the presumed fact beyond a reasonable doubt, independently of the presumption."

Justice Souter concluded by stating that there was clear evidence of Davis's attempt to kill Wood because he could have left the store with Yates but stayed to pursue Wood with a deadly weapon. The evidence that Davis intended to kill Helen Wood was not as clear. The record also showed that Yates heard a woman scream as he left the store but did not attempt to return and kill her.

The jury could have interpreted Yates's behavior to confirm his claim that he and Davis had not originally intended to kill anyone. Even the prosecutor, in summation, conceded that Helen Wood could have been killed inadvertently by Davis.

APPEALS BASED ON NEW EVIDENCE
Newly Discovered Evidence Does Not Stop Execution

On an evening in late September 1981, the body of Texas Department of Public Safety Officer David Rucker was found lying beside his patrol car. He had been shot in the head. At about the same time, Officer Enrique Carri-salez saw a vehicle speeding away from the area where Rucker's body had been found. Carrisalez and his partner chased the vehicle and pulled it over. Carrisalez walked to the car. The driver opened his door and exchanged a few words with the police officer before firing at least one shot into Carrisalez's chest. The officer died nine days later.

Leonel Torres Herrera was arrested a few days after the shootings and charged with capital murder. In January 1982 he was tried and found guilty of murdering Carri-salez. In July 1982 he pleaded guilty to Rucker's murder.

At the trial Officer Carrisalez's partner identified Herrera as the person who fired the gun. He also testified that there was only one person in the car. In a statement by Carrisalez before he died, he also identified Herrera. The speeding car belonged to Herrera's girlfriend, and Herrera had the car keys in his pocket when he was arrested. Splatters of blood on the car and on Herrera's clothes were the same type as Rucker's. Strands of hair found in the car also belonged to Rucker. Finally, a handwritten letter, which strongly implied that he had killed Rucker, was found on Herrera when he was arrested.

In 1992, 10 years after the initial trial, Herrera appealed to the federal courts, alleging that he was innocent of the murders of Rucker and Carrisalez and that his execution would violate the Eighth and Fourteenth Amendments. He presented affidavits (sworn statements) claiming that he had not killed the officers but that his now dead brother had. The brother's attorney, one of Herrera's cellmates, and a school friend all swore that the brother had killed the police officers. The dead brother's son also said that he had witnessed his father killing the police officers.

In *Herrera v. Collins* (506 U.S. 390, 1993), the U.S. Supreme Court ruled 6–3 that executing Herrera would not violate the Eighth and Fourteenth Amendments. The high court said that the trial—not the appeals process—judges a defendant's innocence or guilt. Appeals courts determine only the fairness of the proceedings.

Writing for the majority, Chief Justice Rehnquist stated:

> A person when first charged with a crime is entitled to a presumption of innocence, and may insist that his guilt be established beyond a reasonable doubt.... Once a defendant has been afforded a fair trial and convicted of the offense for which he was charged, the presumption of innocence disappears.... Here, it is not disputed that the State met its burden of proving at trial that petitioner was guilty of the capital murder of Officer Carrisalez beyond a reasonable doubt. Thus, in the eyes of the law, petitioner does not come before the Court as one who is "innocent," but on the contrary as one who has been convicted by due process of two brutal murders.

Based on affidavits here filed, petitioner claims that evidence never presented to the trial court proves him innocent....

Claims of actual innocence based on newly discovered evidence have never been held to state a ground for [court] relief absent an independent constitutional violation occurring in the course of the underlying state criminal proceedings....

This rule is grounded in the principle that [appeals] courts sit to ensure that individuals are not imprisoned in violation of the Constitution—not to correct errors of fact.

Rehnquist continued that states all allow the introduction of new evidence. Texas was 1 of 17 states that require a new trial motion based on new evidence within 60 days. Herrera's appeal came 10 years later. The chief justice, however, emphasized that Herrera still had options, saying, "For under Texas law, petitioner may file a request for executive clemency.... Executive clemency has provided the "fail safe" in our criminal justice system.... It is an unalterable fact that our judicial system, like the human beings who administer it, is fallible. But history is replete with examples of wrongfully convicted persons who have been pardoned in the wake of after-discovered evidence establishing their innocence."

The majority opinion found the information presented in the affidavits inconsistent with the other evidence. The justices questioned why the affidavits were produced at the very last minute. The justices also wondered why Herrera had pleaded guilty to Rucker's murder if he had been innocent. They did note that some of the information in the affidavits might have been important to the jury, "but coming 10 years after petitioner's trial, this showing of innocence falls far short of that which would have to be made in order to trigger the sort of constitutional claim [to decide for a retrial]."

Speaking for the minority, Justice Blackmun wrote:

We really are being asked to decide whether the Constitution forbids the execution of a person who has been validly convicted and sentenced but who, nonetheless, can prove his innocence with newly discovered evidence. Despite the State of Texas' astonishing protestation to the contrary.... I do not see how the answer can be anything but "yes."

The Eighth Amendment prohibits "cruel and unusual punishments." This proscription is not static but rather reflects evolving standards of decency. I think it is crystal clear that the execution of an innocent person is "at odds with contemporary standards of fairness and decency."... The protection of the Eighth Amendment does not end once a defendant has been validly convicted and sentenced.

Claim of Miscarriage of Justice

Lloyd Schlup, a Missouri prisoner, was convicted of participating in the murder of a fellow inmate in 1984 and sentenced to death. He had filed one petition for habeas corpus, arguing that he had inadequate counsel. He claimed

the counsel did not call fellow inmates and other witnesses to testify that could prove his innocence. He filed a second petition, alleging that constitutional error at his trial deprived the jury of crucial evidence that would again have established his innocence.

Using a previous U.S. Supreme Court ruling (*Sawyer v. Whitley*, 505 U.S. 333, 1992), the district court claimed that Schlup had not shown "by clear and convincing evidence that but for a constitutional error no reasonable jury would have found him guilty." Schlup's lawyers argued that the district court should have used another ruling (*Murray v. Carrier*, 477 U.S. 478, 1986), in which a petitioner need only to show that "a constitutional violation has probably resulted in the conviction of one who is actually innocent." The appellate court affirmed the district court's ruling, noting that Schlup's guilt, which had been proven at the trial, barred any consideration of his constitutional claim.

The U.S. Supreme Court, on appeal, reviewed the case to determine whether the *Sawyer* standard provides enough protection from a miscarriage of justice that would result from the execution of an innocent person. In *Schlup v. Delo* (513 U.S. 298, 1995), the court observed, "If a petitioner such as Schlup presents evidence of innocence so strong that a court cannot have confidence in the outcome of the trial... the petitioner should be allowed to... argue the merits of his underlying claims."

The justices concluded that the less stringent *Carrier* standard, as opposed to the rigid *Sawyer* standard, focuses the investigation on the actual innocence, allowing the court to review relevant evidence that might have been excluded or unavailable during the trial.

Schlup v. Delo Revisited in *House v. Bell*

In 2006 the Supreme Court heard a case involving the Tennessee prisoner Paul House, who had been convicted in 1985 of murdering Carolyn Muncey. The prosecution alleged that House, a paroled sex offender, murdered Muncey during an attempted rape. He was convicted based on circumstantial evidence and forensics tests that showed semen stains on Muncey's clothing were of House's blood type. More incriminating were small blood stains found on House's blue jeans that matched Muncey's blood type.

In 1996 House's lawyers filed a habeas corpus petition in U.S. District Court and presented new evidence, including deoxyribonucleic acid tests showing the semen on Muncey's clothing was from her husband, not House. Several witnesses testified that Hubert Muncey Jr. had since confessed while drunk to committing the murder and had a history of beating his wife. In addition, the original blood evidence came into question, due to allegations of the mishandling of blood collected during the autopsy. The defense attorneys argued that some of the autopsy blood spilled on House's pants before they were tested at the FBI laboratory in Washington, D.C. The state admitted that the autopsy blood was improperly sealed and transported and spilled, but argued that the spill occurred after the pants were tested. The district court ruled that the new evidence did not demonstrate actual innocence as required under *Schlup v. Delo* and failed to show that House was ineligible for the death penalty under *Sawyer v. Whitley*. The ruling was eventually upheld on appeal.

In *House v. Bell* (No. 04-8990, 2006), the U.S. Supreme Court ruled 5–3 that House's habeas petition should proceed, because the new evidence constituted a "stringent showing" under *Schlup v. Delo*. The court concluded:

> This is not a case of conclusive exoneration. Some aspects of the State's evidence—Lora Muncey's memory of a deep voice, House's bizarre evening walk, his lie to law enforcement, his appearance near the body, and the blood on his pants—still support an inference of guilt. Yet the central forensic proof connecting House to the crime—the blood and the semen—has been called into question, and House has put forward substantial evidence pointing to a different suspect. Accordingly, and although the issue is close, we conclude that this is the rare case where—had the jury heard all the conflicting testimony—it is more likely than not that no reasonable juror viewing the record as a whole would lack reasonable doubt.

Supporters of House's innocence, including members of the state legislature, petitioned the governor for a pardon. Eventually, in 2008, the U.S. Supreme Court determined that the jury that convicted House did not hear testimony at the time that could have cleared him of the murder. In spring 2009 prosecutors dropped their charges against House, who had contracted multiple sclerosis and was confined to a wheelchair. Shortly thereafter he was released from prison and moved in with his mother.

Suppressed Evidence Means a New Trial

Curtis Lee Kyles was convicted by a Louisiana jury of the first-degree murder of a woman in a grocery store parking lot in 1984. He was sentenced to death. It was revealed on review that the prosecutor had never disclosed certain evidence favorable to the defendant. Among the evidence were conflicting statements by an informant who, the defense believed, wanted to get rid of Kyles to get his girlfriend. The state supreme court, the federal district court, and the Fifth Circuit Court denied Kyles's appeals. The U.S. Supreme Court, in *Kyles v. Whitley* (514 U.S. 419, 1995), reversed the lower courts' decisions. The high court ruled, "Favorable evidence is material, and constitutional error results from its suppression by the government, if there is a 'reasonable probability' that, had the evidence been disclosed to the defense, the result of the proceeding would have been different. . . . [The] net effect of the state-suppressed evidence favoring Kyles raises a reasonable probability that its disclosure would have produced a different result at trial."

The conviction was overturned. Four mistrials followed. On February 18, 1998, after his fifth and final trial ended with a hung jury, Kyles was released from prison. He had spent 14 years on death row.

CHALLENGING THE ANTITERRORISM AND EFFECTIVE DEATH PENALTY ACT OF 1996

The Antiterrorism and Effective Death Penalty Act (AEDPA) became law in April 1996, shortly after the first anniversary of the Oklahoma City bombing. The AEDPA aims in part to "provide for an effective death penalty." After passage of the law the lower courts differed in their interpretations of certain core provisions. For the first time, on April 18, 2000, the U.S. Supreme Court addressed these problems.

Federal Habeas Corpus Relief and the AEDPA

The AEDPA restricts the power of federal courts to grant habeas corpus relief to state inmates who have exhausted their state appeals. Through the writ of habeas corpus, an inmate could have a court review his or her conviction or sentencing. The AEDPA bars a federal court from granting an application for a writ of habeas corpus unless the state court's decision "was contrary to, or involved an unreasonable application of, clearly established federal law, as determined by the Supreme Court of the United States." The idea was to curtail the amount of habeas reviews filed by convicts and thus save the overbooked federal courts time and money.

In 1986 Terry Williams, while incarcerated in a Danville, Virginia, city jail, wrote to police that he had killed two people and that he was sorry for his acts. He also confessed to stealing money from one of the victims. He was subsequently convicted of robbery and capital murder.

During the sentencing hearing the prosecutor presented many crimes Williams had committed besides the murders for which he was convicted. Two state witnesses also testified to the defendant's future dangerousness.

Williams's lawyer, however, called on his mother to testify to his being a nonviolent person. The defense also played a taped portion of a psychiatrist's statement, who said that Williams admitted to him that he had removed bullets from a gun used during robbery so as not to harm anyone. During his closing statement, however, the lawyer noted that the jury would probably find it hard to give his client mercy because he did not show mercy to his victims. The jury sentenced Williams to death, and the trial judge imposed the sentence.

In 1988 Williams filed a state habeas corpus petition. The Danville Circuit Court found Williams's conviction valid. The court found, however, that the defense lawyer's failure to present several mitigating factors at the sentencing phase violated Williams's right to effective assistance of counsel as prescribed by *Strickland v. Washington* (466

U.S. 668, 1984). The mitigating circumstances included early childhood abuse and borderline mental retardation. The habeas corpus hearing further revealed that the state expert witnesses had testified that if Williams were kept in a "structured environment," he would not be a threat to society. The circuit court recommended a new sentencing hearing.

In 1997 the Virginia Supreme Court rejected the district court's recommendation for a new sentencing hearing, concluding that the omitted evidence would not have affected the sentence. In making their ruling, the state supreme court relied on what it considered to be an established U.S. Supreme Court precedent.

Next, Williams filed a federal habeas corpus petition. The federal trial judge ruled not only that the death sentence was "constitutionally infirm" but also that defense counsel was ineffective. However, the Fourth Circuit Court of Appeals reversed the federal trial judge's decision, holding that the AEDPA prohibits a federal court from granting habeas corpus relief unless the state court's decision "was contrary to, or involved an unreasonable application of, clearly established federal law, as determined by the Supreme Court of the United States."

On April 18, 2000, the U.S. Supreme Court, in *Williams v. Taylor* (529 U.S. 362, 2000), reversed the Fourth Circuit Court's ruling by a 6–3 decision. The court concluded that the Virginia Supreme Court's decision rejecting Williams's claim of ineffective assistance was contrary to a Supreme Court–established precedent (*Strickland v. Washington*), as well as an unreasonable application of that precedent. This was the first time the Supreme Court had granted relief on such a claim.

On November 14, 2000, during a court hearing, Williams accepted a plea agreement of a life sentence without parole after prosecutors agreed not to seek the death penalty.

Federal Evidentiary Hearings for Constitutional Claims

Under an AEDPA provision, if the petitioner has failed to develop the facts of his or her challenges of a constitutional claim in state court proceedings, the federal court shall not hold a hearing on the claim unless the facts involve an exception listed by the AEDPA.

In 1993, after robbing the home of Morris Keller Jr. and his wife, Mary Elizabeth, Michael Wayne Williams and his friend Jeffrey Alan Cruse raped the woman and then killed the couple. In exchange for the state's promise not to seek capital punishment, Cruse described details of the crimes. Williams received the death sentence for the capital murders. The prosecution told the jury about the plea agreement with Cruse. The state later revoked the plea agreement after discovering that Cruse had also raped the wife and failed to disclose it. After Cruse's court testimony against Williams, however, the state gave Cruse a life sentence, which Williams alleged amounted to a second, informal plea agreement.

Williams filed a habeas petition in state court, claiming he was not told of the second plea agreement between the state and his codefendant. The Virginia Supreme Court dismissed the petition (1994), and the U.S. Supreme Court refused to review the case (1995).

In 1996, on appeal, a federal district court agreed to an evidentiary hearing of Williams's claims of the undisclosed second plea agreement. The defendant had also claimed that a psychiatric report about Cruse, which was not revealed by the prosecution, could have shown that Cruse was not credible. Moreover, a certain juror might have had possible bias, which the prosecution failed to disclose. Before the hearing could be held, the state concluded that the AEDPA prohibited such a hearing. Consequently, the federal district court dismissed Williams's petition.

When the case was brought before the U.S. Court of Appeals for the Fourth Circuit, the court, interpreting the AEDPA, concluded that the defendant had failed to develop the facts of his claims. On April 18, 2000, in *Williams v. Taylor* (529 U.S. 420), a unanimous U.S. Supreme Court did not address Williams's claim of the undisclosed plea agreement between Cruse and the state. Instead, the high court held that the defendant was entitled to a federal district court evidentiary hearing regarding his other claims. According to the court, "Under the [AEDPA], a failure to develop the factual basis of a claim is not established unless there is lack of diligence, or some greater fault, attributable to the prisoner or the prisoner's counsel. . . . We conclude petitioner has met the burden of showing he was diligent in efforts to develop the facts supporting his juror bias and prosecutorial misconduct claims in collateral proceedings before the Virginia Supreme Court."

High Court Upholds Restriction on Federal Appeals

Even though the Supreme Court ruled in favor of new resentencing hearings for Terry Williams and Michael Williams, it stressed that the AEDPA places a new restriction on federal courts with respect to granting habeas relief to state inmates. The court noted in *Williams v. Taylor* (529 U.S. 362) that under the AEDPA:

> The writ may issue only if one of the following two conditions is satisfied—the state-court adjudication resulted in a decision that (1) "was contrary to . . . clearly established Federal law, as determined by the Supreme Court of the United States," or (2) "involved an unreasonable application of . . . clearly established Federal law, as determined by the Supreme Court of the United States." Under the "contrary to" clause, a federal habeas court may grant the writ if the state court arrives at a conclusion opposite to that reached by this court on a question of law or if the state court decides a case differently than this court has on a set of materially indistinguishable facts. Under the "unreasonable application"

clause, a federal habeas court may grant the writ if the state court identifies the correct governing legal principle from this court's decisions but unreasonably applies that principle to the facts of the prisoner's case.

METHODS OF EXECUTION

The Role of the U.S. Food and Drug Administration

The injection of a deadly combination of drugs has become the method of execution in most states permitting capital punishment. Condemned prisoners from Texas and Oklahoma, two of the first states to introduce this method, brought suit claiming that even though the drugs used had been approved by the U.S. Food and Drug Administration (FDA) for medical purposes, they had never been approved for use in nor tested for human executions.

The FDA commissioner refused to act, claiming serious questions whether the agency had jurisdiction in the area. The U.S. District Court for the District of Columbia disagreed with the condemned prisoners that the FDA had a responsibility to determine if the lethal mixture used during execution was safe and effective. The court noted that decisions by a federal agency not to take action were not reviewable in court.

A divided Court of Appeals for the District of Columbia reversed the lower court ruling. A generally irritated U.S. Supreme Court agreed to hear the case "to review the implausible result that the FDA is required to exercise its enforcement power to ensure that States only use drugs that are 'safe and effective' for human execution."

In *Heckler v. Chaney* (470 U.S. 821, 1985), the unanimous court agreed that, in this case, the FDA did not have jurisdiction.

Is Execution by Hanging Constitutional?

Washington state law imposes capital punishment either by "hanging by the neck" or, if the condemned chooses, by lethal injection. Charles Rodham Campbell was convicted of three counts of murder in 1982 and sentenced to death. Campbell, in challenging the constitutionality of hanging under the Washington statute, claimed that execution by hanging violated his Eighth Amendment right because it was a cruel and unusual punishment. Furthermore, the direction that he be hanged unless he chose lethal injection was a cruel and unusual punishment. He claimed that such instruction further violated his First Amendment right by forcing him to participate in his own execution to avoid hanging.

In *Campbell v. Wood* (18 F.3d. 662, 9th Cir. 1994), the U.S. Court of Appeals for the Ninth Circuit noted, "We do not consider hanging to be cruel and unusual simply because it causes death, or because there may be some pain associated with death.... As used in the Constitution, 'cruel' implies 'something inhuman and barbarous, something more than the mere extinguishment of life.' . . . Camp-

bell is entitled to an execution free only of 'the unnecessary and wanton infliction of pain.'"

According to the court, just because the defendant was given a choice of a method of execution did not mean that he was being subjected to a cruel and unusual punishment: "We believe that benefits to prisoners who may choose to exercise the option and who may feel relieved that they can elect lethal injection outweigh the emotional costs to those who find the mere existence of an option objectionable."

Campbell argued that the state was infringing on his First Amendment right of free exercise of his religion. He claimed that it was against his religion to participate in his own execution by being allowed to elect lethal injection over hanging.

The court contended that Campbell did not have to choose an execution method or participate in his own execution. "He may remain absolutely silent and refuse to participate in any election." The death penalty statute does not require him to choose the method of execution; it simply offers a choice. On appeal (*Campbell v. Wood*, 511 U.S. 1119, 1994), the U.S. Supreme Court decided not to hear the case. In 1994 Campbell was executed by hanging. He refused to cooperate during the execution and had to be pepper sprayed and strapped to a board to carry out the hanging.

Is Execution by Lethal Gas Constitutional?

On April 17, 1992, three California death row inmates—David Fierro, Alejandro Gilbert Ruiz, and Robert Alton Harris—filed a suit on behalf of themselves and all others under sentence of execution by lethal gas. In *Fierro v. Gomez* (790 F. Supp. 966 [N.D. Cal. 1992]), the inmates alleged that California's method of execution by lethal gas violated the Eighth and Fourteenth Amendments. Harris was scheduled to be executed four days later, on April 21, 1992—an execution that was carried out.

The district court prohibited James Gomez, the director of the California Department of Corrections, and Arthur Calderon, the warden of San Quentin Prison, from executing any inmate until a hearing was held. On appeal from Gomez and Calderon, the U.S. Court of Appeals for the Ninth Circuit vacated (annulled) the district court's ruling. On his execution day Harris had filed a habeas corpus petition with the California Supreme Court, challenging the constitutionality of the gas chamber. The court declined to review the case, and Harris was put to death that day. In the aftermath of Harris's execution, the California legislature amended in 1993 its death penalty statute, providing that, if lethal gas "is held invalid, the punishment of death shall be imposed by the alternative means," lethal injection.

In October 1994 a federal district judge, Marilyn Hall Patel (1938–), ruled that execution by lethal gas "is inhumane and has no place in civilized society" (865 F. Supp.

at 1415). She then ordered California's gas chamber closed and that lethal injection be used instead. This was the first time a federal judge had ruled that any method of execution violated the Eighth and Fourteenth Amendments. Even though the state of California maintained that cyanide gas caused almost instant unconsciousness, the judge referred to doctors' reports and witnesses' accounts of gas chamber executions, which indicated that the dying inmates stayed conscious for 15 seconds to a minute or longer and suffered "intense physical pain."

Gomez and Calderon appealed Judge Patel's ruling on the unconstitutionality of the gas chamber before the U.S. Court of Appeals for the Ninth Circuit. The court also appealed the permanent injunction against the use of lethal gas as a method of execution. In February 1996, in *Fierro v. Gomez* (77 F.3d. 301, 9th Cir.), the appellate court affirmed Judge Patel's ruling.

Gomez and Calderon appealed the case to the U.S. Supreme Court. In October 1996 a 7–2 Supreme Court, in *Gomez v. Fierro* (519 U.S. 918), vacated the appellate court's ruling and returned the case to the appellate court for additional proceedings, citing the death penalty statute amended in 1993 (lethal injection as an alternative to lethal gas). As of October 2009 Fierro remained on death row. Ruiz died of natural causes in early 2007.

Does Electrocution Constitute a Cruel and Unusual Punishment?

In the 1990s, even though Florida had three botched executions using the electric chair, the state supreme court ruled each time that electrocution does not constitute a cruel and unusual punishment. In 1990 and 1997 flames shot out from the headpiece worn by the condemned man. On July 8, 1999, Allen Lee Davis developed a nosebleed during his execution in the electric chair.

Thomas Provenzano, who was scheduled to be electrocuted after Davis, challenged the use of the electric chair as Florida's sole method of execution. In *Provenzano v. Moore* (No. 95973, 1999), the Florida Supreme Court ruled 4–3 that the electric chair was not a cruel and unusual punishment. The court further reported that Davis's nosebleed occurred before the execution and did not result from the electrocution.

Subsequently, the court, as it routinely does with all its rulings, posted the *Provenzano* decision on the Internet. Three photographs of Davis covered with blood were posted as part of the dissenting opinion of Justice Leander J. Shaw Jr. (1930–). The photographs brought public outcry worldwide. Justice Shaw claimed that Davis was "brutally tortured to death."

In October 1999, for the first time, the U.S. Supreme Court agreed to consider the constitutionality of electrocution. The death row inmate Anthony Braden Bryan asked the court to review his case, based on the unreliability of the

electric chair. Before the high court could hear the case, however, the Florida legislature voted in a special session to replace electrocution with lethal injection as the primary method of execution, but allowed a condemned person to choose the electric chair as an alternative.

On January 24, 2000, the Supreme Court dismissed *Bryan v. Moore* (No. 99-6723) as moot (irrelevant), based on Florida's new legislation. Governor Jeb Bush (1953–) agreed to sign the bill in conjunction with a second bill that limits, in most cases, death row inmates to two appeals in state courts, with the second appeal to be filed within six months of the first. This provision cut in half the time limit for the second appeal.

In 2001 the Georgia Supreme Court became the first appellate court to rule a method of execution unconstitutional. On October 5 the court held that electrocution was a cruel and unusual punishment in violation of the state constitution. In 2000 the Georgia legislature had passed a law making lethal injection the sole method of execution. Before the state supreme court ruling in October 2001, that law applied only to those sentenced after May 1, 2000.

Challenges to Lethal Injection

In April 2006 the U.S. Supreme Court considered a case in which the Florida inmate Clarence E. Hill challenged the state's form of lethal injection as unnecessarily painful and thus a violation of his Eighth Amendment rights. Hill was convicted in 1983 for the capital murder of Officer Stephen Taylor and sentenced to death. After exhausting his state appeals, he filed for a federal writ of habeas corpus, which was denied. As Hill's execution loomed in January 2006, his lawyers filed a new challenge, this time against the lethal injection procedure itself. A trial court dismissed the claim, because Hill had already exhausted his federal habeas corpus appeals. Federal law prohibits multiple appeals of this type. The ruling was upheld by the Florida Supreme Court.

In *Hill v. McDonough* (No. 05-8794, 2006), the U.S. Supreme Court issued a unanimous 9–0 opinion that Hill's challenge of the form of execution did not constitute a second habeas corpus appeal, but was a new action of a different type. The decision came only minutes before Hill was to be executed. He was already strapped to a gurney and hooked up to intravenous lines. However, the reprieve proved to be temporary. Florida courts refused to hear Hill's challenge, arguing that it was presented too late. His execution date was reset, and the Supreme Court denied a second appeal. In September 2006 Hill was executed by lethal injection.

In September 2007 the U.S. Supreme Court agreed to hear another case pertaining to lethal injection. Two Kentucky death row inmates—Ralph Baze and Thomas Bowling—petitioned the court after lower courts rejected their challenges to the three-drug protocol used for lethal injection in Kentucky. Neither of the men, who had been convicted in separate double murders, had execution dates set at that time. Because the lethal injection protocol in question was widely used by other death penalty states, the court's agreement to hear the case triggered a national moratorium (suspension) on pending executions. In April 2008 the court issued its opinion in *Baze et al. v. Rees* (553 U.S. ___). The court ruled 7–2 that Kentucky's three-drug protocol for lethal injection did not violate the Eighth Amendment's ban on cruel and unusual punishment.

The protocol included administration of sodium thiopental (to render the prisoner unconscious) followed by pancuronium bromide (a paralyzing agent) and potassium chloride, which causes cardiac arrest resulting in death. Although the court acknowledged that improper administration of the drugs (particularly the sodium thiopental) could result in a painful death, it rejected the petitioners' claim that there was a "significant risk" that the protocol would not be properly followed. The court also refused to consider the petitioners' claim that an alternative single-drug protocol for lethal injection offered far less risk of pain. It noted that pursuing such claims in numerous death row cases "would embroil the courts in ongoing scientific controversies beyond their expertise, and would substantially intrude on the role of state legislatures in implementing execution procedures." However, the court warned that states that refused to adopt suitable alternative protocols in the future might violate the Eighth Amendment. The court noted that an alternative protocol would be considered suitable if it was "feasible, readily implemented, and in fact significantly reduces substantial risk of severe pain."

In May 2008 the temporary moratorium on executions ended with the execution of William Lynd in Georgia. Lynd had been convicted of kidnapping and shooting his girlfriend, Virginia Moore, in 1988. The Supreme Court's ruling in *Baze et al. v. Rees* has prompted death penalty states with slightly different lethal injection protocols from that used in Kentucky to adjust their protocols to ensure their constitutionality. According to the Death Penalty Information Center, in "Recent Legislative Activity" (2009, http://www.deathpenaltyinfo.org/recent-legislative-activity), Idaho passed legislation in 2009 to conform its lethal injection protocol to that used in Kentucky. The state also eliminated a firing squad as an alternative method of execution. In 2008 Nebraska's sole reliance upon the electric chair as a means of execution was ruled unconstitutional by the state's Supreme Court. In 2009 a new state law established lethal injection as Nebraska's sole means of execution and directed corrections officials to develop a suitable protocol for carrying it out.

DOES EXTENDED STAY ON DEATH ROW CONSTITUTE A CRUEL AND UNUSUAL PUNISHMENT?

In 2002 Charles Kenneth Foster, a Florida inmate, asked the U.S. Supreme Court to consider whether his long wait for execution constitutes a cruel and unusual punishment prohibited by the Eighth Amendment. Foster had been on death row since 1975 for a murder conviction. In 1981 and again in 1984 the defendant was granted a stay of execution to allow his federal habeas corpus petition.

Justice Stephen G. Breyer (1938–) dissented from the court's refusal to hear the case (*Foster v. Florida*, No. 01-10868, 2002). Justice Breyer pointed out that the defendant's long wait on death row resulted partly from Florida's repeated errors in proceedings. The justice added, "Death row's inevitable anxieties and uncertainties have been sharpened by the issuance of two death warrants and three judicial reprieves. If executed, Foster, now 55, will have been punished both by death and also by more than a generation spent in death row's twilight. It is fairly asked whether such punishment is both unusual and cruel."

Concurring with the court opinion not to hear Foster's case, Justice Clarence Thomas (1948–) observed that the defendant could have ended the "anxieties and uncertainties" of death row had he submitted to execution, which the people of Florida believe he deserves. As of October 2009 Foster remained in Florida prison on death row.

In March 2009 the Supreme Court refused to hear a similar case involving a Florida man who had been on death row for 32 years. William Thompson was sentenced to death for the kidnapping, torture, and murder of Sally Ivester in 1976. Justices Breyer and Stevens expressed their displeasure with the court's decision. Breyer noted that the State of Florida "was in significant part responsible" for Thompson's long stay on death row due to judicial errors during his sentencing trial. Stevens described "the especially severe conditions of confinement" in which Thompson had been held on death row and remarked on the psychological toll that an impending execution takes when a prisoner experiences a long wait for the execution to be administered. He concluded, "Executing defendants after such long delays is unacceptably cruel." However, Justice Thomas noted that Thompson had taken advantage of the many appeals processes allowed under the law and was now complaining about a delayed execution. Thomas recounted the gruesome details of Thompson's crime and the brutal manner in which Ivester was tortured to death. He notes "Three juries recommended that petitioner receive the death penalty for this heinous murder, and petitioner has received judicial review of his sentence on at least 17 occasions." He concluded, "It is the crime" and not the punishment imposed by the jury or the delay in petitioner's execution—that was 'unacceptably cruel.'"

CHAPTER 4
SUPREME COURT RULINGS III: MITIGATING CIRCUMSTANCES, YOUTH, INSANITY, MENTAL RETARDATION, THE ADMISSIBILITY OF VICTIM IMPACT STATEMENTS, AND THE INFLUENCE OF RACE IN CAPITAL CASES

MITIGATING CIRCUMSTANCES

Mitigating circumstances may lessen the responsibility for a crime, whereas aggravating circumstances may add to the responsibility for a crime. In 1978 an Ohio case highlighted the issue of mitigating circumstances before the U.S. Supreme Court after Sandra Lockett was convicted of capital murder for her role in a pawnshop robbery that resulted in the shooting death of the storeowner. Lockett helped plan the robbery, drove the getaway car, and hid her accomplices in her home, but she was not present in the store at the time the storeowner was shot. According to the Ohio death penalty statute, capital punishment had to be imposed on Lockett unless "(1) the victim induced or facilitated the offense; (2) it is unlikely that the offense would have been committed but for the fact that the offender was under duress, coercion, or strong provocation; or (3) the offense was primarily the product of the offender's psychosis or mental deficiency." Lockett was found guilty and sentenced to die.

Lockett appealed, claiming that the Ohio law did not give the sentencing judge the chance to consider the circumstances of the crime, the defendant's criminal record, and the defendant's character as mitigating factors, lessening her responsibility for the crime. In July 1978 the Supreme Court, in *Lockett v. Ohio* (438 U.S. 586), upheld Lockett's contention. Chief Justice Warren Burger (1907–1995) observed, "A statute that prevents the sentencer in capital cases from giving independent mitigating weight to aspects of the defendant's character and record and to the circumstances of the offense proffered in mitigation creates the risk that the death penalty will be imposed in spite of factors that may call for a less severe penalty, and when the choice is between life and death, such risk is unacceptable and incompatible with the commands of the Eighth and Fourteenth Amendments."

Mitigating Circumstances Must Always Be Considered

In *Hitchcock v. Dugger* (481 U.S. 393, 1987), a unanimous Supreme Court further emphasized that all mitigating circumstances had to be considered before the convicted murderer could be sentenced. A Florida judge had instructed the jury not to consider evidence of mitigating factors that were not specifically indicated in the Florida death penalty law. Writing for the court, Justice Antonin Scalia (1936–) stressed that a convicted person had the right "to present any and all relevant mitigating evidence that is available."

CAN A MINOR BE SENTENCED TO DEATH?

On April 4, 1977, 16-year-old Monty Lee Eddings and several friends were pulled over by a police officer as they traveled in a car in Oklahoma. Eddings had several guns in the car, which he had taken from his father. When the police officer approached the car, Eddings shot and killed him. Eddings was tried as an adult even though he was 16 at the time of the murder. He was convicted of first-degree murder for killing a police officer and was sentenced to death.

At the sentencing hearing following the conviction, Eddings's lawyer presented substantial evidence of a turbulent family history, beatings by a harsh father, and serious emotional disturbance. The judge refused, as a matter of law, to consider the mitigating circumstances of Eddings's unhappy upbringing and emotional problems. He ruled that the only mitigating circumstance was the petitioner's youth, which was insufficient to outweigh the aggravating circumstances.

In *Eddings v. Oklahoma* (455 U.S. 104, 1982), the Supreme Court, in a 5–4 opinion, ordered the case remanded (sent back to the lower courts for further proceedings). The justices based their ruling on *Lockett v. Ohio*, which required the trial court to consider and weigh all the mitigating evidence concerning the petitioner's family background and personal history.

By implication, because the majority did not reverse the case on the issue of age, the decision let stand Oklahoma's decision to try Eddings as an adult. Meanwhile, Chief Justice Burger, who filed the dissenting opinion in which Justices Byron R. White (1917–2002), Harry A. Blackmun (1908–1999), and William H. Rehnquist (1924–2005) joined, observed, "the Constitution does not authorize us to determine whether sentences imposed by state courts are sentences we consider 'appropriate'; our only authority is to decide whether they are constitutional under the Eighth Amendment. The Court stops far short of suggesting that there is any constitutional proscription against imposition of the death penalty on a person who was under age 18 when the murder was committed."

Hence, even though the high court did not directly rule on the question of minors being sentenced to death, the sense of the court would appear to be that it would uphold such a sentencing. Eddings's sentence was subsequently changed to life in prison.

Not at 15 Years Old

With three adults, William Thompson brutally murdered a former brother-in-law in Oklahoma. Thompson was 15 at the time of the murder, but the state determined that Thompson, who had a long history of violent assault, had "virtually no reasonable prospects for rehabilitation ... within the juvenile system and ... should be held accountable for his acts as if he were an adult and should be certified to stand trial as an adult." Thompson was tried as an adult and found guilty. As in *Eddings*, Thompson's age was considered a mitigating circumstance, but the jury still sentenced him to death.

Thompson appealed, and even though the Court of Criminal Appeals of Oklahoma upheld the decision, the U.S. Supreme Court, in *Thompson v. Oklahoma* (487 U.S. 815, 1988), did not. In a 5–3 majority vote, with Justice Sandra Day O'Connor (1930–) agreeing to vacate (annul) the sentence but not agreeing with the majority reasoning, the case was reversed. (Justice Anthony M. Kennedy [1936–] took no part in the decision.)

Writing for the majority, Justice John Paul Stevens (1920–) observed that "inexperience, less education, and less intelligence make the teenager less able to evaluate the consequences of his or her conduct while at the same time he or she is much more apt to be motivated by mere emotion or peer pressure than is an adult. The reasons why juveniles are not trusted with the privileges and responsibilities of an adult also explain why their irresponsible conduct is not as morally reprehensible as that of an adult."

Justice Stevens noted that 18 states required the age of at least 16 years before the death penalty could be considered.

Counting the 14 states prohibiting capital punishment, a total of 32 states did not execute people under age 16.

Justice O'Connor agreed with the judgment of the court that the appellate court's ruling should be reversed. O'Connor pointed out, however, that even though most 15-year-old criminals are generally less blameworthy than adults who commit the same crimes, some may fully understand the horrible deeds they have done. Individuals, after all, have different characteristics, including their capability to distinguish right from wrong.

Writing for the minority, Justice Scalia found no national consensus forbidding the execution of a person who was 16 years old at the commission of the murder. The justice could not understand the majority's calculations establishing a "contemporary standard" that forbade the execution of young minors. He reasoned that abolitionist states (states with no death penalty) should not be considered in the issue of executing minors because they did not have executions in the first place. Rather, the 18 states that prohibited the execution of offenders who were younger than 16 when they murdered should be compared with the 19 states that applied the death penalty to young offenders.

For a Number of Years Minors Could Be Sentenced to Death at Age 16 or 17

In 1989 a majority of the court, with Justice O'Connor straddling the fence, found the death penalty unacceptable for an offender who was less than 16 years old when he or she committed murder. A majority of the court, however, found the death sentence acceptable for a minor who was aged 16 or 17 during the commission of murder. The Supreme Court, in two jointly considered cases, *Stanford v. Kentucky* and *Wilkins v. Missouri* (492 U.S. 361, 1989), ruled that inmates who committed their crimes at ages 16 or 17 could be executed for murder.

In January 1981, 17-year-old Kevin Stanford and an accomplice raped Barbel Poore, an attendant at a Kentucky gas station they were robbing. They then took the woman to a secluded area near the station, where Stanford shot her in the face and in the back of the head. Stressing the seriousness of the offense and Stanford's long history of criminal behavior, the court certified him as an adult. He was tried, found guilty, and sentenced to death.

In July 1985, 16-year-old Heath Wilkins stabbed Nancy Allen to death while he was robbing the convenience store where she worked. Wilkins indicated he murdered Allen because "a dead person can't talk." Based on his long history of juvenile delinquency, a Missouri court ordered Wilkins to be tried as an adult. He was found guilty and sentenced to death.

Writing for the majority, Justice Scalia could find no national consensus that executing minors aged 16 and 17 constituted a cruel and unusual punishment. Scalia observed that of the 37 states whose statutes allowed the death penalty, just 12 refused to impose it on 17-year-old offenders, and besides those 12, only three more states refused to impose it on 16-year-old offenders.

Furthermore, Justice Scalia saw no connection between the defendant's argument that those under 18 were denied the right to drive, drink, or vote because they were not considered mature enough to do so responsibly and whether this standard of maturity should be applied to a minor's understanding that murder is terribly wrong. Scalia added, "Even if the requisite degrees of maturity were comparable, the age statutes in question would still not be relevant.... These laws set the appropriate ages for the operation of a system that makes its determinations in gross, and that does not conduct individualized maturity tests for each driver, drinker, or voter.... In the realm of capital punishment in particular, 'individualized consideration [is] a constitutional requirement,' and one of the individualized mitigating factors that sentencers must be permitted to consider is the defendant's age."

Writing for the minority, Justice William J. Brennan (1906–1997) found a national consensus among 30 states when he added the 12 states forbidding the execution of a person who was 16 years old during the commission of the crime to those with no capital punishment, and the states that, in practice if not in law, did not execute minors. Justice Brennan, taking serious exception to the majority's observation that they had to find a national consensus in the laws passed by the state legislatures, stated, "Our judgment about the constitutionality of a punishment under the Eighth Amendment is informed, though not determined... by an examination of contemporary attitudes toward the punishment, as evidenced in the actions of legislatures and of juries. The views of organizations with expertise in relevant fields and the choices of governments elsewhere in the world also merit our attention as indicators whether a punishment is acceptable in a civilized society."

In 1996 Wilkins was retried in Missouri and sentenced to three life terms. Stanford remained on Kentucky's death row until 2003, when his sentence was commuted to life without parole by Governor Paul E. Patton (1937–).

The Supreme Court Reverses Its Decision Regarding Minors

For 15 years the nation's highest court held fast on its decision to allow for the execution of minors who committed capital crimes. The Supreme Court even rejected another appeal by Stanford in 2002. In *Roper v. Simmons* (543 U.S. 633, 2005), however, the court reversed its earlier opinion when it ruled that executing Christopher Simmons was cruel and unusual based on the fact that Simmons was a minor when he committed murder.

In 1993, 17-year-old Simmons and two friends, John Tessmer and Charles Benjamin, planned the elaborate bur-glary and murder of Shirley Cook, who lived in Fenton, Missouri. The three teenagers wanted to experience the thrill of the crime, reasoning that they would not be held accountable because they were under the age of 18. On the night of the murder, Tessmer and Simmons broke into Cook's house. (Benjamin backed out.) When Cook identified who the boys were, they covered her eyes and mouth with duct tape and bound her hands. The teenagers drove Cook to a state park, wrapped more duct tape over her entire face, tied her hands and feet with electrical wire, and threw her off a railroad trestle into a river.

The next day Simmons began bragging about the murder at school and was picked up by the police along with the two other teenagers. Simmons confessed on videotape and was tried and sentenced to death. He made a number of unsuccessful appeals and pleas for habeas corpus (a petition to be heard in federal court). Just weeks before he was scheduled to die, the Missouri Supreme Court called off the execution and reopened the debate in light of the U.S. Supreme Court's *Atkins* decision. (In *Atkins v. Virginia* [536 U.S. 304], the court ruled that executing mentally retarded criminals was a violation of the Eighth Amendment because the mentally retarded do not have as strong a sense of lasting consequences or of right and wrong as normal adults.) The state court overturned Simmons's death sentence 6–3, stating that a national consensus had developed against executing minors since *Stanford* and *Wilkins* were decided. Simmons was resentenced to life without parole.

The U.S. Supreme Court upheld the Missouri court's decision in a 5–4 vote, reversing *Stanford*. The majority reasoned that adolescents do not have the emotional maturity and understanding of lasting consequences that adults have. As such, they cannot be held to as high of a standard and should not be sentenced to death. The majority also agreed with the Missouri court in that a national and international consensus had changed over the past 15 years. The court noted, "To implement this framework we have established the propriety and affirmed the necessity of referring to 'the evolving standards of decency that mark the progress of a maturing society.'"

Justices O'Connor, Scalia, Rehnquist, and Clarence Thomas (1948–) dissented, claiming that the guidelines for executing minors should not be inflexible and that a great many U.S. citizens still favor the death penalty for teenagers who commit especially heinous crimes. Scalia stated that the majority was bowing to international pressures. In his dissent, he wrote, "Though the views of our own citizens are essentially irrelevant to the Court's decision today, the views of other countries and the so-called international community take center stage."

Youth: A Mitigating Circumstance Even for Those over Age 18

On March 23, 1986, Dorsie Lee Johnson Jr. and an accomplice staked out a convenience store in Snyder, Texas, with the intention of robbing it. They learned that only one employee worked during the predawn hours. Agreeing to leave no witnesses to the crime, the 19-year-old Johnson shot and killed the clerk, Jack Huddleston. They then emptied the cash register and stole some cigarettes.

The following month Johnson was arrested and subsequently confessed to the robbery and murder. During jury selection the defense attorneys asked potential jurors whether they believed that people were capable of change and whether they, the potential jurors, had ever done things in their youth that they would not now do.

The only witness the defense called was Johnson's father, who told of his son's drug use, grief over the death of his mother two years before the crime, and the murder of his sister the following year. He spoke of his son's youth and the fact that, at age 19, he did not evaluate things the way a person of 30 or 35 would.

Johnson was tried and convicted of capital murder. Under Texas law the homicide qualified as a capital offense because Johnson intentionally or knowingly caused Huddleston's death. Moreover, the murder was carried out in the course of committing a robbery.

In the sentencing phase of the trial, the judge instructed the jury to answer two questions: (1) whether Johnson's actions were deliberate and intended to kill, and (2) whether there was a possibility that he would continue to commit violent crimes and be a threat to society. If the jury answered "yes" to both questions, Johnson would be sentenced to death. If the jury returned a "no" answer to either question, the defendant would be sentenced to life in prison. The jury was not to consider or discuss the possibility of parole.

Of equal importance was the instruction that the jury could consider all the evidence, both aggravating and mitigating, in either phase of the trial. The jury unanimously answered yes to both questions, and Johnson was sentenced to death.

Five days after the state appellate court denied Johnson's motions for a rehearing, the U.S. Supreme Court issued its opinion in *Penry v. Lynaugh* (492 U.S. 302, 1989), in which it held that the jury should have been instructed that it could consider mental retardation as a mitigating factor during the penalty phase. Based on the *Penry* ruling, Johnson appealed once more, claiming that a separate instruction should have been given to the jurors that would have allowed them to consider his youth. Again, the appellate court rejected his petition.

Affirming the Texas appellate court decision, Justice Kennedy delivered the opinion of the Supreme Court in *Johnson v. Texas* (509 U.S. 350, 1993). He was joined by Justices Rehnquist, White, Scalia, and Thomas. Kennedy noted that the Texas special-issues system (two questions asked of the jury and instruction to consider all evidence) allowed for adequate consideration of Johnson's youth. Justice Kennedy stated:

> Even on a cold record, one cannot be unmoved by the testimony of petitioner's father urging that his son's actions were due in large part to his youth. It strains credulity to suppose that the jury would have viewed the evidence of petitioner's youth as outside its effective reach in answering the second special issue. The relevance of youth as a mitigating factor derives from the fact that the signature qualities of youth are transient; as individuals mature, the impetuousness and recklessness that may dominate in younger years can subside.... As long as the mitigating evidence is within "the effective reach of the sentencer," the requirements of the Eighth Amendment are satisfied.

Justice O'Connor, in a dissenting opinion joined by Justices Blackmun, Stevens, and David H. Souter (1939–), stated that the jurors were not allowed to give full effect to his strongest mitigating circumstance: his youth. Hearing of his less than exemplary youth, a jury might easily conclude, as Johnson's did, that he would continue to be a threat to society.

In 1997 Johnson was executed by lethal injection in the state of Texas.

ROLE OF PSYCHIATRISTS

Validity of a Psychiatrist's Testimony

In 1978 Thomas Barefoot was convicted of murdering a police officer in Bell County, Texas. During the sentencing phase of his trial the prosecution put two psychiatrists on the stand. Neither psychiatrist had actually interviewed Barefoot, nor did either ask to do so. Both psychiatrists agreed that an individual with Barefoot's background and who had acted as Barefoot had in murdering the policeman represented a future threat to society. Partially based on their testimony, the jury sentenced Barefoot to death.

Barefoot's conviction and sentence were appealed many times, and in 1983 his case was argued before the U.S. Supreme Court. Among the issues debated was the validity of the testimony of psychiatrists. Barefoot's lawyers questioned whether it was necessary for the psychiatrists to have interviewed Barefoot or if it was enough for them to answer hypothetical questions that pertained to a hypothetical individual who acted like Barefoot.

Barefoot's attorneys claimed that psychiatrists could not reliably predict that a particular offender would commit other crimes in the future and be a threat to society. They further argued that psychiatrists should also not be allowed to testify about an offender's future dangerousness in response to hypothetical situations presented by the prosecutor and without having first examined the offender.

In *Barefoot v. Estelle* (463 U.S. 880, 1983), the Supreme Court ruled 6–3 that local juries were in the best position to decide guilt and impose a sentence. The court referred to *Jurek v. Texas* (428 U.S. 262, 1976), an earlier case that, among other things, upheld the testimony of laypeople concerning a defendant's possible future actions. Therefore, the court looked on psychiatrists as just another group of people presenting testimony to the jury for consideration. The court claimed that like all evidence presented to the jury, a psychiatric observation "should be admitted and its weight left to the factfinder, who would have the benefit of cross-examination and contrary evidence by the opposing party. Psychiatric testimony predicting dangerousness may be countered not only as erroneous in a particular case but also as generally so unreliable that it should be ignored. If the jury may make up its mind about future dangerousness unaided by psychiatric testimony, jurors should not be barred from hearing the views of the State's psychiatrists along with opposing views of the defendant's doctors."

The high court dismissed the amicus curiae brief (a friend-of-the-court brief prepared to enlighten the court) presented by the American Psychiatric Association (APA), indicating that psychiatric testimony was "almost entirely unreliable" in determining future actions. The court countered that such testimony had been traditionally accepted. The high court also observed that arguments, such as the APA brief, were founded "on the premise that a jury will not be able to separate the wheat from the chaff," a sentiment with which the court did not agree.

The high court also dismissed Barefoot's contention that the psychiatrists should have personally interviewed him. Such methods of observation and conclusion were quite normal in courtroom procedures, and the psychiatric observations had been based on established facts. Barefoot's appeal was denied.

Justice Blackmun strongly dissented from the majority decision. He declared, "In the present state of psychiatric knowledge, this is too much for me. One may accept this in a routine lawsuit for money damages, but when a person's life is at stake—no matter how heinous his offense—a requirement of greater reliability should prevail. In a capital case, the specious testimony of a psychiatrist, colored in the eyes of an impressionable jury by the inevitable untouchability of a medical specialist's words, equates with death itself."

The state of Texas executed Barefoot by lethal injection in 1984.

A Prisoner Maintains Rights during Psychiatric Examination

During the commission of a robbery in 1973, Ernest Smith's accomplice fatally shot a grocery clerk (Smith had tried to shoot the clerk, but his weapon had jammed). The state of Texas sought the death penalty against Smith based on the Texas law governing premeditated murder.

Thereafter, the judge ordered a psychiatric examination of Smith by James P. Grigson to determine if Smith was competent to stand trial. Without permission from Smith's lawyer, Grigson interviewed Smith in jail for about 90 minutes and found him competent. Grigson then discussed his conclusions and diagnosis with the state attorney. Smith was eventually found guilty. During the sentencing phase of the trial, over the protests of the defendant's lawyers, Grigson testified that Smith was a "very severe sociopath," who would continue his previous behavior, which would get worse. The jury sentenced Smith to death.

Smith appealed his sentence, claiming he was not informed of his rights. Both the federal district court and the appeals court agreed. So did a unanimous Supreme Court. In *Estelle v. Smith* (451 U.S. 454, 1981), the court ruled that the trial court had the right to determine if Smith was capable of standing trial. It had no right, however, to use the information gathered without first advising him of his Fifth Amendment right against self-incrimination. According to the court, the psychiatrist was "an agent of the state" about whom the defendant had not been warned, but who was reporting about the defendant. Noting *Miranda v. Arizona* (384 U.S. 436, 1966), the court continued, "The Fifth Amendment privilege is available outside of criminal court proceedings and serves to protect persons in all settings in which their freedom of action is curtailed in any significant way from being compelled to incriminate themselves."

The court reiterated that the prosecution may not use any statements made by a suspect under arrest "unless it demonstrates the use of procedural safeguards effective to secure the privilege against self-incrimination."

In 1981 Smith was convicted of a lesser charge and sentenced to life in prison.

Needing a Psychiatrist to Prove Insanity

In 1979 Glen Burton Ake and Steven Hatch shot and killed the Reverend Richard Douglass and Marilyn Douglass and wounded their children, Brooks and Leslie, in Canadian County, Oklahoma. Before the trial, because of Ake's bizarre behavior, the trial judge ordered him examined by a psychiatrist to determine if he should be put under observation. The psychiatrist diagnosed Ake as a probable paranoid schizophrenic and reported that his client claimed "to be the 'sword of vengeance' of the Lord." The physician recommended a long-term psychiatric examination to determine Ake's competency to stand trial.

Ake's psychiatric evaluation confirmed his paranoid schizophrenia. Consequently, the court pronounced him incompetent to stand trial and ordered him committed to the state mental hospital.

Six weeks later the hospital psychiatrist informed the court that Ake had become competent to stand trial. Under daily treatment with an antipsychotic drug, he could stand trial. The state of Oklahoma resumed proceedings against the accused murderer.

Before the trial Ake's lawyer told the court of his client's insanity defense. He also informed the court that for him to defend Ake adequately, he needed to have Ake examined by a psychiatrist to determine his mental condition at the time he committed murder. During his stay at the mental hospital, Ake was evaluated as to his "present sanity" to stand trial but not his mental state during the murder. Because Ake could not afford a psychiatrist, his counsel asked the court to provide a psychiatrist or the money to hire one. The trial judge refused his request, claiming the state is not obligated to provide a psychiatrist, even to poor defendants in capital cases.

Ake was tried for two counts of first-degree murder and for two counts of shooting with intent to kill. During the trial Ake's only defense was insanity; however, none of the psychiatrists at the state mental hospital could testify to his mental state at the time of the crime.

The judge instructed the jurors that Ake could be found not guilty by reason of insanity if he could not distinguish right from wrong when he committed murder. The jurors were told they could presume Ake sane at the time of the crime unless he presented sufficient evidence to raise a reasonable doubt about his sanity during the crime. The jury found him guilty on all counts. The jury sentenced Ake to death based on the earlier testimony of the psychiatrist, who concluded that Ake was a threat to society. On appeal, the Oklahoma Court of Appeals agreed with the trial court that the state did not have the responsibility to provide an impoverished defendant with a psychiatrist to help with his defense.

The U.S. Supreme Court disagreed. In *Ake v. Oklahoma* (470 U.S. 68, 1985), the court ruled 8–1 to reverse the lower court's ruling, finding that "there was no expert testimony for either side on Ake's sanity at the time of the offense." The high court further observed, "This Court has long recognized that when a State brings its judicial power to bear on an indigent [poor] defendant in a criminal proceeding, it must take steps to assure that the defendant has a fair opportunity to present his defense. This elementary principle, grounded in significant part on the Fourteenth Amendment's due process guarantee of fundamental fairness, derives from the belief that justice cannot be equal where, simply as a result of his poverty, a defendant is denied the opportunity to participate meaningfully in a judicial proceeding in which his liberty is at stake."

In 1986 Ake was retried, found guilty, and sentenced to life in prison.

INSANITY AND EXECUTION
Can an Insane Person Be Executed?

In 1974 Alvin Ford was convicted of murder and sentenced to death in Florida. There was no question that he was completely sane at the time of his crime, at the trial, and at the sentencing. Eight years later Ford began to show signs of delusion—from thinking that people were conspiring to force him to commit suicide to believing that family members were being held hostage in prison.

Ford's lawyers had a psychiatrist examine their client. After 14 months of evaluation and investigation, the doctor concluded that Ford suffered from a severe mental disorder that would preclude him from assisting in the defense of his life. A second psychiatrist concluded that Ford did not understand why he was on death row.

Florida law required the governor to appoint a panel of three psychiatrists to determine whether Ford was mentally capable of understanding the death penalty and the reasons he was being sentenced to death. The three state-appointed doctors met with Ford once for about 30 minutes and then filed separate reports. Ford's lawyers were present but were ordered by the judge not to participate in the examination "in any adversarial manner."

The three psychiatrists submitted different diagnoses, but all agreed that Ford was sane enough to be executed. Ford's lawyers attempted to submit to the governor the reports of the first two psychiatrists along with other materials. However, the governor refused to inform the lawyers whether he would consider these reports. He eventually signed Ford's death warrant.

Ford's appeals were denied in state and federal courts, but a 7–2 Supreme Court, in *Ford v. Wainwright* (477 U.S. 399, 1986), reversed the earlier judgments. In light of the fact that there had been no precedent formed for such a case in U.S. history, the justices turned to English law. Writing for the majority, Justice Thurgood Marshall (1908–1993) observed that even though the reasons appear unclear, English common law forbade the execution of the insane. The English jurist Sir William Blackstone (1723–1780) had labeled such a practice "savage and inhuman." Likewise, the other noted English judicial resource, Sir Edward Coke (1552–1634), observed that even though the execution of a criminal was to serve as an example, the execution of a madman was considered "of extreme inhumanity and cruelty, and can be no example to others." Consequently, because the Eighth Amendment forbidding a cruel and unusual punishment was prepared by men who accepted English common law, there could be no question that the Eighth Amendment prohibited the execution of the insane.

The issue then became the method the state used to determine Ford's insanity. The high court noted that Florida did not allow the submission of materials that might be relevant to the decision whether or not to execute the condemned man. In addition, Ford's lawyers were not given the chance to question the state-appointed psychiatrists about the basis for finding their client competent. Questions the defense could have asked included the possibility of personal bias on the doctors' part toward the death penalty, any history of error in their judgment, and their degree of certainty in reaching their conclusions. Finally, the justices pointed out that the greatest defect in Florida's practice is its entrusting the ultimate decision about the execution entirely to the executive branch. The high court observed, "Under this procedure, the person who appoints the experts and ultimately decides whether the State will be able to carry out the sentence that it has long sought is the Governor, whose subordinates have been responsible for initiating every stage of the prosecution of the condemned from arrest through sentencing. The commander of the State's corps of prosecutors cannot be said to have the neutrality that is necessary for reliability in the factfinding proceeding."

The high court further observed that even though a prisoner has been sentenced to death, he is still protected by the Constitution. Therefore, ascertaining his sanity as a basis for a legal execution is as important as other proceedings in a capital case.

In dissent, Justice Rehnquist, joined by Chief Justice Burger, thought the Florida procedure consistent with English common law, which had left the decision to the executive branch. Rehnquist warned, "A claim of insanity may be made at any time before sentence and, once rejected, may be raised again; a prisoner found sane two days before execution might claim to have lost his sanity the next day, thus necessitating another judicial determination of his sanity and presumably another stay of his execution."

Ford remained on Florida's death row until 1991, when he died of natural causes.

Can an Insane Person Stabilized by Drugs Be Executed?

In 1979 Charles Singleton stabbed Mary Lou York twice in the neck after robbing her grocery store in Hamburg, Arkansas. He was tried, convicted, and sentenced to death. He was sane during the murder and throughout the trial.

However, Singleton developed schizophrenia while in prison. At one point during his incarceration, Singleton claimed his prison cell was possessed by demons. When given antipsychotic medication, however, Singleton regained his sanity. Fearing a psychotic outburst from Singleton, the prison forced medication on him when he refused to take it. Singleton filed several habeas corpus petitions in state and federal courts, claiming that in light of *Ford*, he was not

competent enough to be executed. He also argued that the forcible administration of antipsychotic medication was a violation of the Eighth Amendment, which forbids a cruel and unusual punishment.

The case was taken up by the U.S. Court of Appeals for the Eighth Circuit. In *Singleton v. Norris* (319 F.3d 1018 [8th Cir., 2003]), the appellate court upheld the death penalty for Singleton in a 5–4 decision. The majority felt that as long as Singleton was on medication and in full control of his faculties, his execution was not a violation of the Eighth Amendment. Singleton appealed to the U.S. Supreme Court, but the high court turned the case down, effectively endorsing the decision of the appellate court. Singleton was executed by the state of Arkansas on January 6, 2004.

CAN A MENTALLY RETARDED PERSON BE EXECUTED?
Penry I

In 1979 Pamela Carpenter was brutally raped, beaten, and stabbed with a pair of scissors in Livingston, Texas. Before she died, she was able to describe her attacker, and as a result, Johnny Paul Penry was arrested for, and later confessed to, the crime. At the time of the crime, Penry was out on parole for another rape. He was found guilty for the murder of Carpenter and sentenced to death.

Among the issues considered in his appeal was whether the state of Texas could execute a mentally retarded person. At Penry's competency hearing a psychiatrist testified that the defendant had an intelligence quotient (IQ) of 54. Penry had been tested in the past as having an IQ between 50 and 63, indicating mild to moderate retardation. According to the psychiatrist, during the commission of the crime the 22-year-old Penry had the mental age of a child 6-and-a-half years old and the social maturity of someone who was 9 to 10 years old. Penry's attorneys argued, "Because of their mental disabilities, mentally retarded people do not possess the level of moral culpability to justify imposing the death sentence.... There is an emerging national consensus against executing the mentally retarded."

Writing for the majority regarding the execution of mentally retarded people, Justice O'Connor, in *Penry v. Lynaugh* (492 U.S. 302, 1989), found no emerging national consensus against such executions. Furthermore, even though profoundly retarded people had not been executed for murder historically, Penry did not fall into this group.

Justice O'Connor noted that Penry was found competent to stand trial. He was able to consult rationally with his lawyer and understood the proceedings against him. She thought that the defense was guilty of lumping all mentally retarded people together, ascribing, among other things, a lack of moral capacity to be culpable for actions that call for the death punishment. O'Connor wrote:

Mentally retarded persons are individuals whose abilities and experiences can vary greatly. [If the mentally retarded were not treated as individuals, but as an undifferentiated group,] a mildly mentally retarded person could be denied the opportunity to enter into contracts or to marry by virtue of the fact that he had a "mental age" of a young child.... In light of the diverse capacities and life experiences of mentally retarded persons, it cannot be said on the record before us today that all mentally retarded people, by definition, can never act with the level of culpability associated with the death penalty.

Furthermore, the majority could find no national movement toward any type of consensus on this issue. Even though *Penry* produced several public opinion polls that indicated strong public opposition to executing the retarded, almost none of this public opinion was reflected in death penalty legislation. Only the federal Anti-Drug Abuse Act of 1988 and the states of Georgia and Maryland at the time banned the execution of retarded people found guilty of a capital crime.

Justice Brennan disagreed. Even though he agreed that lumping mentally retarded people together might result in stereotyping and discrimination, he believed there are characteristics that fall under the clinical definition of mental retardation. Citing the amicus curiae brief prepared by the American Association on Mental Retardation, he noted, "Every individual who has mental retardation—irrespective of his or her precise capacities or experiences—has 'a substantial disability in cognitive ability and adaptive behavior.'...Though individuals, particularly those who are mildly retarded, may be quite capable of overcoming these limitations to the extent of being able to 'maintain themselves independently or semi-independently in the community,' nevertheless, the mentally retarded by definition 'have a reduced ability to cope with and function in the everyday world.'"

Justice Brennan did not believe that executing a person not fully responsible for his or her actions would serve the "penal goals of deterrence or retribution." What is the point of executing someone who did not fully recognize the terrible evil that he or she had done? Furthermore, he argued, executing a mentally retarded person would not deter nonretarded people, those who would be aware of the possibility of an execution.

Even though the Supreme Court held that executing people with mental retardation was not a violation of the Eighth Amendment, it ruled that Penry's Eighth Amendment right was violated because the jury was not instructed that it could consider mental retardation as a mitigating factor during sentencing. The case was sent back to the lower court. In 1990 Texas retried Penry, and he was again found guilty of capital murder. During the sentencing phase the prosecution used a specific portion of a psychiatric report to point out the doctor's opinion that, if released from custody, Penry would be a threat to society. Penry appealed

his case all the way to the Supreme Court. Ten years later, in November 2000, with Penry less than three hours from being put to death, the Supreme Court granted a stay of execution to hear Penry's claims.

Penry II

Penry once again appealed to the Supreme Court after his case was retried. In his appeal to the Supreme Court, Penry argued that the use of a portion of an old psychiatric report at his 1990 retrial violated his Fifth Amendment right against self-incrimination. In 1977 Penry was arrested in connection with another rape. During this rape case the state of Texas provided Penry with a psychiatrist at the request of his lawyer. The psychiatrist was to determine the defendant's competency to stand trial. In 2000 Penry argued that the psychiatrist was an "agent of the state" and that the prosecution's use of his report in the 1990 retrial for murder violated Penry's right against self-incrimination. Penry also claimed jury instructions were inadequate.

On June 4, 2001, the Supreme Court ruled 6–3 in *Penry v. Johnson* (532 U.S. 782) that the admission of the psychiatrist's report did not violate Penry's Fifth Amendment right. The court held that this case was different from *Estelle v. Smith*, discussed earlier, in which the justices found that the psychiatrist's testimony about the defendant's future dangerousness based on the defendant's statements without his lawyer present violated his Fifth Amendment right. The justices emphasized that *Estelle* was restricted to that particular case.

The justices, however, sent the case back to the trial court for resentencing because, as in the original *Penry* case, the state did not give the sentencing jury adequate instructions about how to weigh mental retardation as a mitigating factor.

The Court Revisits Mental Retardation

Daryl Renard Atkins was convicted and sentenced to death for a 1996 abduction, armed robbery, and capital murder. On appeal to the Virginia Supreme Court, Atkins argued that he could not be executed because he was mentally retarded. Relying on *Penry v. Lynaugh*, the court affirmed the conviction. The court ordered a sentencing retrial because the trial court had used the wrong verdict form. As with the first penalty trial, a psychologist testified that Atkins was "mildly mentally retarded," having an IQ of 59. The jury sentenced Atkins to death for a second time. Atkins again appealed to the Virginia Supreme Court, which upheld the trial court ruling.

The U.S. Supreme Court unanimously agreed to hear Atkins's case. Thirteen years after ruling that executing the mentally retarded does not violate the Constitution, the Supreme Court, in a 6–3 decision, reversed its 1989 *Penry* decision. On June 20, 2002, in *Atkins v. Virginia* (536 U.S.

304), most of the court held that "executions of mentally retarded criminals are 'cruel and unusual punishments' prohibited by the Eighth Amendment."

Justice Stevens delivered the opinion of the court. Justices O'Connor, Kennedy, Souter, Ruth Bader Ginsburg (1933–), and Stephen G. Breyer (1938–) joined the opinion. According to the court, since *Penry*, many states had concluded that death is not a suitable punishment for mentally retarded offenders, reflecting society's sentiments that these individuals are less culpable than average offenders. The court observed, "Mentally retarded persons...have diminished capacities to understand and process information, to communicate, to abstract from mistakes and learn from experience, to engage in logical reasoning, to control impulses, and to understand the reactions of others.... Their deficiencies do not warrant an exemption from criminal sanctions, but they do diminish their personal culpability."

The justices also noted that even though the theory is that capital punishment would serve as deterrence to those contemplating murder, this theory does not apply to the mentally retarded because their diminished mental capacities prevent them from appreciating the possibility of execution as punishment. Moreover, the lesser culpability of mentally retarded criminals does not warrant the severe punishment of death.

Justice Scalia disagreed with the ruling that a person who is slightly mentally retarded does not possess the culpability to be sentenced to death. He claimed that the ruling finds "no support in the text or history of the Eighth Amendment." The justice also noted that current social attitudes do not support the majority decision. He pointed out that the state laws that the majority claimed reflect society's attitudes against executing the mentally retarded are still in their infancy and have not undergone the test of time.

On the relationship between a criminal's culpability and the deserved punishment, Justice Scalia stated:

> Surely culpability, and deservedness of the most severe retribution, depends not merely (if at all) upon the mental capacity of the criminal (above the level where he is able to distinguish right from wrong) but also upon the depravity of the crime—which is precisely why this sort of question has traditionally been thought answerable not by a categorical rule of the sort the Court today imposes upon all trials, but rather by the sentencer's weighing of the circumstances (both degree of retardation and depravity of crime) in the particular case. The fact that juries continue to sentence mentally retarded offenders to death for extreme crimes shows that society's moral outrage sometimes demands execution of retarded offenders. By what principle of law, science, or logic can the Court pronounce that this is wrong? There is none. Once the Court admits (as it does) that mental retardation does not render the offender morally *blameless*...there is no basis for saying that the death penalty

is *never* appropriate retribution, no matter *how* heinous the crime.

Penry's Sentence Revisited

On July 3, 2002, about two weeks after the Supreme Court ruled that it is unconstitutional to execute a mentally retarded person, a Texas jury concluded that Penry was not mentally retarded. He was resentenced to death. Three years later the Texas Court of Criminal Appeals ruled that the jury had not fully considered Penry's claim of mental retardation and ordered a new sentencing hearing. The Texas attorney general appealed the decision. In 2008 Penry's sentence was converted to three life terms in prison without the chance of parole. As part of a plea deal agreement, Penry had to apologize to the victim's family and concede that he was not mentally retarded.

COMPETENCY STANDARD

In Las Vegas, Nevada, on August 2, 1984, Richard Allen Moran fatally shot a bartender and a patron four times each. Several days later he went to the home of his former wife and fatally shot her, then turned the gun on himself. However, his suicide attempt failed, and Moran confessed to his crimes. Later, the defendant pleaded not guilty to three counts of first-degree murder. Two psychiatrists examined Moran and concluded that he was competent to stand trial. Approximately 10 weeks after the evaluations, the defendant decided to dismiss his attorneys and change his plea to guilty. After review of the psychiatric reports, the trial court accepted the waiver for counsel and the guilty plea. The defendant was later sentenced to death.

Seven months later Moran appealed his case, claiming that he had been "mentally incompetent to represent himself." The appellate court reversed the conviction, ruling that "competency to waive constitutional rights requires a higher level of mental functioning than that required to stand trial." A defendant is considered competent to stand trial if he can understand the proceedings and help in his defense. Yet, for a defendant to be considered competent to waive counsel or to plead guilty, he has to be capable of "'reasoned choice' among the alternatives available to him." The appellate court found Moran mentally incapable of the reasoned choice needed to be in a position to waive his constitutional rights.

The Supreme Court ruled 7–2 in *Godinez v. Moran* (509 U.S. 389, 1993) to reverse the judgment of the court of appeals, holding that the standard for measuring a criminal defendant's competency to plead guilty or to waive his right to counsel is not higher than the standard for standing trial. The high court then sent the case back to the lower courts for further proceedings. Moran was executed in March 1996.

VICTIM IMPACT STATEMENTS

First, They Are Not Constitutional

John Booth and Willie Reid stole money from elderly neighbors to buy heroin in 1983. Booth, knowing his neighbors could identify him, tied up the elderly couple and then repeatedly stabbed them in the chest with a kitchen knife. The couple's son found their bodies two days later. Booth and Reid were found guilty.

The state of Maryland permitted a victim impact statement to be read to the jury during the sentencing phase of the trial. The victim impact statement prepared in this case explained the tremendous pain caused by the murder of the parents and grandparents to the family. A 5–4 Supreme Court, in *Booth v. Maryland* (482 U.S. 496, 1987), while recognizing the agony caused to the victim's family, ruled that victim impact statements, as required by Maryland's statute, were unconstitutional and could not be used during the sentencing phase of a capital murder trial.

Writing for the majority, Justice Lewis F. Powell Jr. (1907–1998) indicated that a jury must determine whether the defendant should be executed, based on the circumstances of the crime and the character of the offender. These factors had nothing to do with the victim. The high court noted that it is the crime and the criminal that are at issue. Had Booth and Reid viciously murdered a drunken bum, the crime would have been just as horrible. Furthermore, some families could express the pain and disruption they suffered as a result of the murder better than other families, and a sentencing should not depend on how well a family could express its grief.

Willie Reid's sentence was later converted to two life terms. As of October 2009 Booth remained on Maryland's death row.

...And Then They Are

Pervis Tyrone Payne of Tennessee spent the morning and early afternoon of June 27, 1987, injecting cocaine and drinking beer. Later, he drove around the town with a friend, each of them taking turns reading a pornographic magazine. In mid-afternoon, Payne went to his girlfriend's apartment, who was away visiting her mother in Arkansas. Charisse Christopher lived across the hall from the apartment. Payne entered Christopher's apartment and made sexual advances toward Christopher, who resisted. Payne became violent.

When the police arrived, they found Christopher on the floor with 42 direct knife wounds and 42 defensive wounds on her arms and hands. Her two-year-old daughter had suffered stab wounds to the chest, abdomen, back, and head. The murder weapon, a butcher knife, was found at her feet. Christopher's three-year-old son, despite several stab wounds that went completely through his body, was still alive. Payne was arrested, and a Tennessee jury convicted him of the first-degree murders of Christopher and her daughter and of the first-degree assault, with intent to murder, of Christopher's son, Nicholas.

During the sentencing phase of the trial, Payne called his parents, his girlfriend, and a clinical psychologist to testify about the mitigating aspects of his background and character. The prosecutor, however, called Nicholas's grandmother, who testified how much the child missed his mother and baby sister. In arguing for the death penalty, the prosecutor commented on the continuing effects the crime was having on Nicholas and his family. The jury sentenced Payne to death on each of the murder counts. The state supreme court agreed, rejecting Payne's claim that the admission of the grandmother's testimony and the state's closing argument violated his Eighth Amendment rights under *Booth v. Maryland.*

On hearing the appeal, the U.S. Supreme Court ruled 6–3 in *Payne v. Tennessee* (501 U.S. 808, 1991) to uphold the death penalty and overturned *Booth v. Maryland.* In *Payne,* the court ruled that the Eighth Amendment does not prohibit a jury from considering, at the sentencing phase of a capital trial, victim impact evidence relating to a victim's personal characteristics and the emotional impact of the murder on the victim's family. The Eighth Amendment also does not bar a prosecutor from arguing such evidence at the sentencing phase.

The court reasoned that the assessment of harm caused by a defendant as a result of a crime has long been an important concern of criminal law in determining both the elements of the offense and the appropriate punishment. Victim impact evidence is simply another form or method of informing the sentencing jury or judge about the specific harm caused by the crime in question.

The *Booth* case unfairly weighted the scales in a capital trial. No limits were placed on the mitigating evidence the defendant introduced relating to his own circumstances. The state, however, was potentially barred from offering a glimpse of the life of the victim or from showing the loss to the victim's family or to society. *Booth* was decided by narrow margins, the court continued, and had been questioned by members of the Supreme Court as well as by the lower courts.

Dissenting, Justice Stevens stated that a victim impact statement "sheds no light on the defendant's guilt or moral culpability, and thus serves no purpose other than to encourage jurors to decide in favor of death rather than life on the basis of their emotions rather than their reason."

As of October 2009 Payne remained on Tennessee's death row.

THE ISSUE OF RACE IN CAPITAL CASES

In 1978 Willie Lloyd Turner, an African-American, robbed a jewelry store in Franklin, Virginia. Angered because the owner had set off a silent alarm, Turner first shot the owner in the head, wounding him, and then shot him twice in the chest, killing him for "snitching." Turner's lawyer submitted to the judge the following question for the jurors: "The defendant, Willie Lloyd Turner, is a member of the Negro race. The victim, W. Jack Smith, Jr., was a white Caucasian. Will these facts prejudice you against Willie Lloyd Turner or affect your ability to render a fair and impartial verdict based solely on the evidence?"

The judge refused to allow this question to be asked. A jury of eight whites and four African-Americans convicted Turner and then, in a separate sentencing hearing, recommended the death sentence, which the judge imposed.

Turner appealed his conviction, claiming that the judge's refusal to ask prospective jurors about their racial attitudes deprived him of his right to a fair trial. Even though his argument failed to convince state and federal appeals courts, the U.S. Supreme Court heard his case. The high court ruled 7–2 in *Turner v. Murray* (476 U.S. 28, 1986) to overturn Turner's death sentence, but not his conviction.

Writing for the majority, Justice White noted that, in considering a death sentence, the jury makes a subjective decision that is uniquely his or her own regarding what punishment should be meted out to the offender. White further stated:

> Because of the range of discretion entrusted to a jury in a capital sentencing hearing, there is a unique opportunity for racial prejudice to operate but remain undetected. On the facts of this case, a juror who believes that blacks are violence prone or morally inferior might well be influenced by that belief in deciding whether petitioner's crime involved the aggravating factors specified under Virginia law. Such a juror might also be less favorably inclined toward petitioner's evidence of mental disturbance as a mitigating circumstance. More subtle, less consciously held racial attitudes could also influence a juror's decision in this case. Fear of blacks, which could easily be stirred up by the violent facts of petitioner's crime, might incline a juror to favor the death penalty.

The high court recognized that the death sentence differs from all other punishments and, therefore, requires a more comprehensive examination of how it is imposed. The lower court judge, by not asking prospective jurors about their racial attitudes, had not exercised this thorough examination. Consequently, the Supreme Court reversed Turner's death sentence. Justice Powell, in his dissent, observed that the court ruling seemed to be "based on what amounts to a constitutional presumption that jurors in capital cases are racially biased. Such presumption unjustifiably suggests that criminal justice in our courts of law is meted out on racial grounds." In 1995 Turner was executed by the state of Virginia.

Limits to Consideration of Racial Attitudes

On May 13, 1978, Warren McCleskey and three armed men robbed a furniture store in Fulton County, Georgia. A police officer, responding to a silent alarm, entered the store, was shot twice, and died. McCleskey was African-American; the officer was white. McCleskey admitted taking part in the robbery but denied shooting the police officer. The state proved that at least one shot came from the weapon McCleskey was carrying and produced two witnesses who had heard McCleskey admit to the shooting. A jury found him guilty, and McCleskey, offering no mitigating circumstances during the sentencing phase, received the death penalty.

McCleskey eventually appealed his case all the way to the U.S. Supreme Court. Part of his appeal was based on two major statistical studies of more than 2,000 Georgia murder cases that occurred during the 1970s. Prepared by David C. Baldus, Charles A. Pulanski Jr., and George Woodworth, the statistical analyses were referred to as the Baldus study. (The two studies were "Comparative Review of Death Sentences: An Empirical Study of the Georgia Experience" [*Journal of Criminal Law and Criminology*, vol. 74, no. 3, 1983] and "Monitoring and Evaluating Contemporary Death Sentencing Systems: Lessons from Georgia" [*University of California Davis Law Review*, vol. 18, no. 1375, 1985].)

The Baldus study found that defendants charged with killing white people received the death penalty in 11% of cases, but defendants charged with killing African-Americans received the death penalty in only 1% of the cases. The study also found a reverse racial difference, based on the defendant's race—4% of the African-American defendants received the death penalty, as opposed to 7% of the white defendants.

Furthermore, the Baldus study reported on the cases based on the combination of the defendant's race and that of the victim. The death penalty was imposed in 22% of the cases involving African-American defendants and white victims, in 8% of the cases involving white defendants and white victims, in 3% of the cases involving white defendants and African-American victims, and in 1% of the cases involving African-American defendants and African-American victims.

The Baldus study also found that prosecutors sought the death penalty in 70% of the cases involving African-American defendants and white victims, in 32% of the cases involving white defendants and white victims, in 19% of the cases involving white defendants and African-American victims, and in 15% of the cases involving African-American defendants and African-American victims.

Finally, after taking account of variables that could have explained the differences on nonracial grounds, the study concluded that defendants charged with killing white victims were 4.3 times as likely to receive the death penalty as defendants charged with killing African-Americans. In addition, African-American defendants were 1.1 times as likely to get a death sentence as other defendants were. Therefore, McCleskey, who was African-American and killed a white victim, had the greatest likelihood of being sentenced to death.

In court testimony, Baldus testified that in really brutal cases where there is no question the death penalty should be imposed, racial discrimination on the part of the jurors tends to disappear. The racial factors usually come into play in midrange cases, such as McCleskey's, where the jurors were faced with choices.

Even though the federal district court did not accept the Baldus study, both the court of appeals and the U.S. Supreme Court accepted the study as valid. However, a 5–4 Supreme Court, in *McCleskey v. Kemp* (481 U.S. 279, 1987), rejected McCleskey's appeal. McCleskey had to show that the state of Georgia had acted in a discriminatory manner in his case, and the Baldus study was not enough to support the defendant's claim that any of the jurors had acted with discrimination.

Justice Powell noted that statistics, at most, may show that a certain factor might likely enter some decision-making processes. The court recognized that a jury's decision could be influenced by racial prejudice, but the majority believed previous rulings had built in enough safeguards to guarantee equal protection for every defendant. The court declared, "At most, the Baldus study indicates a discrepancy that appears to correlate with race. Apparent disparities in sentencing are an inevitable part of our criminal justice system. . . . We hold that the Baldus study does not demonstrate a constitutionally significant risk of racial bias affecting the Georgia capital sentencing process."

The court expressed concern that if it ruled that Baldus's findings did represent a risk, the findings might well be applied to lesser cases. It further noted that it is the job of the legislative branch to consider these findings and incorporate them into the laws to guarantee equal protection in courts of law.

Justice Brennan, who, along with Justice Marshall, believed capital punishment constitutes a cruel and unusual punishment and, therefore, is unconstitutional, thought the Baldus study powerfully demonstrated that it is impossible to eliminate arbitrariness in the imposition of the death penalty. Therefore, he argued, the death penalty must be abolished altogether because the court cannot rely on legal safeguards to guarantee an African-American defendant a fair sentencing. Even though the Baldus study did not show that racism necessarily led to McCleskey's death sentence, it had surely shown that McCleskey faced a considerably greater likelihood of

being sentenced to death because he was an African-American man convicted of killing a white man.

Also writing in dissent, Justice Blackmun thought the court majority had concentrated too much on the potential racial attitudes of the jury. As important, he thought, were the racial attitudes of the prosecutor's office, which the Baldus study found to be much more likely to seek the death penalty for an African-American person who had killed a white person than for other categories.

The district attorney for Fulton County had testified that no county policy existed on how to prosecute capital cases. Decisions to seek the death penalty were left to the judgment of the assistant district attorneys who handled the cases. Blackmun thought that such a system was certainly open to abuse. Without guidelines, the prosecutors could let their racial prejudices influence their decisions.

Blackmun also noted that the court majority had totally dismissed Georgia's history of racial prejudice as past history. Even though it should not be the overriding factor, this bias should be considered in any case presented to the high court, he thought. Justice Blackmun found most disturbing the court's concern that, if the Baldus findings were upheld, they might be applied to other cases, leading to constitutional challenges. Blackmun thought that a closer scrutiny of the effects of racial discrimination would benefit the criminal justice system and, ultimately, society.

In 1991 McCleskey was executed in the electric chair by the state of Georgia.

Prosecutor's Racially Based Use of Peremptory Challenges in Jury Selection

James Ford, an African-American, was charged with the kidnapping, rape, and murder of a white woman on February 29, 1984. The state of Georgia informed Ford that it planned to seek the death penalty. Before the trial, Ford filed a "Motion to Restrict Racial Use of Peremptory Challenges," claiming that the prosecutor had consistently excluded African-Americans from juries where the victims were white.

At a hearing on the defendant's motion, Ford's lawyer noted that it had been his experience that the district attorney and his assistants had used their peremptory challenges (the right to reject a juror without giving a reason) to excuse potential African-American jurors. Ford's lawyer asked the trial judge to prevent this from happening by ordering the district attorney to justify on the record his reasons for excusing potential African-American jurors.

The prosecutor denied any discrimination on his part. He referred to the U.S. Supreme Court decision in *Swain v. Alabama* (380 U.S. 202, 1965), which said, in part, "It would be an unreasonable burden to require an attorney for either side to justify his use of peremptory challenges." The judge denied the defense attorney's motion because he had previously seen the district attorney passing over prospective white jurors in favor of potential African-American jurors.

During jury selection the prosecutor used 9 of his 10 peremptory challenges to dismiss prospective African-American jurors, leaving only one African-American member seated on the jury. In closed sessions, the judge allowed Ford's attorney's observation, for the record, that 9 of the 10 African-American prospective members had been dismissed on peremptory challenges by the prosecutor. The judge, however, told the prosecutor that he did not have to offer any reasons for his peremptory actions.

Ford was convicted on all counts and sentenced to death. His attorney, believing that the jury did not represent a fair cross-section of the community, called for a new trial and claimed that Ford's "right to an impartial jury as guaranteed by Sixth Amendment to the United States Constitution was violated by the prosecutor's exercise of his peremptory challenges on a racial basis." On appeal, the Georgia Supreme Court affirmed the conviction.

Ford appealed to the U.S. Supreme Court. In *Ford v. Georgia* (498 U.S. 411, 1991), the high court reversed the decision of the Georgia Supreme Court. The court vacated Ford's conviction and ruled that its decision in *Batson v. Kentucky* (476 U.S. 79, 1986) could be applied retroactively to Ford's case, which had been tried in 1984. In 1986 the high court had superseded *Swain* when it ruled in *Batson* that a defendant could make a case claiming the denial of equal protection of the laws solely on evidence that the prosecutor had used peremptory challenges to exclude members of the defendant's race from the jury.

Delivering the opinion for a unanimous court, Justice Souter held that the Georgia Supreme Court had erred when it ruled that Ford had failed to present a proper equal protection claim. Even though Ford's pretrial motion did not mention the Equal Protection Clause (of the Fourteenth Amendment), and his new trial motion had cited the Sixth Amendment rather than the Fourteenth, the motion referring to a pattern of excluding African-American members "'over a long period of time' constitutes the assertion of an equal protection claim." As of October 2009 Ford was in the Georgia State Prison serving a sentence of life without the possibility of parole.

Using Race/Ethnicity to Obtain a Death Sentence

On June 5, 2000, the Supreme Court, in a summary disposition, ordered the Texas Court of Criminal Appeals to hold a new sentencing hearing for Victor Saldano, an Argentine national on death row. In a summary disposition, the court decides a case in a simple proceeding without a jury. Generally, a summary disposition is rare in criminal cases. In this instance, the crime was committed by a foreign national and thus fell outside of a trial jury's mandate. In *Saldano v. Texas* (No. 99-8119), the court cited the confession of error by the Texas attorney general John Cornyn (1952–) regarding the use of race as a factor in sentencing the defendant.

Texas death penalty statutes require that the jury consider a defendant's future dangerousness to determine whether or not to impose the death penalty. At the sentencing hearing Walter Quijano, the court-appointed psychologist, testified that Saldano was "a continuing threat to society" because he is Hispanic. Quijano told the jury that because Hispanics are "over-represented" in prisons they are more likely to be dangerous. Following this decision, other death row inmates whose cases reflected similar circumstances were granted new sentencing hearings. Saldano's own case continued in the courts; in March 2004 the Fifth U.S. Circuit Court of Appeals refused to reinstate Saldano's death sentence. As of October 2009, Saldano remained on Texas's death row.

CHAPTER 5
DEATH PENALTY LAWS: STATE, FEDERAL, AND U.S. MILITARY

STATE DEATH PENALTY LAWS

Before the late 1960s U.S. death penalty laws varied considerably from state to state and from region to region. Few national standards existed on how a murder trial should be conducted or which types of crimes deserved the death penalty. In South Carolina, for instance, a person could be executed for rape or robbery. In Georgia and in a number of other states, juries were given complete discretion in delivering a sentence along with the conviction. Though verdicts were swift, the punishments such juries meted out could be arbitrary and discriminatory.

In the late 1960s and early 1970s the U.S. Supreme Court undertook a series of cases that questioned the constitutionality of state capital punishment laws. In *Furman v. Georgia* (408 U.S. 238, 1972), the court ruled that the death penalty, as it was then being administered, constituted a cruel and unusual punishment in violation of the Eighth and Fourteenth Amendments to the U.S. Constitution. According to the court, the state laws that were then in effect led to arbitrary sentencing of the death penalty. As a result, many states changed their laws to conform to standards set by the *Furman* decision. Since *Furman*, review of individual state statutes has continued as appeals of capital sentences reach state courts or the U.S. Supreme Court. In particular, the use of capital punishment against the insane (*Ford v. Wainwright*), the mentally retarded (*Atkins v. Virginia*), and juveniles (*Roper v. Simmons*) has been found to be unconstitutional by the U.S. Supreme Court.

Court decisions have also affected state trial and sentencing procedures. Under revised laws, most states now use a bifurcated (two-part) trial system, where the first trial is used to determine a defendant's guilt, and the second trial determines the sentence of a guilty defendant. In most trials, jurors are usually only given the option of either sentencing a convicted felon to life in prison or to death. During a sentencing hearing, juries must consider all the aggravating circumstances presented by the prosecution and the mitigat-

ing circumstances presented by the defense. Mitigating circumstances may lessen responsibility for a crime, whereas aggravating circumstances may add to responsibility for a crime.

Capital Offenses under State Laws

State laws, statutes, and criminal codes specifically lay out which crimes are to be handled as capital cases. Table 5.1 lists capital offenses by state in 2007 per the U.S. Department of Justice's Bureau of Justice Statistics. Note that New Mexico eliminated the death penalty in 2009. In addition, New York's capital punishment law has been found, in part, to be unconstitutional, which will be described in Chapter 8.

CAPITAL MURDER OFFENSES. Different types of capital murder are specified by legal definition. Even though varying somewhat from one jurisdiction to another, the types of homicide most commonly specified are murder carried out during the commission of a felony (serious offense such as rape, robbery, or arson); murder of a peace officer, corrections employee, or firefighter engaged in the performance of official duties; murder by an inmate serving a life sentence; and murder for hire (contract murder). Different statutory terminology may be used in different states to designate essentially similar crimes. Terms such as *capital murder*, *first-degree murder*, *capital felony*, or *murder Class 1 felony* may indicate the same offense in different states.

NON-HOMICIDE CRIMES. As described in Chapter 3, the imposition of the death penalty for some non-homicide crimes has been ruled unconstitutional by the courts. The notable examples are rape and kidnapping in which the victim survives. However, other offenses (such as treason and air piracy or hijacking) that carry the death penalty under law have not yet had their constitutionality tested. In addition, some states are slow to change their statutes to be in accordance with Supreme Court findings. Thus, some offenses are still listed as capital offenses under state laws even though those offenses have been ruled noncapital crimes by the courts.

TABLE 5.1

Capital offenses, by state, 2007

State	Offense
Alabama	Intentional murder with 18 aggravating factors (Ala. Stat. Ann. 13A-5-40 (a)(1)-(18)).
Arizona	First-degree murder accompanied by at least 1 of 14 aggravating factors (A.R.S. § 13-703(F)).
Arkansas[a]	Capital murder (Ark. Code Ann. 5-10-101) with a finding of at least 1 of 10 aggravating circumstances; treason. **Revision:** Amended the definition of capital murder to include murder committed in the course of robbery, aggravated robbery, residential burglary, or commercial burglary (Ark. Cod Ann. § 5-10-101 (Supp. 2007)), effective 7/31/2007.
California	First-degree murder with special circumstances; train wrecking; treason; perjury causing execution.
Colorado[b]	First-degree murder with at least 1 of 17 aggravating factors; first-degree kidnapping resulting in death; treason.
Connecticut	Capital felony with 8 forms of aggravated homicide (C.G.S. § 53a-54b).
Delaware	First-degree murder with at least 1 statutory aggravating circumstance (11 Del. C. § 4209).
Florida	First-degree murder; felony murder; capital drug trafficking; capital sexual battery.
Georgia	Murder; kidnapping with bodily injury or ransom when the victim dies; aircraft hijacking; treason.
Idaho	First-degree murder with aggravating factors; aggravated kidnapping; perjury resulting in death.
Illinois	First-degree murder with 1 of 21 aggravating circumstances.
Indiana	Murder with 16 aggravating circumstances (IC 35-50-2-9).
Kansas	Capital murder with 8 aggravating circumstances (KSA 21-3439, KSA 21-4625).
Kentucky	Murder with aggravating factors; kidnapping with aggravating factors (KRS 32.025).
Louisiana	First-degree murder; aggravated rape of victim under age 13; treason (La. R.S. 14:30, 14:42, and 14:113).
Maryland	First-degree murder, either premeditated or during the commission of a felony, provided that certain death eligibility requirements are satisfied.
Mississippi	Capital murder (Miss. Code Ann. § 97-3-19(2)); aircraft piracy (Miss. Code Ann. § 97-25-55(1)).
Missouri[a]	First-degree murder (565.020 RSMO 2000). **Revision:** Added to the capital statute provisions for selecting members of the execution team and prohibiting disclosure of the identity of anyone who has been on the execution team (Mo. Rev. Stat § 546.720), effective 8/28/2007.
Montana	Capital murder with 1 of 9 aggravating circumstances (Mont. Code Ann. § 46-18-303); aggravated sexual intercourse without consent (Mont. Code Ann. § 45-5-503).
Nebraska	First-degree murder with a finding of at least 1 statutorily-defined aggravating circumstance.
Nevada	First-degree murder with at least 1 of 15 aggravating circumstances (NRS 200.030, 200.033, 200.035).
New Hampshire	Six categories of capital murder (RSA 630:1, RSA 630:5).
New Mexico	First-degree murder with at least 1 of 7 statutorily-defined aggravating circumstances (Section 30-2-1 A, NMSA).
New York	First-degree murder with 1 of 13 aggravating factors (NY Penal Law §125.27).
North Carolina	First-degree murder (NCGS §14-17).
Ohio	Aggravated murder with at least 1 of 10 aggravating circumstances (O.R.C. secs. 2903.01, 2929.02, and 2929.04).
Oklahoma	First-degree murder in conjunction with a finding of at least 1 of 8 statutorily-defined aggravating circumstances; sex crimes against a child under 14 years of age.
Oregon	Aggravated murder (ORS 163.095).
Pennsylvania	First-degree murder with 18 aggravating circumstances.
South Carolina[a]	Murder with 1 of 12 aggravating circumstances (§ 16-3-20(C)(a)); criminal sexual conduct with a minor with 1 of 9 aggravators (§ 16-3-655). **Revision:** Added as an aggravating circumstance murder committed while in the commission of first-degree arson (§16-3-20(C)(a)(1)(j)), effective 6/18/2007.
South Dakota[a]	First-degree murder with 1 of 10 aggravating circumstances. **Revision:** Amended the code of criminal procedure to allow for use of a 3-drug protocol in administering lethal injection (SDCL § 23A-27A-32), effective 7/1/2007.
Tennessee[a]	First-degree murder with 1 of 15 aggravating circumstances (Tenn. Code Ann. § 39-13-204). **Revision:** Amended the definition of first-degree murder to include killing in the perpetration of rape or aggravated rape of a child (Tenn Code Ann. § 39-13-202 (a)(2)), effective 7/1/2007.
Texas[a]	Criminal homicide with 1 of 9 aggravating circumstances (Tex. Penal Code § 19.03); super aggravated sexual assault (Tex. Penal Code § 12.42(c)(3)). **Revision:** Revised the penal code and the code of criminal procedure to allow the death penalty for aggravated sexual assault of victims under the age of 14 when the offender has a previous conviction for a similar offense (TX Penal Code § 12.42(c)(3) and Tex. Code Crim. Proc. Art. 37.072), effective 9/1/2007.
Utah[a]	Aggravated murder (76-5-202, Utah Code Annotated). **Revision:** Amended the criminal code to allow for an automatic sentence of life without parole if the death penalty is ruled unconstitutional (Utah Code Ann. § 76-3-207) and added to the definition of aggravated murder intentional killing when the victim is younger than 14 years of age (Utah Code Ann. § 76-5-202(t)). Both changes became effective 4/30/07.

THE TEXAS "LAW OF PARTIES." Under Texas law a person who is party to, but does not actually commit, a murder can receive the death penalty. Section 7.02 of the Texas Penal Code took effect in 1974 and allows prosecutors to charge an accomplice with capital murder if the accomplice should have anticipated that the murder was going to occur. This is known informally as "the law of parties" and is explained by Jordan Smith, in "Wrong Place, Wrong Time" (*Austin Chronicle*, February 11, 2005). The law of parties received national attention when it was used in 1997 to impose a death sentence against Kenneth Foster for his role as the getaway driver in a murder. Foster and three other men were arrested in 1996. They had been robbing people at gunpoint when they saw an attractive woman in a suburban neighborhood. One of the men, Mauriceo Brown, left the car to talk to the woman

TABLE 5.1

Capital offenses, by state, 2007 [CONTINUED]

State	Offense
Virginia[a]	First-degree murder with 1 of 15 aggravating circumstances (VA Code § 18.2-31). **Revision:** Added to the definition of capital murder willful, deliberate, and premeditated killing of a judge or a witness when the killing is for the purpose of interfering with the person's duties in a criminal case (Va. Code § 18.2-31(14) and (15)), effective 7/1/2007.
Washington	Aggravated first-degree murder.
Wyoming[a]	First-degree murder. **Revision:** Added as a capital offense murder during the commission of sexual abuse of a minor (W.S. § 6-2-101), effective 7/1/2007.

Notes: New Jersey enacted legislation repealing the death penalty (P.L. 2007, c.204 (NJSA2C:11-3)), effective 12/17/2007. In 2004, New York's statute was ruled in part to be unconstitutional. In 2009, New Mexico abolished the death penalty.
[a]Nine states revised statutory provisions relating to the death penalty during 2007.
[b]The Colorado Supreme Court struck a portion of that state's capital statute on April 23, 2007 (*People v. Montour*, 157 P.3d 489 (Colo. 2007)). The statute (*Colo. Rev. Stat.* § 18-1.3-1201(1)(a)) specified that defendants pleading guilty to a class 1 felony be sentenced by the judge, thereby requiring defendants to waive their right to a jury trial on all facts essential to determining death penalty eligibility as established in *Ring v. Arizona*. The court ruled that this was unconstitutional under Sixth and Fourteenth Amendments.

SOURCE: Tracy L. Snell, "Table 1. Capital Offenses, by State, 2007," in *Capital Punishment, 2007—Statistical Tables*, U.S. Department of Justice, Office of Justice Programs, Bureau of Justice Statistics, December 23, 2008, http://www.ojp.usdoj.gov/bjs/pub/html/cp/2007/cp07st.pdf (accessed August 24, 2009)

and wound up shooting and killing her boyfriend, Michael LaHood Jr. Allegedly, Brown was at least 80 feet away from the car when the shooting occurred. He fled back to the car containing the other three men and they sped from the scene. Brown was sentenced to death; he was executed in 2006. The other two men involved were not charged with capital murder.

Foster garnered the support of abolitionists who argued that a death sentence was too harsh a penalty for his crime. After exhausting all appeals Foster faced execution on August 31, 2007. Just hours before the scheduled execution the Texas governor Rick Perry (1950–) granted clemency— a very rare occurrence in the state. Foster's sentence was changed to life imprisonment with a possibility for parole.

ACTS OF TERRORISM. In the aftermath of the September 11, 2001, attacks on the World Trade Center and the Pentagon, several states expanded their death penalty statutes to apply to acts of terrorism. Because acts of terrorism generally include "regular" criminal offenses already defined by state law, terrorism statutes include additional criteria to define terrorist acts. For example, Florida Criminal Code 775.30 (2009, http://www.leg.state.fl.us/STATUTES/index.cfm?App_mode=Display_Statute&Search_String=&URL=Ch0775/SEC30.HTM&Title=->2009->Ch0775->Section%2030#0775.30) defines terrorism as an activity that violates the state's criminal code *and* "is intended to intimidate, injure, or coerce a civilian population; [i]nfluence the policy of a government by intimidation or coercion; or [a]ffect the conduct of government through destruction of property, assassination, murder, kidnapping, or aircraft piracy."

As of October 2009, however, all defendants accused of terrorist acts in relation to the September 11, 2001, attacks and the nation's subsequent "war on terror" have been prosecuted by federal or military authorities.

LEGISLATIVE MEASURES IN 2009. According to the Death Penalty Information Center (DPIC) 2009 report "Smart on Crime: Reconsidering the Death Penalty in a Time of Economic Crisis" by Richard C. Dieter (October 2009, http://www.deathpenaltyinfo.org/documents/CostsRptFinal.pdf), 11 states—Colorado, Connecticut, Illinois, Kansas, Maryland, Montana, Nebraska, New Hampshire, New Mexico, Texas, and Washington—considered bills during 2009 to repeal their capital penalty statutes. As of October 2009 only the measure in New Mexico had passed. The DPIC also reports that legislation in Virginia that would have expanded the number of offenses subject to the death penalty was vetoed by that state's governor.

The Appeals Process in State Capital Cases

The appeals process in capital cases varies slightly from state to state but generally includes the steps shown in Figure 5.1.

The appeals process begins with the direct appeal. In *Gregg v. Georgia* (428 U.S. 153, 1976), the U.S. Supreme Court ruled that any death sentence must be appealed from the trial court directly to the highest court in the state with criminal jurisdiction. The highest court of the state may be either the state supreme court or the highest court of criminal appeals. The state high court evaluates the trial court records for constitutional or legal errors. If the high court upholds the conviction and sentence, the defendant can appeal directly to the U.S. Supreme Court using a writ of certiorari. A writ of certiorari is a petition to the Supreme Court to review only the issues brought up in the direct appeal in the state's high court. If the Supreme Court denies certiorari, the trial court's ruling stands.

If the first round of direct appeals is denied, the inmate may then seek state habeas corpus appeals (federal appeals by which state and federal inmates request a federal court to determine whether they are being held in violation of their

FIGURE 5.1

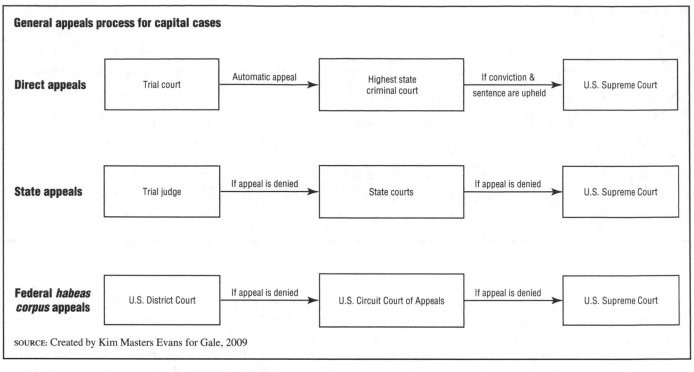

General appeals process for capital cases

Direct appeals	Trial court	Automatic appeal →	Highest state criminal court	If conviction & sentence are upheld →	U.S. Supreme Court
State appeals	Trial judge	If appeal is denied →	State courts	If appeal is denied →	U.S. Supreme Court
Federal *habeas corpus* appeals	U.S. District Court	If appeal is denied →	U.S. Circuit Court of Appeals	If appeal is denied →	U.S. Supreme Court

SOURCE: Created by Kim Masters Evans for Gale, 2009

constitutional rights), starting with the trial judge. Habeas corpus review, which affords state and federal prisoners the chance to challenge the constitutionality of their convictions or sentences, has long been considered an important safeguard in all criminal trials, especially those involving the death penalty. If turned down by the trial judge, the convict may petition the first level of state appellate courts and finally the state's highest court. This second round of appeals differs from the direct appeal in that the condemned may raise issues that were not and could not have been raised during the direct appeal. These issues include the incompetence of the defense lawyer, jury bias, or the suppression of evidence by police or prosecution. If the state review is denied, the condemned can again appeal directly to the U.S. Supreme Court.

A death row inmate who has exhausted all state appeals can then file a petition for a federal habeas corpus review on grounds of violation of his or her constitutional rights. The right may involve a violation of the Sixth Amendment to the U.S. Constitution (the right to have the assistance of counsel for defense), the Eighth Amendment (the ban against a cruel and unusual punishment), or the Fourteenth Amendment (the right to due process). The inmate files the appeal with the district court in the state in which he or she was convicted. If the district court denies the appeal, the inmate can proceed to the U.S. Circuit Court of Appeals in the region. As of 2009 there were 94 federal judicial districts and 12 U.S. Circuit Courts of Appeal around the United States. (See Figure 5.2.) Finally, if the circuit court denies the appeal, the condemned can for a third time ask the U.S. Supreme Court for a certiorari review.

If a convict comes to the end of all appeals and is still on death row, the only way the sentence can be altered is through the power of clemency. The power of clemency may rest solely with a state's governor, with a clemency board, or with the governor and a board of advisers. (See Table 5.2.) All states provide for clemency, which may take the form of a reprieve, a commutation, or a pardon. A reprieve, which typically involves a stay of execution, is just a temporary measure to allow further investigation of a case. A commutation involves the reduction of a criminal sentence after a criminal conviction. In the context of capital punishment, a commutation typically means replacing the death sentence with a lesser sentence, such as life without parole. Table 5.3 lists the number of death sentences that were commuted between 1973 and 2008 by each jurisdiction. Illinois had the most commutations (156), followed by Texas (52) and Florida (18). Neither a reprieve nor a commutation removes a person's responsibility for the crime. A pardon, however, frees from punishment a person convicted of a crime, as well as removes his or her criminal record as if the conviction never happened. Pardons are generally only given if investigators can prove beyond any doubt that a death row inmate did not commit the crime of which he or she was convicted.

According to the DPIC, 245 clemencies were granted by states and the federal government "for humanitarian reasons" between 1976 and September 2009. (See Table 5.4.) The DPIC notes that humanitarian reasons include "doubts about the defendant's guilt or conclusions of the governor regarding the death penalty process." The vast majority (172) of the humanitarian-based clemencies occurred in Illinois. In 2003 Illinois Governor George Ryan (1934–)

FIGURE 5.2

Geographic boundaries of United States Courts of Appeals and United States District Courts

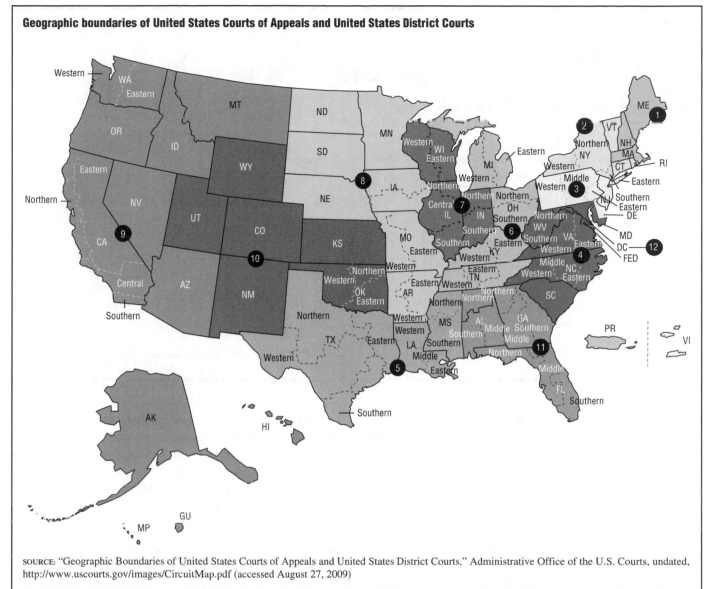

SOURCE: "Geographic Boundaries of United States Courts of Appeals and United States District Courts," Administrative Office of the U.S. Courts, undated, http://www.uscourts.gov/images/CircuitMap.pdf (accessed August 27, 2009)

commuted the death sentences or pardoned all of the state's death row prisoners. Despite this event, clemencies are rarely granted. As shown in Table 5.4, all other states (and the federal government) reported a small number of clemencies granted for humanitarian reasons between 1976 and September 2009. Texas, a state with an active death penalty process, had only two clemencies during this period.

State Death Penalty Methods

The U.S. Department of Justice reports in *Capital Punishment, 2007—Statistical Tables* (December 23, 2008) that 36 states used lethal injection as the primary method of execution in 2007. (See Table 5.5.) Some states also authorized one or more alternative methods—electrocution, lethal gas, hanging, or death by firing squad. As described in the notes to Table 5.5, the choice of method is generally left up to the condemned, depending on when the sentence was imposed. As of 2007

electrocution was the only method used to administer the death penalty in Nebraska. However, in 2008 the state's supreme court found that method to be unconstitutional. In 2009 Nebraska lawmakers authorized lethal injection as the state's sole method of execution. Also in 2009 the state of Idaho eliminated the firing squad as an optional execution method, leaving lethal injection as its sole execution method.

Witnesses to State Executions

Death penalty states have statutes or policies (or both) that specify which witnesses may be present at an execution. Witnesses usually include prison officials, physicians, the condemned person's relatives, the victim's relatives, spiritual advisers, selected state citizens, and reporters. In celebrated cases, however, such as that of Julius Rosenberg (1918–1953) and Ethel Rosenberg (1915–1953), who were convicted spies, the notorious California killer Caryl

TABLE 5.2

Clemency process by state

States in which the governor has sole authority (14)

Alabama	Kansas	New Mexico	Oregon	Washington
California[a]	Kentucky	New York[c]	South Carolina	Wyoming
Colorado	New Jersey[c]	North Carolina	Virginia	

States in which the governor must have the recommendation of clemency from a board or advisory group (8)

Arizona	Louisiana	Oklahoma
Delaware	Montana	Pennsylvania
Florida[b]		Texas

States in which the governor may receive a non-binding recommendation of clemency from a board or advisory group (10)

Arkansas	Mississippi	Ohio
Illinois	Missouri	South Dakota
Indiana	New Hampshire	Tennessee
Maryland		

States in which a board or advisory group determines clemency (3)

Connecticut	Georgia	Idaho

States in which the governor sits on a board or advisory group that determines clemency (3)

Nebraska	Nevada	Utah

Note: For federal death row inmates, the president alone has pardon power.
[a]California—The governor may not grant a pardon or commutation to a person twice convicted of a felony except on recommendation of the state Supreme Court, with at least four judges concurring.
[b]Florida's governor must have recommendation of board, on which s/he sits.
[c]New York and New Jersey no longer have the death penalty, as of 2007.

SOURCE: "Clemency Process by State," in *Clemency*, Death Penalty Information Center, 2009, http://www.deathpenaltyinfo.org/clemency (accessed August 24, 2009)

Chessman (1921–1960), and the convicted Oklahoma City bomber Timothy McVeigh (1968–2001), the witnesses made up a larger group.

FEDERAL DEATH PENALTY LAWS

In modern times, capital punishment has generally fallen under the states' purview. Each year, the federal government pursues the death penalty in far fewer cases than most states with death penalty statutes. The reason for this is simple: Most crimes are state crimes. Generally speaking, the federal government is only involved in prosecuting a relatively small number of crimes—those that cross state boundaries, those that are committed on federal property, or crimes that affect federal officials or the working of the federal government. Table 5.6 lists federal capital offenses by law as of October 2008.

The federal government, however, has been executing criminals almost since its formation. In 1790 Thomas Bird became the first inmate executed under the federal death penalty. He was hanged in Maine for murder. The DPIC reports that 34 people were executed by the federal government between 1927 and 1963 (2009, http://www.deathpenaltyinfo.org/federal-executions-1927-2003). On February 15, 1963, Victor Feguer was hanged in Iowa for kidnapping and murder. This was the last execution by the federal government until nearly 40 years later.

Expansion of the Federal Death Penalty

In 1988 Congress enacted the first of several laws that broadened the scope of the federal death penalty. The Anti-Drug Abuse Act included a drug-kingpin provision, allowing the death penalty for murder resulting from large-scale illegal drug dealing. The act did not specify the method of federal execution. In 1993 President George H. W. Bush (1924–) authorized the use of lethal injection under this law.

In 1994 the Violent Crime Control and Law Enforcement Act (also known as the Federal Death Penalty Act) added more than 50 crimes punishable by death. Among these federal crimes are murder of certain government officials, kidnapping resulting in death, murder for hire, fatal drive-by shootings, sexual abuse crimes resulting in death, carjacking resulting in death, and other crimes not resulting in death, such as running a large-scale drug enterprise. The method of execution would be the same as that used in the state where the sentencing occurred. If the state did not allow the death penalty, the judge would choose a state with the death penalty.

Antiterrorism legislation came about in the wake of the Oklahoma City bombing in 1995 and the September 11, 2001, terrorist attacks. In 1996 Congress passed and President Bill Clinton (1946–) signed the Antiterrorism and Effective Death Penalty Act (AEDPA). Another capital crime was added on June 25, 2002, as part of the Terrorist Bombings Convention Implementation Act of 2002. The law makes punishable by death the bombing of places of public use, government facilities, public transportation systems, and infrastructure facilities with the intent to cause death or serious physical injury or with intent to cause

TABLE 5.3

Number of death sentences commuted, 1973–2008

	Sentence commuted
Federal	1
Alabama	2
Arizona	6
Arkansas	2
California	15
Colorado	1
Connecticut	0
Delaware	0
Florida	18
Georgia	9
Idaho	3
Illinois	156
Indiana	6
Kansas	0
Kentucky	2
Louisiana	7
Maryland	4
Massachusetts	2
Mississippi	0
Missouri	2
Montana	1
Nebraska	2
Nevada	4
New Jersey	8
New Mexico	5
New York	0
North Carolina	8
Ohio	12
Oklahoma	3
Oregon	0
Pennsylvania	6
Rhode Island	0
South Carolina	3
South Dakota	0
Tennessee	4
Texas	52
Utah	1
Virginia	11
Washington	0
Wyoming	0
Total	**356**

Note: Data for 2006–2008 from Death Penalty Information Center

SOURCE: Adapted from "Appendix Table 4. Number Sentenced to Death and Number of Removals, by Jurisdiction and Reason for Removal, 1973–2005," in *Capital Punishment, 2005*, U.S. Department of Justice, Office of Justice Programs, Bureau of Justice Statistics, December 2006, http://www.ojp.usdoj.gov/bjs/pub/pdf/cp05.pdf (accessed August 24, 2009) and text in *The Death Penalty in 2007: Year End Report*, Death Penalty Information Center, December 2007, http://www.deathpenaltyinfo.org/2007YearEnd.pdf (accessed August 27, 2008) and text in *The Death Penalty in 2008: Year End Report*, Death Penalty Information Center, December 2008, http://www.deathpenaltyinfo.org/2008YearEnd.pdf (accessed August 27, 2008)

TABLE 5.4

Clemencies granted, by state, 1976–2009

Clemencies granted by state since 1976	Number of clemencies
Illinois	172
Ohio	11
New Jersey	8
Virginia	8
Florida	6
Georgia	7
New Mexico	5
North Carolina	5
Indiana	3
Kentucky	2
Maryland	2
Missouri	2
Louisiana	2
Oklahoma	3
Texas	2
Alabama	1
Arkansas	1
Idaho	1
Montana	1
Nevada	1
Tennessee	1
Federal	1
Total	**245**

SOURCE: "Clemencies Granted by State since 1976," in *Clemency*, Death Penalty Information Center, 2009, http://www.deathpenaltyinfo.org/clemency (accessed August 24, 2009)

mation helpful to defense attorneys appointed in federal death penalty cases. According to Dick Burr, David Bruck, and Kevin McNally of the FDPRCP, in "An Overview of the Federal Death Penalty Process" (August 3, 2009, http://www.capdefnet.org/fdprc/contents/shared_files/docs/1__overview_of_fed_death_process.asp), between 1988, when the Anti-Drug Abuse Act was signed into law, and August 3, 2009, the U.S. attorney general authorized the government to seek the death penalty against 461 defendants. Of these, 261 were tried, of which three were executed—McVeigh and Juan Raul Garza in 2001 and Louis Jones Jr. in 2003. Most of the rest of the defendants received life sentences from juries or judges or through plea bargain agreements.

The federal government's death row and execution chamber are located in Terre Haute, Indiana. According to the DPIC, 58 inmates were on federal death row as of September 30, 2009 (http://www.deathpenaltyinfo.org/federal-death-row-prisoners). In federal cases, the president alone has clemency power.

Federal Government Resumes Executions

Timothy McVeigh was sentenced to death for conspiracy and murder in 1997 for the bombing of the Alfred P. Murrah Federal Building in Oklahoma City, Oklahoma, on April 19, 1995, which killed 168 people. McVeigh received an execution date of May 16, 2001. Then–U.S. Attorney General John D. Ashcroft (1942–), however, delayed the execution following the discovery that the

destruction resulting in major economic loss. The USA Patriot Act of 2001 and the USA Patriot Act Improvement and Reauthorization Act of 2005 expanded the list of terrorist acts deemed federal crimes that could be subject to the death penalty.

New Laws Lead to an Increase in Federal Capital Cases

In 1992 the Administrative Office of the United States Court established the Federal Death Penalty Resource Counsel Project (FDPRCP) to serve as a clearinghouse for infor-

TABLE 5.5

Method of execution, by state, 2007

Lethal injection	Electrocution	Lethal gas	Hanging	Firing squad
Alabama[a]	Alabama[a]	Arizona[a,b]	Delaware[a,c]	Idaho[a]
Arizona[a,b]	Arkansas[a,d]	California[a]	New Hampshire[a,e]	Oklahoma[f]
Arkansas[a,d]	Florida[a]	Missouri[a]	Washington[a]	Utah[g]
California[a]	Illinois[a,h]	Wyoming[j]		
Colorado	Kentucky[a,i]			
Connecticut	Nebraska			
Delaware[a,c]	Oklahoma[f]			
Florida[a]	South Carolina[a]			
Georgia	Tennessee[a,k]			
Idaho[a]	Virginia[a]			
Illinois[a]				
Indiana				
Kansas				
Kentucky[a,i]				
Louisiana				
Maryland				
Mississippi				
Missouri[a]				
Montana				
Nevada				
New Hampshire[a]				
New Mexico				
New York				
North Carolina				
Ohio				
Oklahoma[a]				
Oregon				
Pennsylvania				
South Carolina[a]				
South Dakota				
Tennessee[a,k]				
Texas				
Utah[a]				
Virginia[a]				
Washington[a]				
Wyoming[a]				

Notes: The method of execution of federal prisoners is lethal injection, pursuant to 28 CFR, Part 26. For offenses under the Violent Crime Control and Law Enforcement Act of 1994, the execution method is that of the state in which the conviction took place (18 U.S.C. 3596). In 2004, New York's statute was ruled in part to be unconstitutional. In 2009 New Mexico abolished the death penalty.

[a]Authorizes two methods of execution.
[b]Authorizes lethal injection for persons sentenced after November 15, 1992; inmates sentenced before that date may select lethal injection or gas.
[c]Authorizes lethal injection for those whose capital offense occurred on or after June 13, 1986; those who committed the offense before that date may select lethal injection or hanging.
[d]Authorizes lethal injection for those whose offense occurred on or after July 4, 1983; inmates whose offense occurred before that date may select lethal injection or electrocution.
[e]Authorizes hanging only if lethal injection cannot be given.
[f]Authorizes electrocution if lethal injection is held to be unconstitutional, and firing squad if both lethal injection and electrocution are held to be unconstitutional.
[g]Authorizes firing squad if lethal injection is held unconstitutional. Inmates who selected execution by firing squad prior to May 3, 2004, may still be entitled to execution by that method.
[h]Authorizes electrocution only if lethal injection is held illegal or unconstitutional.
[i]Authorizes lethal gas if lethal injection is held to be unconstitutional.
[j]Authorizes lethal injection for persons sentenced on or after March 31, 1998; inmates sentenced before that date may select lethal injection or electrocution.
[k]Authorizes lethal injection for those whose capital offense occurred after December 31, 1998; those who committed the offense before that date may select electrocution by written waiver.

SOURCE: Tracy L. Snell, "Table 2. Method of Execution, by State, 2007," in *Capital Punishment, 2007—Statistical Tables*, U.S. Department of Justice, Office of Justice Programs, Bureau of Justice Statistics, December 23, 2008, http://www.ojp.usdoj.gov/bjs/pub/html/cp/2007/cp07st.pdf (accessed August 24, 2009)

Federal Bureau of Investigation (FBI) had failed to turn over more than 3,000 documents to the defense and prosecution during the trial. McVeigh appealed for a second stay of execution, but the U.S. Court of Appeals for the Tenth Circuit denied his request, affirming a U.S. District Court's ruling that there was no evidence that the federal government intentionally hid the FBI files from the defense. On June 11, 2001, the execution was carried out.

Eight days later, on June 19, 2001, the Texas drug boss Juan Raul Garza became the second federal prisoner to be executed since 1963. He was the first person to be executed under the Anti-Drug Abuse Act of 1988 for murders result-ing from a drug enterprise. Garza received the death sentence in 1993 for the 1990 murders of three associates.

Garza was initially scheduled to be executed in August 2000. In July 2000 President Clinton granted a four-month reprieve (a stay of execution for a short time to resolve an issue) to allow the Department of Justice to establish clemency guidelines by which a death row inmate could plead for his or her life after exhausting all appeals. Some critics noted that the Clinton administration, which had been running the government for seven years, should have previously taken the time to put in place a clemency protocol for capital cases. Others claimed the government could have

TABLE 5.6

Federal crimes punishable by death

7 U.S.C. 2146 (murder of a federal animal transportation inspector)
8 U.S.C. 1324 (death resulting from smuggling aliens into the United States)
15 U.S.C. 1825(a)(2)(C) (killing those enforcing the Horse Protection Act)
18 U.S.C. 32 (death resulting from destruction of aircraft or their facilities)
18 U.S.C. 33 (death resulting from destruction of motor vehicles or their facilities used in United States foreign commerce)
18 U.S.C. 36 (murder by drive-by shooting)
18 U.S.C. 37 (death resulting from violence at international airports)
18 U.S.C. 115(a)(1)(A) (murder of a family member of a United States officer, employee or judge with intent to impede or retaliate for performance of federal duties)
18 U.S.C. 115(a)(1)(B) (murder of a former United States officer, employee or judge or any member of their families in retaliation for performance of federal duties)
18 U.S.C. 229 (death resulting from chemical weapons offenses)
18 U.S.C. 241 (death resulting from conspiracy against civil rights)
18 U.S.C. 242 (death resulting from deprivation of civil rights under color of law)
18 U.S.C. 245 (death resulting from deprivation of federally protected activities)
18 U.S.C. 247 (death resulting from obstruction of religious beliefs)
18 U.S.C. 351 (killing a member of Congress, cabinet officer, or Supreme Court justice)
18 U.S.C. 794 (espionage)
18 U.S.C. 844(d) (death resulting from the unlawful transportation of explosives in United States foreign commerce)
18 U.S.C. 844(f) (death resulting from bombing federal property)
18 U.S.C. 844(i) (death resulting from bombing property used in or used in an activity which affects United States foreign commerce)
18 U.S.C. 924(c) (death resulting from carrying or using a firearm during and in relation to a crime of violence or a drug trafficking offense)
18 U.S.C. 930(c) (use of a firearm or dangerous weapon a firearm or other dangerous weapon in a federal facility)
18 U.S.C. 1091 (genocide when the offender is a United States national)
18 U.S.C. 1111 (murder within the special maritime jurisdiction of the United States)
18 U.S.C. 1114 (murder of a federal employee, including a member of the United States military, or anyone assisting a federal employee or member of the United States military during the performance of (or on account of) the performance of official duties)
18 U.S.C. 1116 (murder of an internationally protected person)
18 U.S.C. 1119 (murder of a U.S. national by another outside the United States)
18 U.S.C. 1120 (murder by a person who has previously escaped from a federal prison)
18 U.S.C. 1121(a) (murder of another who is assisting or because of the other's assistance in a federal criminal investigation or killing (because of official status) a state law enforcement officer assisting in a federal criminal investigation)
18 U.S.C. 1201 (kidnapping where death results)
18 U.S.C. 1203 (hostage-taking where death results)
18 U.S.C. 1503 (murder to obstruct federal judicial proceedings)
18 U.S.C. 1512 (tampering with a federal witness or informant where death results)
18 U.S.C. 1513 (retaliatory murder of a federal witness or informant)
18 U.S.C. 1716 (death resulting from mailing injurious items)
18 U.S.C. 1751 (murder of the President, Vice President, or a senior White House official)
18 U.S.C. 1958 (murder for hire in violation of U.S. law)
18 U.S.C. 1959 (murder in aid of racketeering)
18 U.S.C. 1992 (attacks on railroad and mass transit systems engaged in interstate or foreign commerce resulting in death)
18 U.S.C. 2113 (murder committed during the course of a bank robbery)
18 U.S.C. 2119 (death resulting from carjacking)
18 U.S.C. 2241, 2245 (aggravated sexual abuse within the special maritime and territorial jurisdiction of the United States where death results)
18 U.S.C. 2242, 2245 (sexual abuse within the special maritime and territorial jurisdiction of the United States where death results)
18 U.S.C. 2243, 2245 (sexual abuse of a minor or ward within the special maritime and territorial jurisdiction of the United States where death results)
18 U.S.C. 2244, 2245 (abusive sexual contact within the special maritime and territorial jurisdiction of the United States where death results)
18 U.S.C. 2251 (murder during the course of sexual exploitation of a child)
18 U.S.C. 2280 (a killing resulting from violence against maritime navigation)
18 U.S.C. 2281 (death resulting from violence against fixed maritime platforms)
18 U.S.C. 2282A (murder using devices or dangerous substances in U.S. waters)
18 U.S.C. 2283 (transportation of explosives, biological, chemical, radioactive or nuclear materials for terrorist purposes on the high seas or aboard a U.S. vessel or in U.S. waters)
18 U.S.C. 2291 (murder in the destruction of vessels or maritime facilities)
18 U.S.C. 2332 (killing an American overseas)
18 U.S.C. 2332a (death resulting from use of weapons of mass destruction)
18 U.S.C. 2322b (multinational terrorism involving murder)
18 U.S.C. 2332f (death resulting from bombing of public places, government facilities, public transportation systems or infrastructure facilities, [effective when the terrorist bombing treaty enters into force for the United States])
18 U.S.C. 2340A (death resulting from torture committed outside the United States)
18 U.S.C. 2381 (treason)
18 U.S.C. 2441 (war crimes)
18 U.S.C. 3261 (murder committed by members of the United States armed forces or accompanying or employed by the United States armed forces overseas)
21 U.S.C. 461(c) (murder of federal poultry inspectors during or because of official duties)
21 U.S.C. 675 (murder of federal meat inspectors during or because of official duties)
21 U.S.C. 848(c), 18 U.S.C. 3592(b) (major drug kingpins and attempted murder by drug kingpins to obstruct justice)
21 U.S.C. 848(e)(1) (drug kingpin murders)
21 U.S.C. 1041(c) (murder of an egg inspector during or because of official duties)
42 U.S.C. 2283 (killing federal nuclear inspectors during or because of official duties)
49 U.S.C. 46502 (air piracy where death results)
49 U.S.C. 46506 (murder within the special aircraft jurisdiction of the United States)

SOURCE: Charles Doyle, "Federal Crimes Punishable by Death," in *The Death Penalty: Capital Punishment Legislation in the 110th Congress*, Congressional Research Service, October 15, 2008, http://wikileaks.org/leak/crs/RL34163.pdf (accessed August 24, 2009)

applied to capital cases the clemency guidelines that it uses for noncapital cases. It should be noted that, even with no formal guidelines in place, Garza could have pleaded for clemency.

On September 13, 2000, Garza asked President Clinton to commute his death sentence to life imprisonment without parole. Garza's lawyer argued that the Department of Justice study of the federal death penalty system, released the day before, showed that federal capital punishment is "plagued by systemic bias, disparity and arbitrariness." The defense counsel claimed that it would be unfair to put Garza to death because the federal death penalty discriminates against members of minorities and is administered unevenly geographically. (Of the 18 men on federal death row at that time, 16 were minorities, and 6 had been convicted in Texas.) Again, the president delayed the execution, this time to December 12, 2000. It took another six months for the U.S. government to carry out Garza's death penalty. George W. Bush (1946–), the newly elected president and formerly the governor of Texas, refused to stay the execution, and Garza was executed June 19, 2001.

Louis Jones Jr., a retired soldier, was executed by the U.S. government on March 18, 2003. In 1995 Jones was convicted of killing a female soldier. He admitted kidnapping Tracie Joy McBride from an air force base in Texas. The federal government prosecuted Jones because his crime originally occurred at a U.S. military facility. As of September 2009, Jones was the last person to have been executed by the federal government.

Federal Capital Punishment in Non–Death Penalty States

According to U.S. Department of Justice policy, federal criminal law can be enacted in any state. Federal law can also be enacted in any U.S. territory. In 2000 federal prosecutors in Puerto Rico sought the death penalty against two men for kidnapping and murder. Puerto Rico had its last execution in 1927 and had banned the death penalty in 1929. In August 2003 a federal jury voted to acquit the defendants.

Massachusetts outlawed capital punishment in 1975, but in 2000 the federal government sought the death penalty in the case of Kristen Gilbert in Massachusetts. Gilbert was charged with killing four patients at the Veterans Affairs Medical Center in Northampton, a federal hospital. The jury found Gilbert guilty of first-degree murder but was deadlocked on the death sentence. As a result, Judge Michael A. Ponsor (1946–) sentenced the defendant to life imprisonment without the possibility of parole.

Michigan has not executed an inmate under state law since it joined the Union in 1837. In 1938 Anthony Cherboris was executed in the state under federal law for killing a bystander during a bank robbery. This was the last federal death sentence in Michigan until March 16, 2002, when

Marvin Gabrion received the death penalty for killing Rachel Timmerman in 1997 on federal property in Manistee National Forest. No execution date had been set for Gabrion as of October 2009.

In September 2003 Massachusetts was once again the scene of a federal death penalty case. The Federal Death Penalty Act of 1994 allowed federal prosecutors to seek the death penalty in the case of Gary Lee Sampson, who killed two men in separate carjacking incidents in 2001. Before the trial phase began, Sampson pleaded guilty to the crimes. The case proceeded to the penalty phase, in which a federal jury sentenced him to death. As of September 2009, Sampson remained on death row.

According to the DPIC (2009, http://www.deathpenalty info.org/federal-death-penalty), 6 of the 58 inmates on federal death row as of September 2, 2009, had been sentenced for crimes that occurred in states that do not have the death penalty—two in Iowa and one each in Massachusetts, Michigan, North Dakota, and Vermont. The sentence in North Dakota was particularly notable, because it involved a crime that began in neighboring Minnesota, also a non–death penalty state. In 2003 Dru Sjodin, a student at the University of North Dakota, was kidnapped, raped, and murdered. Her body was found in Minnesota. Alfonso Rodriguez Jr. was convicted of the crime and sentenced to death. The judge ordered the execution to take place in South Dakota, which allows the death penalty by means of lethal injection.

Federal prisoners in death penalty cases used to be imprisoned in the state where the trial was held, but during the 1990s the U.S. Bureau of Prisons built the 50-cell federal death house in Terre Haute to accommodate the condemned. It started housing death row inmates in 1999.

Limiting Federal Appeals

The Antiterrorism and Effective Death Penalty Act (AEDPA) of 1996 applied new restrictions and filing deadlines regarding appeals by death row inmates. It restricts death row inmates' use of habeas corpus petitions. The law requires death row inmates to file their habeas corpus petitions in the appropriate district courts within six months of the final state appeal. Before the enactment of this law, no filing deadline existed. Under the 1996 law, a defendant who fails to challenge his or her conviction or sentence within the time specified cannot file another petition unless approved by a three-judge appellate court. The AEDPA further dictates that federal judges must defer to the rulings of the state courts, unless the rulings violate the U.S. Constitution or U.S. laws or contradict "the Supreme Court's recognition of a new federal right that is made retroactively applicable."

Some opponents feared that the limitations on federal habeas corpus petitions required by the AEDPA would contribute to the execution of innocent people. In addition, they believed that the unclear language of the AEDPA allowed for varying interpretations in federal appeals courts. For the first time, in 2000, in *Williams v. Taylor* (529 U.S. 362) and *Williams v. Taylor* (529 U.S. 420), the U.S. Supreme Court addressed the lower courts' interpretation of the AEDPA, ultimately ruling that the AEDPA was valid as long as the state appellate courts did not uphold rulings contrary to the precedents laid down by the U.S. Supreme Court.

Federal Death Penalty Methods

The federal government currently authorizes the method of execution under two different laws. Crimes prosecuted under 28 Code of Federal Regulations, Part 26, call for execution by lethal injection, whereas offenses covered by the Violent Crime Control and Law Enforcement Act of 1994 (also known as the Federal Death Penalty Act of 1994) are referred to the state where the conviction occurred.

U.S. MILITARY DEATH PENALTY LAWS

The U.S. military has its own death penalty law: the Uniform Code of Military Justice (UCMJ) found under U.S. Code, Title 10, Chapter 47. Lethal injection is the method of execution. For crimes that occurred on or after November 17, 1997, the UCMJ provides the alternative sentence of life without the possibility of parole. As commander in chief, the president of the United States can write regulations and procedures to implement the UCMJ provisions. The military needs the president's approval to implement a death sentence.

According to the DPIC in "The U.S. Military Death Penalty" (January 1, 2009, http://www.deathpenaltyinfo.org/us-military-death-penalty), the U.S. military executed 135 people between 1916 and 2009. The first U.S. soldier to be executed since the Civil War (1861–1865) was U.S. Army Private Edward Slovik (1920–1945). In 1944 he was charged with desertion while assigned to the European theater during World War II (1939–1945). Even though Slovik was just one of hundreds of U.S. soldiers who were convicted of desertion and sentenced to death, he was the only one executed. It is believed that, among other reasons, the military wanted to use his case as a deterrent to future desertions. Slovik died by firing squad on January 31, 1945, in France. Since then no other soldier has been executed for desertion. The last military execution occurred on April 13, 1961, when U.S. Army Private John A. Bennett (1935–1961) was hanged for the 1954 rape and attempted murder of an 11-year-old Austrian girl.

In "The U.S. Military Death Penalty," the DPIC reports that there were nine men on military death row in 2009: six African-Americans, two whites, and one Asian. All were convicted of premeditated murder or felony murder (murder that occurs during the commission of another serious crime, such as arson). The military's death row is located at the U.S. Disciplinary Barracks at Fort Leavenworth, Kansas.

CHAPTER 6
STATISTICS: DEATH SENTENCES, CAPITAL CASE COSTS, AND EXECUTIONS

STATISTICAL SOURCES

On a nationwide basis there are three primary sources of statistical information regarding death sentences, inmates on death row, and executions. The first is the Bureau of Justice Statistics (BJS), a division of the Office of Justice Programs under the U.S. Department of Justice (DOJ). Since 1993 the BJS has published an annual report titled *Capital Punishment* (http://www.ojp.gov/bjs/cp.htm#publications) that summarizes data collected by the U.S. Census Bureau from state correctional offices as part of the National Prisoner Statistics program. The reports for 1993 through 2005 are available in both paper and electronic format and include detailed information and data analysis. The reports for 2006 and 2007 (the latest available as of October 2009) are electronic versions only and include a limited number of statistical tables with no detailed analysis. *Capital Punishment, 2007: Statistical Tables* (December 23, 2008, http://www.ojp.gov/bjs/pub/html/cp/2007/cp07st.htm) provides statistics on death row inmates and executions conducted through 2007. In many cases in this chapter, the BJS statistics are updated with data for 2008 collected from two other notable sources: the Death Penalty Information Center (DPIC) and the Criminal Justice Project of the NAACP Legal Defense and Educational Fund Inc. (LDF).

The DPIC (http://www.deathpenaltyinfo.org/contact-dpic) is a private nonprofit organization that provides a comprehensive array of news, statistics, and other information about capital punishment and the inmates on death row. Since 1996 the DPIC has published in December an annual report known as its year-end report (http://www.deathpenaltyinfo.org/reports). As of October 2009, the latest report available was *The Death Penalty in 2008: Year End Report* (December 2008, http://www.deathpenaltyinfo.org/2008Yearend.pdf). The LDF calls itself "America's legal counsel on issues of race" (http://www.naacpldf.org/content.aspx?article=1133). Since 2000 the organization's Criminal Justice Project has published a series of reports titled *Death Row U.S.A.* (http://www.naacpldf.org/content.aspx?article=297) that list the names of all inmates known to be on death row or to have been executed. The race and gender of death row defendants is included. Information is also provided on the race and gender of executed defendants and their victims on a state-by-state basis. As of fall 2009, the latest report available was *Death Row U.S.A.: Winter 2009* by Deborah Fins (January 1, 2009, (http://www.naacpldf.org/content/pdf/pubs/drusa/DRUSA_Winter_2009.pdf). The DPIC and LDF are opposed to capital punishment.

DEATH ROW

Table 6.1 lists the cities and states in which death row facilities are located around the country. Most states house men and women inmates under sentence of death in different cities.

It should be noted that the number of inmates on death row is constantly changing. New death sentences increase the number, but existing death sentences may be overturned during the appeals process. Commutations, pardons, executions, and deaths due to causes other than execution also reduce the number of prisoners on death row in any given year.

Death Row Demographics: Year-end 2007

As noted earlier, the BJS publication *Capital Punishment, 2007: Statistical Tables* provides statistics on death row inmates as of year-end 2007. Table 6.2 shows the breakdown of death row entries and exits during 2007 for the state and federal prison systems. At the end of 2006, 3,233 prisoners were under sentence of death. The vast majority of prisoners (3,191) were on state death rows. Only 42 of the inmates were on federal death row. The overall racial makeup of the death row prisoners at that time was 1,806 white inmates (56% of total) and 1,353 black inmates (42% of total). Although the number of death row prisoners of other races is not provided, it made up 2% of the total at year-end 2006.

TABLE 6.1

Death row locations, by state

Alabama	Atmore (Women: Wetumpka)
Arizona	Florence (Women: Perryville)
Arkansas	Grady (Women: Pine Bluff)
California	San Quentin (Women: Chowchilla)
Colorado	Canon City
Connecticut	Somers
Delaware	Smyrna (Women: Claymont)
Federal system	Terre Haute, IN
Florida	Stark (Women: Lowell)
Georgia	Jackson (Women: Atlanta)
Idaho	Boise (Women: Pocatello)
Illinois	Pontiac (Women: Dwight)
Indiana	Michigan City (Women: Indianapolis)
Kansas	El Dorado (Women: Topeka)
Kentucky	Eddyville (Women: Pee Wee Valley)
Louisiana	Angola (Women: St. Gabriel)
Maryland	Baltimore
Mississippi	Parchman (Women: Pearl)
Missouri	Mineral Point (Women: Fulton)
Montana	Deer Lodge (Women: Warm Springs)
Nebraska	Tecumseh
Nevada	Ely (Women: Carson City)
New Hampshire	Concord
New Jersey	Trenton
New Mexico	Santa Fe
North Carolina	Raleigh
Ohio	Youngstown and Mansfield (Women: Marysville)
Oklahoma	McAlester (Women: McLoud)
Oregon	Salem
Pennsylvania	SCI Greene (Waynesburg) or SCI Graterford (Women: Muncy)
South Carolina	Ridgville (Women: Columbia)
South Dakota	Sioux Falls
Tennessee	Nashville
Texas	Livingston (Women: Gatesville)
U.S. Military	Fort Leavenworth—Kansas
Utah	Draper
Virginia	Waverly
Washington	Walla Walla
Wyoming	Rawlins (Women: Lusk)

SOURCE: Adapted from *State by State Database*, Death Penalty Information Center, August 28, 2009, http://www.deathpenaltyinfo.org/state_by_state (accessed August 28, 2009)

As shown in Table 6.2, 115 new prisoners were received by corrections officials under sentence of death during 2007. Another 86 prisoners were removed from death row for causes other than execution. Forty-two prisoners on death row were executed in 2007. As a result, there were 3,220 prisoners under sentence of death at year-end 2007. Nearly all (3,172) were on state death rows, while 48 were on federal death row. Overall, 1,804 (56%) of the condemned prisoners were white, and 1,345 (42%) were black—the same white-to-black ratio reported at the end of 2006. The other 2% of death row prisoners at year-end 2007 were of other races.

NEW ENTRIES DURING 2007. Table 6.3 provides additional details for the 115 inmates that entered death row during 2007. Nearly all (109) were sentenced under state laws. The remaining six prisoners were sentenced under federal laws. Of the 109 inmates sentenced to state death rows in 2007, the largest number (71 inmates, or 65% of the total) were sentenced in the South. The three southern states with the largest number of death row entries were Florida (21 inmates), Texas (14 inmates), and Alabama (13 inmates). Each of the other regions sent far fewer numbers to death row in 2007. The western region of the United States added 21 inmates, or 19% of the total. Nearly all of these prisoners were sentenced in two states—California and Arizona. California added 10 inmates to death row in 2007, while Arizona added 7 inmates. The states of the Midwest had 9 new inmates under sentence of death—5 in Ohio, 3 in Illinois, and 1 in Missouri—for 8% of the total. The northeastern region sent 8 new prisoners to death row in 2007—6 in Pennsylvania and 2 in Connecticut—for 7% of the total.

GENDER, RACE, EDUCATIONAL BACKGROUND, AND MARITAL STATUS. Table 6.4 provides a summary of certain demographic information for the 3,220 state and federal prisoners under sentence of death at year-end 2007. Nearly all (98.3%) were male, while only 1.7%

TABLE 6.2

Prisoners under sentence of death, by race, 2006 and 2007

Region and jurisdiction	Prisoners under sentence of death, 12/31/06			Received under sentence of death			Removed from death row (excluding executions)[a]			Executed			Prisoners under sentence of death, 12/31/07		
	Total[b]	White[c]	Black[c]	Total[b]	White[c]	Black[c]	Total[b]	White[c]	Black[c]	Total[b]	White[c]	Black[c]	Total[b]	White[c]	Black[c]
U.S. total	3,233	1,806	1,353	115	67	47	86	41	41	42	28	14	3,220	1,804	1,345
Federal[d]	42	17	24	6	4	2	0	0	0	0	0	0	48	21	26
State	3,191	1,789	1,329	109	63	45	86	41	41	42	28	14	3,172	1,783	1,319

Note: Some figures shown for year-end 2006 are revised from those reported.

[a]Includes 16 deaths from natural causes (5 in California; 2 each in Alabama and Florida; and 1 each in Pennsylvania, Indiana, Missouri, Georgia, Kentucky, Maryland, and Tennessee); 2 deaths from suicide (1 each in North Carolina and California); and 1 inmate murdered by another inmate (in Mississippi).
[b]Totals include persons of races other than white and black.
[c]In this table white and black inmates include Hispanics.
[d]Excludes persons held under Armed Forces jurisdiction with a military death sentence for murder.

SOURCE: Adapted from Tracy L. Snell, "Table 4. Prisoners under Sentence of Death, by Region, Jurisdiction, and Race, 2006 and 2007," in *Capital Punishment, 2007—Statistical Tables*, U.S. Department of Justice, Office of Justice Programs, Bureau of Justice Statistics, December 23, 2008, http://www.ojp.usdoj.gov/bjs/pub/html/cp/2007/cp07st.pdf (accessed August 24, 2009)

TABLE 6.3

Prisoners received under sentence of death, by region, state, and race, 2006 and 2007

	Received under sentence of death		
Region and jurisdiction	Total[a]	White[b]	Black[b]
U.S. total	115	67	47
Federal[c]	6	4	2
State	109	63	45
Northeast	8	4	4
Connecticut	2	0	2
New Hampshire	0	0	0
New Jersey	0	0	0
New York	0	0	0
Pennsylvania	6	4	2
Midwest	9	3	6
Illinois	3	1	2
Indiana	0	0	0
Kansas	0	0	0
Missouri	1	1	0
Nebraska	0	0	0
Ohio	5	1	4
South Dakota	0	0	0
South	71	39	31
Alabama	13	8	5
Arkansas	2	1	1
Delaware	2	0	2
Florida	21	13	8
Georgia	4	4	0
Kentucky	0	0	0
Louisiana	1	1	0
Maryland	0	0	0
Mississippi	2	2	0
North Carolina	3	0	3
Oklahoma	3	1	2
South Carolina	4	3	1
Tennessee	1	0	1
Texas	14	6	7
Virginia	1	0	1
West	21	17	4
Arizona	7	6	1
California	10	8	2
Colorado	0	0	0
Idaho	0	0	0
Montana	0	0	0
Nevada	2	1	1
New Mexico	0	0	0
Oregon	2	2	0
Utah	0	0	0
Washington	0	0	0
Wyoming	0	0	0

Note: Some figures shown for year-end 2006 are revised from those reported.

[a]Totals include persons of races other than white and black.

[b]In this table white and black inmates include Hispanics.

[c]Excludes persons held under armed forces jurisdiction with a military death sentence for murder.

SOURCE: Adapted from Tracy L. Snell, "Table 4. Prisoners under Sentence of Death, by Region, Jurisdiction, and Race, 2006 and 2007," in *Capital Punishment, 2007—Statistical Tables*, U.S. Department of Justice, Office of Justice Programs, Bureau of Justice Statistics, December 23, 2008, http://www.ojp.usdoj.gov/bjs/pub/html/cp/2007/cp07st.pdf (accessed August 24, 2009)

TABLE 6.4

Sex, race, and Hispanic origin of prisoners under sentence of death, 2007

	Prisoners under sentence of death, 2007
Characteristic	Year-end
Total inmates	3,220
Gender	
Male	98.3%
Female	1.7
Race	
White	56.0%
Black	41.8
All other races*	2.2
Hispanic origin	
Hispanic	12.9%
Non-Hispanic	87.1
Number unknown	413

Note: Calculations are based on those cases for which data were reported. Detail may not add to total due to rounding.

*At yearend 2006, inmates of "other" races consisted of 28 American Indians, 35 Asians, and 11 self-identified Hispanics. During 2007, 1 Asian was admitted; and 2 American Indians, 1 Asian, and 1 self-identified Hispanic were removed.

SOURCE: Adapted from Tracy L. Snell, "Table 5. Demographic Characteristics of Prisoners under Sentence of Death, 2007," in *Capital Punishment, 2007—Statistical Tables*, U.S. Department of Justice, Office of Justice Programs, Bureau of Justice Statistics, December 23, 2008, http://www.ojp.usdoj.gov/bjs/pub/html/cp/2007/cp07st.pdf (accessed August 24, 2009)

The BJS also reports the regional makeup of the death row population. (See Table 7.1 in Chapter 7.) The southern states had the largest number (1,739 prisoners, or 54% of the total), followed by the western states (930 prisoners, or 29% of the total), the Midwest (273 prisoners, or 9% of the total), and the northeastern states (230 prisoners, or 7% of the total). Overall, the five states with the largest numbers of death row inmates at year-end 2007 were California (655 inmates), Florida (389 inmates), Texas (372 inmates), Ohio (182 inmates), and North Carolina (167 inmates).

The educational background of death row inmates at year-end 2007 is shown in Table 6.5. Only 9.2% of the prisoners had attended college. The largest percentage (40.4%) had graduated from high school or received a GED. More than one-third (36.7%) had completed school through the 9th to the 11th grades. Another 13.8% had completed school through the 8th grade or lower. The median grade completed was the 11th grade, meaning that half of the inmates had completed that grade or more, and half had completed that grade or less. It should be noted that the educational status of more than 500 of the death row inmates was unknown.

Table 6.6 provides information about the marital status of death row prisoners at year-end 2007. More than half (54.5%) had never been married. Less than one-fourth (22.2%) of the inmates on death row were married at the time. A slightly smaller percentage (20.4%) were divorced or separated. Only 2.8% of the inmates were widowed.

were female. As indicated above, 56% of the death row prisoners were white, 41.8% were black, and 2.2% were other races. A large majority (87.1%) of the inmates were non-Hispanic, while 12.9% were Hispanic. However, the Hispanic origin of more than 400 of the inmates on death row was unknown.

TABLE 6.5

Educational level of prisoners under sentence of death, 2007

Characteristic	Prisoners under sentence of death, 2007 Year-end
Education	
8th grade or less	13.8%
9th–11th grade	36.7
High school graduate/GED	40.4
Any college	9.2
Median	11th
Number unknown	522

Note: Calculations are based on those cases for which data were reported. Detail may not add to total due to rounding.

SOURCE: Adapted from Tracy L. Snell, "Table 5. Demographic Characteristics of Prisoners under Sentence of Death, 2007," in *Capital Punishment, 2007—Statistical Tables*, U.S. Department of Justice, Office of Justice Programs, Bureau of Justice Statistics, December 23, 2008, http://www.ojp.usdoj.gov/bjs/pub/html/cp/2007/cp07st.pdf (accessed August 24, 2009)

TABLE 6.6

Marital status of prisoners under sentence of death, 2007

Characteristic	Prisoners under sentence of death, 2007 Year-end
Marital status	
Married	22.2%
Divorced/separated	20.4
Widowed	2.8
Never married	54.5
Number unknown	362

Note: Calculations are based on those cases for which data were reported. Detail may not add to total due to rounding.

SOURCE: Adapted from Tracy L. Snell, "Table 5. Demographic Characteristics of Prisoners under Sentence of Death, 2007," in *Capital Punishment, 2007—Statistical Tables*, U.S. Department of Justice, Office of Justice Programs, Bureau of Justice Statistics, December 23, 2008, http://www.ojp.usdoj.gov/bjs/pub/html/cp/2007/cp07st.pdf (accessed August 24, 2009)

The BJS could not determine the marital status of 362 death row inmates.

LENGTH OF TIME ON DEATH ROW. Because the capital punishment appeal process is so lengthy, many condemned inmates at year-end 2007 had been on death row for many years. Table 6.7 lists the mean (average) and median number of months that prisoners had been on death row. Overall, the average amount of time was 141 months (11 years and 9 months). The median amount of time was 133 months (11 years and 1 month). In general, white inmates had the longest average time on death row—144 months (12 years)—compared with black inmates or those of Hispanic origin. Overall, the male occupants of death row at year-end 2007 had been there for an average of 142 months (11 years and 10 months), compared with an average of 102 months (8 years and 6 months) for female inmates.

TABLE 6.7

Elapsed time since sentencing for inmates under sentence of death on 12/31/07, by gender, race, and Hispanic origin

Inmates under sentence of death	Elapsed time since sentencing	
	Mean	Median
Total	**141 mo**	**133 mo**
Male	142	134
Female	102	98
White*	144	138
Black*	142	136
Hispanic	127	114

Note: For those persons sentenced to death more than once, the data are based on the most recent death sentence.
*Excludes persons of Hispanic origin.

SOURCE: Tracy L. Snell, "Table 17. Elapsed Time since Sentencing for Inmates under Sentence of Death on 12/31/07, by Gender, Race, and Hispanic Origin," in *Capital Punishment, 2007—Statistical Tables*, U.S. Department of Justice, Office of Justice Programs, Bureau of Justice Statistics, December 23, 2008, http://www.ojp.usdoj.gov/bjs/pub/html/cp/2007/cp07st.pdf (accessed August 24, 2009)

TABLE 6.8

Time under sentence of death by year of execution, 1977–2007

Year of execution	Average elapsed time from sentence to execution for all inmates
Total	**127 mo**
1977–83	51 mo
1984	74
1985	71
1986	87
1987	86
1988	80
1989	95
1990	95
1991	116
1992	114
1993	113
1994	122
1995	134
1996	125
1997	133
1998	130
1999	143
2000	137
2001	142
2002	127
2003	131
2004	132
2005	147
2006	145
2007	153

Note: Average time was calculated from the most recent sentencing date.

SOURCE: Adapted from Tracy L. Snell, "Table 11. Time under Sentence of Death and Execution, by Race, 1977–2007," in *Capital Punishment, 2007—Statistical Tables*, U.S. Department of Justice, Office of Justice Programs, Bureau of Justice Statistics, December 23, 2008, http://www.ojp.usdoj.gov/bjs/pub/html/cp/2007/cp07st.pdf (accessed August 24, 2009)

The BJS compiles statistics on the length of time that condemned prisoners spend on death row before being executed. (See Table 6.8.) An inmate executed between 1977 and 1983 had spent an average of 51 months (4 years

TABLE 6.9

Age at time of arrest for capital offense and age of prisoners under sentence of death at year-end 2007

| | Prisoners under sentence of death | | | |
| | At time of arrest | | On December 31, 2007 | |
Age	Number*	Percent	Number	Percent
Total number under sentence of death on 12/31/07	**2,955**	**100%**	**3,220**	**100%**
19 or younger	317	10.7	I	—
20–24	812	27.5	42	1.3
25–29	677	22.9	249	7.7
30–34	508	17.2	431	13.4
35–39	321	10.9	574	17.8
40–44	172	5.8	546	17.0
45–49	88	3.0	583	18.1
50–54	34	1.2	357	11.1
55–59	19	0.6	250	7.8
60–64	5	0.2	127	3.9
65 or older	2	0.1	60	1.9
Mean age	29 yrs.		43 yrs.	
Median age	27 yrs.		42 yrs.	

— Less than .05%

Notes: The youngest person under sentence of death was a black male in Texas, born in June 1988 and sentenced to death in June 2007. The oldest person under sentence of death was a white male in Arizona, born in September 1915 and sentenced to death in June 1983.

*Excludes 265 inmates for whom the date of arrest for capital offense was not available.

SOURCE: Tracy L. Snell, "Table 7. Age at Time of Arrest for Capital Offense and Age of Prisoners under Sentence of Death at Year end 2007," in *Capital Punishment, 2007—Statistical Tables*, U.S. Department of Justice, Office of Justice Programs, Bureau of Justice Statistics, December 23, 2008, http://www.ojp.usdoj.gov/bjs/pub/html/cp/2007/cp07st.pdf (accessed August 24, 2009)

and 3 months) on death row. By the late 1990s that time had nearly tripled to 143 months (11 years and 11 months). An inmate executed in 2007 had spent an average of 153 months (12 years and 9 months) on death row.

AGE AT TIME OF ARREST, AT YEAR-END 2007. Table 6.9 shows the age breakdown of condemned inmates at their time of arrest and at year-end 2007. At the time of their arrest, just over half (50.4%) of the inmates were in their 20s. In fact, the age category containing the largest number (812) of inmates was 20–24 years old. The mean (average) age at time of arrest was 29 years old. The median age was 27 years old. Overall, the vast majority (89.2%) of all inmates eventually sentenced to death were less than age 40 when they were arrested for their capital crimes.

By contrast, the population of death row inmates at year-end 2007 was much older. The age category containing the largest number (583) of inmates was 45–49 years old. The mean (average) age on death row was 43 years old. Overall, 59.8% of prisoners on death row at year-end 2007 were 40 or older.

CRIMINAL HISTORY. BJS statistics indicate that most prisoners on death row at year-end 2007 were already convicted felons when they were arrested for their capital crimes. (See Table 6.10.) Nearly two thirds (65.4%) of the prisoners under sentence of death had prior felony convictions. Just over 8% of the death row inmates had prior homicide convictions. However, 60.6% of the inmates had no particular legal status at the time of their

TABLE 6.10

Criminal history profile of prisoners under sentence of death, by race and Hispanic origin, 2007

| | Percent of prisoners under sentence of death[a] | | | |
	All[b]	White[c]	Black[c]	Hispanic
U.S. total	**100%**	**100%**	**100%**	**100%**
Prior felony convictions				
Yes	65.4%	61.8%	71.0%	61.3%
No	34.6	38.2	29.0	38.7
Number unknown	273			
Prior homicide convictions				
Yes	8.4%	8.5%	8.8%	6.7%
No	91.6	91.5	91.2	93.3
Number unknown	54			
Legal status at time of capital offense				
Charges pending	7.9%	9.1%	7.3%	5.2%
Probation	10.6	8.9	12.4	11.4
Parole	15.4	13.3	16.5	20.3
On escape	1.4	1.8	0.9	1.8
Incarcerated	3.6	4.2	3.4	2.5
Other status	0.5	0.4	0.6	0.3
None	60.6	62.5	59.0	58.5
Number unknown	354			

[a]Percentages are based on those offenders for whom data were reported. Detail may not add to total because of rounding.

[b]Includes American Indians, Alaska Natives, Asians, Native Hawaiians, and other Pacific Islanders.

[c]White and black categories exclude Hispanics.

SOURCE: Tracy L. Snell, "Table 8. Criminal History Profile of Prisoners under Sentence of Death, by Race and Hispanic Origin, 2007," in *Capital Punishment, 2007—Statistical Tables*, U.S. Department of Justice, Office of Justice Programs, Bureau of Justice Statistics, December 23, 2008, http://www.ojp.usdoj.gov/bjs/pub/html/cp/2007/cp07st.pdf (accessed August 24, 2009)

TABLE 6.11

Number of inmates received under sentence of death, 1993–2007

Year	Inmates received
1993	295
1994	328
1995	326
1996	323
1997	281
1998	306
1999	284
2000	235
2001	167
2002	169
2003	153
2004	140
2005	138
2006	121
2007	115

SOURCE: Tracy L. Snell, "Table 14. Number of Inmates Received under Sentence of Death, 1993–2007," in *Capital Punishment, 2007—Statistical Tables*, U.S. Department of Justice, Office of Justice Programs, Bureau of Justice Statistics, December 23, 2008, http://www.ojp.usdoj.gov/bjs/pub/html/cp/2007/cp07st.pdf (accessed August 24, 2009)

capital offense. Another 15.4% were on parole, 10.6% were on probation, and 7.9% had charges pending when they were arrested. Small percentages of inmates had committed their capital offenses while they were incarcerated (3.6%) or had escaped from incarceration (1.4%). Note that the legal history and status of some death row inmates at year-end 2007 could not be determined.

DECLINING DEATH ROW ENTRIES. Table 6.11 shows the number of inmates under sentence of death that were received by prisons each year between 1993 and 2007. After peaking in 1994 at 328, the number dropped below 300 over the following three years. In 1998 the number of entries to death row rebounded above 300 but then began a sustained and definite decline. By the early 2000s prisons were regularly receiving less than 200 inmates per year under sentence of death. In 2007 the number of new death row entries dropped to 115, its lowest level in 15 years.

LEAVING DEATH ROW. A number of prisoners are removed from death row each year for reasons other than execution: resentencing, retrial, commutation (replacement of the death sentence with a lesser sentence), or death while awaiting execution (natural death, murder, or suicide). According to the BJS in *Capital Punishment, 2007: Statistical Tables*, 7,547 people were under sentence of death between 1977 and 2007. Of these, 1,099, or 14.6%, were executed, while 3,228, or 42.8%, received other dispositions (were removed from death row for reasons other than execution).

Table 6.12 provides a breakdown by state of the prisoners who died on death row between 1973 and 2007 for reasons other than execution. California, with its large death row population, had the most deaths, 59, followed by Florida with 44 and Texas with 35.

TABLE 6.12

Deaths on death row due to reasons other than execution, 1973–2007

	Died on death row (not executed)
Federal	0
Alabama	24
Arizona	14
Arkansas	3
California	59
Colorado	2
Connecticut	0
Delaware	0
Florida	44
Georgia	14
Idaho	3
Illinois	14
Indiana	4
Kansas	0
Kentucky	5
Louisiana	6
Maryland	3
Massachusetts	0
Mississippi	5
Missouri	10
Montana	2
Nebraska	4
Nevada	13
New Jersey	3
New Mexico	1
New York	0
North Carolina	18
Ohio	19
Oklahoma	12
Oregon	1
Pennsylvania	18
Rhode Island	0
South Carolina	5
South Dakota	1
Tennessee	14
Texas	35
Utah	1
Virginia	6
Washington	1
Wyoming	1
Total	**365**

SOURCE: Adapted from Tracy L. Snell, "Appendix Table 4. Number Sentenced to Death and Number of Removals, by Jurisdiction and Reason for Removal, 1973–2005," in *Capital Punishment, 2005*, U.S. Department of Justice, Office of Justice Programs, Bureau of Justice Statistics, December 2006, http://www.ojp.usdoj.gov/bjs/pub/pdf/cp05.pdf (accessed August 24, 2009); Tracy L. Snell, "Table 4. Prisoners under Sentence of Death, by Region, Jurisdiction and Race, 2005 and 2006," in *Capital Punishment, 2006—Statistical Tables*, U.S. Department of Justice, Office of Justice Programs, Bureau of Justice Statistics, December 2007, http://www.ojp.usdoj.gov/bjs/pub/html/cp/2006/cp06st.htm (accessed August 28, 2009); and Tracy L. Snell, "Table 4. Prisoners under Sentence of Death, by Jurisdiction and Race, 2006 and 2007," in *Capital Punishment, 2007—Statistical Tables*, U.S. Department of Justice, Office of Justice Programs, Bureau of Justice Statistics, December 2008, http://www.ojp.usdoj.gov/bjs/pub/html/cp/2007/cp07st.htm (accessed August 28, 2009)

Death Row Demographics: Year-end 2008

According to Fins in *Death Row U.S.A.: Winter 2009*, there were 3,297 inmates on death row at year-end 2008. (See Table 6.13.) The vast majority of inmates (3,239, or 98% of the total) were male, while only 58 inmates (2% of the total) were female. Fins notes that 1,475 of the inmates (45% of the total) were white, while 1,371 of the inmates

TABLE 6.13

Total number of death row inmates as reported by the NAACP, January 1, 2009

Total known to Legal Defense Fund (LDF) is 3,297

Race of defendant:

White	1,475 (44.74%)
Black	1,371 (41.58%)
Latino/Latina	374 (11.34%)
Native American	36 (1.09%)
Asian	40 (1.21%)
Unknown at this issue	1 (.03%)

Gender:

Male	3,239 (98.24%)
Female	58 (1.76%)

SOURCE: "Total Number of Death Row Inmates Known to LDF," in *Death Row U.S.A.: Winter 2009*, NAACP Legal Defense and Educational Fund, Inc., January 1, 2009, http://www.naacpldf.org/content/pdf/pubs/drusa/DRUSA_Winter_2009.pdf (accessed August 24, 2009)

(42% of the total) were black. Another 374 inmates (11% of the total) were classified as Latino or Latina. Much smaller numbers were Asian or Native American.

DEATH ROW POPULATION OVER TIME. Combining Fins's estimate for year-end 2008 with data provided by the BJS in annual *Capital Punishment* reports for 2004 through 2007 provides the yearly breakdown shown in Figure 6.1. The number of death row inmates at year-end decreased from 3,377 in 2003 to 3,220 in 2007 and then increased to 3,297 in 2008. A much longer period of record is shown in Figure 6.2 using BJS data from *Key Facts at a Glance: Prisoners on Death Row* (December 2008, http://www.ojp.usdoj.gov/bjs/glance/tables/drtab.htm) and Fins's estimate for 2008. In 1953 the nation's death row population was only 131 inmates. By 1971 the number had grown to 642, before plummeting to 134 in 1973. This drop was due to the landmark *Furman v. Georgia* decision by the U.S. Supreme Court in 1972 that ruled the death penalty unconstitutional. The ruling forced states to develop more uniform systems for applying capital punishment. During the late 1970s, the death row population began to grow once more. It underwent a long and steady increase that persisted for more than two decades. In 2000 the number of prisoners under sentence of death reached its highest level ever—3,601 inmates. The number then dipped slightly and hovered between 3,200 and 3,400 over the following eight years.

WOMEN ON DEATH ROW. According to the BJS in *Capital Punishment, 2008: Statistical Tables*, 58 women were on death row at year-end 2008. Table 6.14 provides a breakdown by state of female inmates under sentence of death. California had the largest contingent (15) of women under sentence of death, followed by Texas (10), and Pennsylvania (5).

FIGURE 6.1

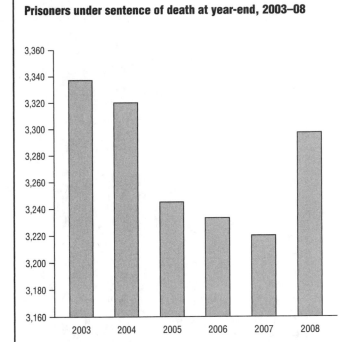

Prisoners under sentence of death at year-end, 2003–08

SOURCE: Adapted from "Table 4. Prisoners under Sentence of Death, by Region, Jurisdiction, and Race, 2003 and 2004," in *Capital Punishment, 2004*, U.S. Department of Justice, Office of Justice Programs, Bureau of Justice Statistics, November 2005, http://www.ojp.usdoj.gov/bjs/pub/pdf/cp04.pdf (accessed August 28, 2009) and "Table 4. Prisoners under Sentence of Death, by Region, State, and Race, 2004 and 2005," in *Capital Punishment, 2005*, U.S. Department of Justice, Office of Justice Programs, Bureau of Justice Statistics, December 2006, http://www.ojp.usdoj.gov/bjs/pub/pdf/cp05.pdf (accessed August 28, 2009) and "Table 4. Prisoners under Sentence of Death, by Region, State, and Race, 2005 and 2006," in *Capital Punishment, 2006—Statistical Tables*, U.S. Department of Justice, Office of Justice Programs, Bureau of Justice Statistics, December 2007, http://www.ojp.usdoj.gov/bjs/pub/html/cp/2006/cp06st.htm (accessed August 28, 2009) and "Table 4. Prisoners under Sentence of Death, by Region, Jurisdiction and Race, 2006 and 2007," in *Capital Punishment, 2007—Statistical Tables*, U.S. Department of Justice, Office of Justice Programs, Bureau of Justice Statistics, December 2008, http://www.ojp.usdoj.gov/bjs/pub/html/cp/2007/cp07st.htm (accessed August 28, 2009) and "Total Number of Death Row Inmates Known to LDF," in *Death Row U.S.A. Winter 2009 (as of January 1, 2009)*, NAACP Legal Defense and Educational Fund, Inc., January 1, 2009, http://www.naacpldf.org/content/pdf/pubs/drusa/DRUSA_Winter_2009.pdf (accessed August 24, 2009)

DEATH SENTENCES DECLINE AS HOMICIDES DECLINE

During the late 1990s the number of defendants sentenced to death each year began to decline. (See Figure 6.3.) In 1973 only 42 death sentences were handed out in the United States. During the 1980s and early 1990s, between 250 and 300 defendants per year were regularly sentenced to die. The number of death sentences peaked in 1996 at 317 and then began a dramatic decline. The DPIC in its 2008 year-end report estimates that only 111 defendants were sentenced to death in 2008, the lowest number in more than three decades. The decline in death sentences beginning in the late 1990s may be linked to the corresponding decrease

FIGURE 6.2

Number of prisoners under sentence of death, 1953–2008

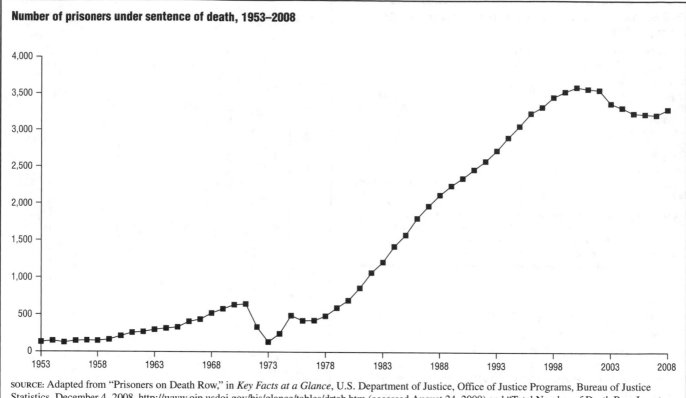

SOURCE: Adapted from "Prisoners on Death Row," in *Key Facts at a Glance*, U.S. Department of Justice, Office of Justice Programs, Bureau of Justice Statistics, December 4, 2008, http://www.ojp.usdoj.gov/bjs/glance/tables/drtab.htm (accessed August 24, 2009) and "Total Number of Death Row Inmates Known to LDF," in *Death Row U.S.A. Winter 2009 (as of January 1, 2009)*, NAACP Legal Defense and Educational Fund, Inc., January 1, 2009, http://www.naacpldf.org/content/pdf/pubs/drusa/DRUSA_Winter_2009.pdf (accessed August 24, 2009)

TABLE 6.14

Women under sentence of death, by race and jurisdiction, year-end 2008

Jurisdiction	All races[a]	White[b]	Black[b]
Total	58	40	15
California	15	11	2
Texas	10	6	4
Pennsylvania	5	2	3
North Carolina	5	2	2
Alabama	4	2	2
Mississippi	3	3	0
Federal	2	2	0
Louisiana	2	1	1
Tennessee	2	2	0
Arizona	2	2	0
Ohio	1	1	0
Florida	1	1	0
Georgia	1	1	0
Kentucky	1	1	0
Oklahoma	1	1	0
Virginia	1	1	0
Idaho	1	1	0
Indiana	1	0	1

[a]Includes American Indians, Alaska Natives, Asians, Native Hawaiians, and other Pacific Islanders.
[b]Excludes persons of Hispanic/Latino origin.

SOURCE: Tracy L. Snell, "Table 12. Women under Sentence of Death, by Race and Jurisdiction, 12/31/08," in *Capital Punishment, 2008—Statistical Tables*, U.S. Department of Justice, Office of Justice Programs, Bureau of Justice Statistics, December 2009, http://bjs.ojp.usdoj.gov/content/pub/pdf/cp08st.pdf (accessed December 19, 2009)

in the nation's homicide rate. As shown in Figure 1.4 in Chapter 1, the homicide rate dropped dramatically from 9.8 homicides per 100,000 population in 1991 to 5.4 homicides per 100,000 population in 2008.

FINANCIAL COSTS OF THE DEATH PENALTY

As noted in Chapter 1, capital cases are more expensive to litigate than noncapital homicides. This is due in part to the lengthy appeals process built in to the death penalty process. An additional expense is the cost of specialized housing and extra security provided on death rows. During the first decade of the 21st century, several studies have been performed to analyze the financial costs associated with capital punishment systems. Some of these studies have been conducted and/or funded by private organizations that may or may not be opposed to the death penalty or take no public stance on it either way. Other studies have been published by government agencies or commissions at the state or federal level. More casual studies on the costs of capital punishment are conducted by journalists for publication by newspapers or other news outlets.

California

In 2004 the California Commission on the Fair Administration of Justice (CCFAJ) was created by the state's legislators to examine California's criminal justice system

FIGURE 6.3

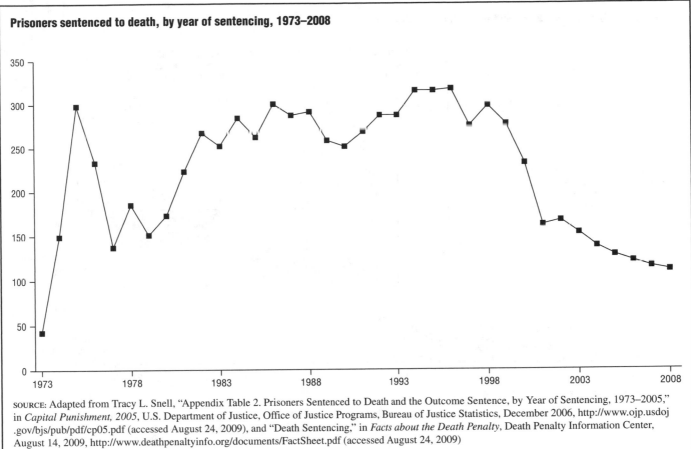

Prisoners sentenced to death, by year of sentencing, 1973–2008

SOURCE: Adapted from Tracy L. Snell, "Appendix Table 2. Prisoners Sentenced to Death and the Outcome Sentence, by Year of Sentencing, 1973–2005," in *Capital Punishment, 2005*, U.S. Department of Justice, Office of Justice Programs, Bureau of Justice Statistics, December 2006, http://www.ojp.usdoj .gov/bjs/pub/pdf/cp05.pdf (accessed August 24, 2009), and "Death Sentencing," in *Facts about the Death Penalty*, Death Penalty Information Center, August 14, 2009, http://www.deathpenaltyinfo.org/documents/FactSheet.pdf (accessed August 24, 2009)

and make recommendations to remedy any problems (2009, http://www.ccfaj.org). The CCFAJ examined numerous issues associated with the state's capital punishment system, many of which have cost implications. In July 2008 it published *California Commission on the Fair Administration of Justice: Final Report* (http://www.ccfaj.org/docume nts/CCFAJFinalReport.pdf) containing the CCFAJ's findings and recommendations.

The CCFAJ notes that one particularly expensive component of the state's capital punishment system is the lengthy amount of time that prisoners spend on death row. As shown in Figure 6.4, the average time between death sentence and execution in California is 20 to 25 years. This is about twice the national average for other death penalty states. The CCFAJ complains, "Just to keep cases moving at this snail's pace, we spend large amounts of taxpayers' money each year: by conservative estimates, well over one hundred million dollars annually." Part of the problem, notes the CCFAJ, is lack of funding for qualified attorneys to handle death sentence appeals and habeas corpus proceedings, which has resulted in a huge backlog of cases. The commission estimates that nearly $100 million per year in additional tax money would have to be injected into the system to reduce the backlog, a substantial cost for a state that, as of fall 2009, had a severe budget problem. The

report provides cost estimates "using conservative rough projections" for the following four options:

- The "present system"—$137 million per year
- The present system after implementation of all recommended reforms—$232.7 million per year
- A revised system that imposes the death penalty in more narrow circumstances—$130 million per year
- A revised system that imposes lifetime incarceration instead of the death penalty—$11.5 million per year

The CCFAJ concludes, "Whether to do nothing, to make the investments needed to fix the current system, to replace the current system with a narrower death penalty law, or to replace capital punishment with lifetime incarceration are ultimately choices that must be made by the California electorate, balancing the perceived advantages gained by each alternative against the potential costs and foreseeable consequences."

After combing through state and federal records, Rone Tempest notes in "Death Row Often Means a Long Life" (*Los Angeles Times*, March 6, 2005) that the death penalty system in California costs taxpayers more than $114 million each year. This amount is more than what it would cost to imprison California's then 640 death row inmates for life

FIGURE 6.4

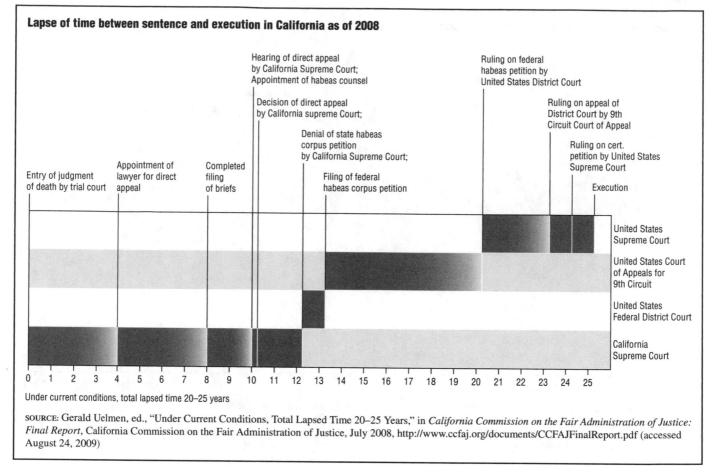

Lapse of time between sentence and execution in California as of 2008

Hearing of direct appeal
by California Supreme Court;
Appointment of habeas counsel

Ruling on federal
habeas petition by
United States District Court

Decision of direct appeal
by California supreme Court;

Ruling on appeal of
District Court by 9th
Circuit Court of Appeal

Denial of state habeas
corpus petition
by California Supreme Court;

Ruling on cert.
petition by United States
Supreme Court

Entry of judgment
of death by trial court

Appointment of
lawyer for direct
appeal

Completed
filing
of briefs

Filing of federal
habeas corpus petition

Execution

United States
Supreme Court

United States Court
of Appeals for
9th Circuit

United States
Federal District Court

California
Supreme Court

0 1 2 3 4 5 6 7 8 9 10 11 12 13 14 15 16 17 18 19 20 21 22 23 24 25

Under current conditions, total lapsed time 20–25 years

SOURCE: Gerald Uelmen, ed., "Under Current Conditions, Total Lapsed Time 20–25 Years," in *California Commission on the Fair Administration of Justice: Final Report*, California Commission on the Fair Administration of Justice, July 2008, http://www.ccfaj.org/documents/CCFAJFinalReport.pdf (accessed August 24, 2009)

without parole. Tempest estimates that every year, the state spends approximately $57.5 million ($90,000 per prisoner) for housing these inmates on death row, where each lives in a private cell and is surrounded by more guards than normal prisoners. Huge costs are also incurred during executions. The article notes that California had executed only 11 inmates since 1977. Each of these executions cost taxpayers approximately $250 million. The death penalty has also burdened the courts. According to Ronald George, the chief justice of the California Supreme Court, the court spent 20% of its resources on capital cases. In the end, the state still did not have enough money to appoint lawyers to 115 death row inmates for their first direct appeal. As of October 2009, as noted in the DPIC's *Smart on Crime: Reconsidering the Death Penalty in a Time of Economic Crisis* (http://www.deathpenaltyinfo.org/documents/CostsRptFinal.pdf), Richard C. Dieter confirmed the CCFAJ findings that the death penalty was costing California approximately $137 million annually.

Maryland

In March 2008 the Urban Institute published *The Cost of the Death Penalty in Maryland* (John Roman et al., http://www.urban.org/UploadedPDF/411625_md_death_penalty.pdf). The Urban Institute is a nonprofit organization based in Washington, D.C., that describes itself as a provider of "nonpartisan economic and social policy research" (2009, http://www.urban.org/about/). The research was funded by the Abell Foundation of Baltimore, Maryland, a private organization devoted to helping "the disadvantaged in the Baltimore community and the region" (2009, http://www.abell.org/aboutthefoundation/index.html).

Roman et al. note that since 1978 Maryland had 56 cases resulting in a death sentence. Five of these inmates were executed. As of 2008 the state had five inmates on death row. The authors examined the costs of adjudication (the process of judging) and incarceration for 1,136 cases that occurred between 1978 and 1999 in which the defendant was eligible for the death penalty. Note this does not mean that the prosecution sought a death sentence, only that the defendant was eligible for capital punishment under state law. The authors conclude that an average case in which a death sentence was not sought cost more than $1.1 million. An average case in which a death sentence was sought, but not imposed, cost $1.8 million. An average case in which a death sentence was sought and imposed cost just over $3 million. The breakdown for the latter was about $1.7 million for adjudication costs and about $1.3 million for incarceration costs.

New Jersey

In 2006 the governor of New Jersey appointed the New Jersey Death Penalty Study Commission (NJDPSC) to assess the state's capital punishment system and issue recommendations regarding its continued usage. At that time, New Jersey had only eight prisoners on death row and had not executed anyone in more than two decades. In January 2007 the NJDPSC published the *New Jersey Death Penalty Study Commission Report* (http://www.njleg.state.nj.us/committees/dpsc_final.pdf), in which it recommended replacing the state's death sentence with a sentence of life imprisonment without the chance of parole. The decision was based on a number of factors, including costs. The commission notes, "The costs of the death penalty are greater than the costs of life in prison without parole, but it is not possible to measure these costs with any degree of precision." However, estimates are provided from state agencies indicating that eliminating the death penalty in favor of lifetime incarceration would save nearly $1.5 million per year in public defender costs for the 19 capital cases active at that time and save approximately $1 million per death row inmate in incarceration costs. The potential cost savings in court-related expenses could not be estimated, and it was concluded that no cost savings would be achieved by prosecutor offices in the state.

In December 2007 New Jersey abolished the death penalty in the state and replaced it with lifetime incarceration without parole.

Washington

In December 2006 the Washington State Bar Association (WSBA) published *Final Report of the Death Penalty Subcommittee of the Committee on Public Defense* (http://www.wsba.org/lawyers/groups/finalreport.pdf). At that time there had been 79 death penalty cases in Washington in the previous 25 years. However, only four executions had taken place, the most recent in 2001. The WSBA reviewed previous statistical reports on costs associated with the state's death penalty and surveyed prosecutors and defense attorneys who had been involved in capital cases regarding trial costs and attorney compensation. Data were also collected on state and federal costs during the appeal process.

The WSBA notes that quantifying and comparing costs between criminal cases is very difficult. It estimates that trying a death penalty case in Washington costs an average of $467,000 more than a comparable noncapital case. This figure includes the extra expenses incurred by the prosecutor and the defense. Fees and costs at the appellate level were estimated to be at least $100,000 more for a capital case than for a comparable noncapital case. The WSBA concludes, "It costs significantly more to try a capital case to final verdict than to try the same case as an aggravated murder case where the penalty sought is life without possibility of parole." However, the WSBA does not foresee that eliminating the death penalty in Washington would reduce the budgets of prosecutor offices. Instead the cost savings would likely be devoted to other cases.

In "Death Penalty Hangs in Balance as Debate Heats Up," Terry McConn in the *Walla Walla Union-Bulletin* (November 7, 2009, http://union-bulletin.com/articles/2009/11/07/local_news/091108adeathpenalty.txt) notes that two bills were introduced during 2009 in the Washington legislature to abolish the death penalty. Both bills were reportedly motivated, at least in part, by excessive costs in the state's capital punishment system. Neither bill was passed into law.

Kansas

In *Performance Audit Report: Costs Incurred for Death Penalty Cases* (December 2003, http://www.kslegislature.org/postaudit/audits_perform/04pa03a.pdf), the state of Kansas finds that death penalty murder cases cost an average of $1.2 million from when the murder investigation begins to when the sentence is carried out. Murder cases where the death penalty is neither sought nor given cost $740,000.

The state itemizes these costs for each stage of a death penalty case. The cost of investigating a case in which the defendant is sentenced to death is $145,000, compared with $66,000 for a death penalty case in which the defendant receives a lesser sentence and $47,000 for a non–death penalty case. The average price tag for a trial that results in a death sentence is nearly 16 times greater than for a non–death penalty trial ($508,000 as opposed to $32,000), and the appeal is 21 times greater ($401,000 as opposed to $19,000). Keeping a convict on death row in Kansas costs roughly half as much as detaining a murderer for whom the death penalty is never sought ($350,000 versus $659,000). Kansas, however, did not have a large death row population at the time the study was performed. Only six inmates were on death row in December 2003. As of winter 2009, according to *Death Row U.S.A.*, that number had increased to ten, but no one had been executed in Kansas since the death penalty was reinstated in 1994.

Connecticut

In *Study Pursuant to Public Act No. 01-151 of the Imposition of the Death Penalty in Connecticut* (January 8, 2003, http://www.cga.ct.gov/olr/Death%20Penalty%20Commission%20Final%20Report.pdf), Connecticut's Commission on the Death Penalty addresses the cost of prosecuting capital cases. As of January 2002 Connecticut had seven death row inmates and had not executed any. The last execution occurred in 1960. Because Connecticut had not carried out an execution, the commission did not present any comparison between the cost of implementing the death penalty and keeping an inmate in prison without the possibility of parole. Nonetheless, the commission was able to illustrate the defense costs for defendants sentenced to death (following trial and sentencing), compared with the defense costs incurred by defendants receiving life imprisonment without parole (also following trial and sentencing).

The commission reviewed the cases of the seven men on death row from 1973 to 2002. The defense costs ranged from nearly $102,000 to $1.1 million, with an average cost of about $380,000 per case. The prisoners serving life sentences without parole included those incarcerated from 1989 to 2001. Their defense costs ranged from $86,000 to $321,000, with an average cost of about $202,000 per inmate. Between 2006 and 2007 the Connecticut Division of Public Defender Services reports in "Cost of Public Defender Services: Cost Attributable to the Death Penalty" (February 21, 2008, http://www.ocpd.state.ct.us/Content/Annual2007/2007Chap4.htm#Cost Attributable to the Death Penalty) that it spent approximately $2.3 million for capital cases.

New York

In "Capital Punishment Proves to Be Expensive" (*New York Law Journal*, April 30, 2002), Daniel Wise investigates the costs of the death penalty in New York since its reinstatement in 1995. Between 1995 and 2001 defense costs had amounted to $68.4 million by that time. No national system has been in place to track prosecution costs; however, the state Division of Criminal Justice Services paid counties that prosecuted capital cases $5.1 million between 1995 and 2001. Each year the allocation for the New York Court of Appeals increased by more than $533,000 to allow for the salary of an extra clerk for each of the seven judges. The New York Prosecutors Training Institute, which assists district lawyers in capital cases, costs $1.2 million annually to operate. The defense for Darrel Harris, the first person to be sentenced to death under New York's 1995 law, had spent about $1.7 million, and the Capital Defender Office spent $1.2 million just to prepare the brief. (Harris's conviction was subsequently ruled unconstitutional.) The Department of Correctional Services spent $1.3 million to construct a new death row, allocating another $300,000 annually to guard it.

In "Costly Price of Capital Punishment: Restoration of the Death Penalty in New York State Has Cost $160 Million as Wheels of Justice Turn Slowly" (September 21, 2003, http://archives.timesunion.com/mweb/wmsql.wm.request?oneimage&imageid=6230644), Andrew Tilghman in the *Albany Times Union* estimates that trying capital cases cost the state more than $160 million between 1995 and 2003. He reports that the capital defender office spent at least $79 million over this period to defend people charged with capital crimes. Tilghman doubles that amount to obtain the estimate of at least $160 million in total costs. He notes that only seven people received death sentences in New York between 1995 and 2003, and no executions took place.

In "Switch by Former Supporter Shows Evolution of Death Law," Sam Roberts in the *New York Times* (February 28, 2005, http://www.nytimes.com/2005/02/28/nyregion/28death.html?pagewanted=2&_r=1&sq=capital%20punishment&st=nyt&scp=3) discusses the views of state assemblywoman Helene Weinstein on capital punishment. Weinstein was chairwoman of the state judiciary committee at the time and had developed serious reservations about the fairness of the death penalty given the number of death row inmates that had been exonerated around the country and concerns about racial biases in death sentencing. She estimated that more than $170 million had been spent on death penalty cases in New York, but no executions had taken place in the state. (Weinstein does not specify a time for her cost estimate; presumably she is referring to costs incurred since 1995 when the death penalty was reinstated in New York.)

In 2004 a state court of appeals found parts of New York's death penalty law to be unconstitutional. As will be described in Chapter 8, the state legislature has declined to change the law. As a result, all of New York's death row inmates have been resentenced to life in prison without the chance of parole.

Federal Death Penalty Costs

Since the passage of the Anti-Drug Abuse Act in 1988 and the Violent Crime Control and Law Enforcement Act of 1994 (also known as the Federal Death Penalty Act), the number of federal prosecutions, including crimes punishable by death, has risen. As described in Chapter 5, between 1988 and August 3, 2009, the U.S. attorney general authorized the government to seek the death penalty against 461 defendants. Two hundred sixty-one of the defendants were tried, of which three were executed. Most of the rest of the defendants received life sentences from juries or judges or through plea bargain agreements. In the federal system defendants are deemed death-eligible if their crime is considered a death penalty crime under federal law. The U.S. Attorney General chooses which death-eligible defendants will face a death sentence at trial. These cases are called death-authorized cases.

In June 2008 the Office of Defender Services (ODS) of the Administrative Office of the U.S. Courts published *Update on the Cost, Quality, and Availability of Defense Representation in Federal Death Penalty Cases: Preliminary Report on Phase One of the Research* by Jon B. Gould and Lisa Greenman (http://www.uscourts.gov/defenderservices/FDPC_Contents.cfm). The report was an update of a 1998 study on the federal death penalty system that specifically examined funding for defense services provided to defendants in capital cases. For the 2008 report the ODS analyzed cost data for federal death penalty cases from 1998 to 2004 in which the government provided public defenders (at taxpayer expense) for the defendants. The results included medians for total costs of defense representation, meaning half the values were less than the median value and the other half were greater than the median value. The median cost for a death-authorized case was $353,185. The median cost for a death-eligible but non-death-authorized case was $44,809.

During the second phase of the ODS investigation, the agency will conduct a comprehensive examination of the data collected in the first phase described earlier and issue recommendations on the federal death penalty system. As of October 2009 that report had not been published.

EXECUTIONS

Until 1930 the U.S. government did not keep any record of the number of people executed under the death penalty. As shown in Table 6.15, from 1930 through 2008 a total of 4,995 executions were conducted under civil authority in the United States. Military authorities carried out an additional 160 executions between 1930 and 1961, the date of the last military execution.

From 1930 to 1939 a total of 1,667 inmates were executed, the highest number of people put to death in any decade. The number of executions generally declined between the 1930s and the 1960s. In 1930, 155 executions took place, reaching a high of 199 in 1935. By 1950 executions were down to 82, further dropping to 49 each in 1958 and 1959, and then rising slightly to 56 in 1960. In 1967 a 10-year moratorium (temporary suspension) of the death penalty began as states waited for the U.S. Supreme Court to determine a constitutionally acceptable procedure for carrying out the death penalty. (See Figure 1.2 in Chapter 1.)

The moratorium ended in 1976, but no executions occurred that year. The first execution following the moratorium occurred in Utah in January 1977. In 1999, 98 inmates were put to death, the most in a one-year period after the death penalty was reinstated. As shown in Table 6.15, between 1977 and the end of 2008, 1,136 people were put to death. Figure 6.5 shows the number of executions conducted by year between 1977 and 2008. Figure 6.6 shows the cumulative number of executions over that same time.

Locations of Executions

Table 6.15 shows the number of prisoners executed by state between 1930 and 2008 and between 1977 and 2008. Texas, by far, had the most executions during both periods—720 executions between 1930 and 2008 and 423 executions between 1977 and 2008.

Overall, 35 jurisdictions carried out executions between 1977 and 2008. The federal government executed three men. As mentioned previously, the largest number of executions in a single state occurred in Texas,

TABLE 6.15

Number of persons executed, by jurisdiction, 1930–2007 and 1977–2007

Jurisdiction	Since 1930	Since 1977
U.S. total	**4,995**	**1,136**
Texas	720	423
Georgia	409	43
New York	329	0
North Carolina	306	43
California	305	13
Florida	236	66
South Carolina	202	40
Ohio	200	28
Virginia	194	102
Alabama	173	38
Mississippi	164	10
Louisiana	160	27
Pennsylvania	155	3
Oklahoma	148	88
Arkansas	145	27
Missouri	128	66
Kentucky	106	3
Illinois	102	12
Tennessee	97	4
New Jersey	74	0
Maryland	73	5
Arizona	61	23
Indiana	60	19
Washington	51	4
Colorado	48	1
Nevada	41	12
District of Columbia	40	0
West Virginia	40	0
Federal system	36	3
Massachusetts	27	0
Delaware	26	14
Connecticut	22	1
Oregon	21	2
Utah	19	6
Iowa	18	0
Kansas	15	0
Montana	9	3
New Mexico	9	1
Wyoming	8	1
Nebraska	7	3
Vermont	4	0
Idaho	4	1
South Dakota	2	1
New Hampshire	1	0

Note: Military authorities carried out an additional 160 executions between 1930 and 1961.

SOURCE: Adapted from Tracy L. Snell, "Table 9. Number of Persons Executed, by Jurisdiction, 1930–2007," in *Capital Punishment, 2007—Statistical Tables*, U.S. Department of Justice, Office of Justice Programs, Bureau of Justice Statistics, December 23, 2008, http://www.ojp.usdoj.gov/bjs/pub/html/cp/2007/cp07st.pdf (accessed August 24, 2009)

followed by Virginia (102), Oklahoma (88), Missouri and Florida (both 66), Georgia and North Carolina (both 43), and South Carolina (40). Together, these eight states carried out just over three-quarters of all executions during this 31-year period. (See Figure 6.7.) The breakdown by state for executions from 2006 through 2008 is shown in Table 6.16. Texas again had, by a wide margin, the most executions of any state over this period.

In Table 6.17 the DPIC calculates an execution rate (the number of executions per 10,000 persons living in the state) based on population data from 2008 and execution

FIGURE 6.5

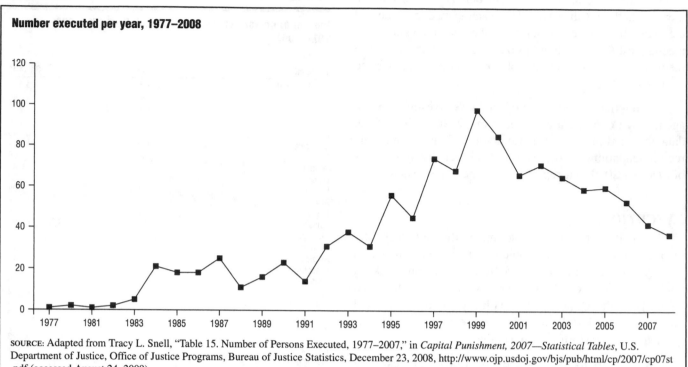

Number executed per year, 1977–2008

SOURCE: Adapted from Tracy L. Snell, "Table 15. Number of Persons Executed, 1977–2007," in *Capital Punishment, 2007—Statistical Tables*, U.S. Department of Justice, Office of Justice Programs, Bureau of Justice Statistics, December 23, 2008, http://www.ojp.usdoj.gov/bjs/pub/html/cp/2007/cp07st .pdf (accessed August 24, 2009)

FIGURE 6.6

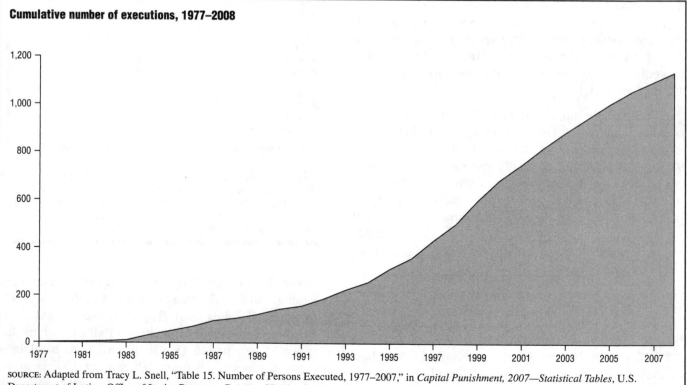

Cumulative number of executions, 1977–2008

SOURCE: Adapted from Tracy L. Snell, "Table 15. Number of Persons Executed, 1977–2007," in *Capital Punishment, 2007—Statistical Tables*, U.S. Department of Justice, Office of Justice Programs, Bureau of Justice Statistics, December 23, 2008, http://www.ojp.usdoj.gov/bjs/pub/html/cp/2007/cp07st .pdf (accessed August 24, 2009)

FIGURE 6.7

Number of persons executed, by jurisdiction, 1977–2008

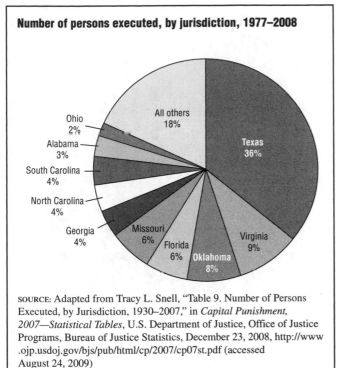

SOURCE: Adapted from Tracy L. Snell, "Table 9. Number of Persons Executed, by Jurisdiction, 1930–2007," in *Capital Punishment, 2007—Statistical Tables*, U.S. Department of Justice, Office of Justice Programs, Bureau of Justice Statistics, December 23, 2008, http://www .ojp.usdoj.gov/bjs/pub/html/cp/2007/cp07st.pdf (accessed August 24, 2009)

TABLE 6.16

Number of executions, 2006–08

State	2006	2007	2008
Texas	24	26	18
Ohio	5	2	2
Oklahoma	4	3	2
Virginia	4		4
Florida	4		2
South Carolina	1	1	3
North Carolina	4		
Alabama	1	3	
Georgia		1	3
Indiana	1	2	
Mississippi	1		2
Tennessee	1	2	
California	1		
Montana	1		
Nevada	1		
Arizona		1	
South Dakota		1	
Kentucky			1
Total:	**53**	**42**	**37**

SOURCE: Adapted from Tracy L. Snell, "Table 9. Number of Persons Executed, by Jurisdiction, 1930–2006," and "Advance Count of Executions: January 1, 2007–December 31, 2007," in *Capital Punishment, 2006—Statistical Tables*, U.S. Department of Justice, Office of Justice Programs, Bureau of Justice Statistics, December 2007, http://www.ojp.usdoj.gov/bjs/ pub/html/cp/2006/cp06st.pdf (accessed August 24, 2009); and Tracy L. Snell, "Advance Count of Executions, January 1, 2008–December 31, 2008," in *Capital Punishment, 2007—Statistical Tables*, U.S. Department of Justice, Office of Justice Programs, Bureau of Justice Statistics, December 2008, http://www.ojp.usdoj.gov/bjs/pub/html/cp/2007/cp07st.pdf (accessed August 24, 2009)

data covering 1976 through April 17, 2009. The states are ranked from largest to smallest rates. The data indicate that Oklahoma had the highest execution rate—0.244 executions

TABLE 6.17

State execution rates, 1976–April 17, 2009

State/rank	2008 population	Cumulative executions: 1976–April 17, 2009	Executions per capita (×10,000)
1. Oklahoma	3,642,361	89	0.244
2. Texas	24,326,974	437	0.179
3. Delaware	873,092	14	0.160
4. Virginia	7,760,000	103	0.133
5. Missouri	5,911,605	66	0.112
6. Arkansas	2,855,390	27	0.095
7. South Carolina	4,479,800	41	0.092
8. Alabama	4,661,900	41	0.088
9. Louisiana	4,410,796	27	0.061
10. North Carolina	9,222,414	43	0.047
11. Nevada	2,600,167	12	0.046
12. Georgia	9,685,744	44	0.045
13. Florida	18,328,340	67	0.037
14. Arizona	6,500,180	23	0.035
15. Mississippi	2,938,618	10	0.034
16. Montana	967,440	3	0.031
17. Indiana	6,376,792	19	0.030
18. Ohio	11,485,910	28	0.024
19. Utah	2,736,424	6	0.022
20. Wyoming	532,668	1	0.019
21. Nebraska	1,783,432	3	0.017
22. South Dakota	804,194	1	0.012
23. Illinois	12,901,563	12	0.009
24. Maryland	5,633,597	5	0.009
25. Tennessee	6,214,888	5	0.008
26. Kentucky	4,269,245	3	0.007
27. Idaho	1,523,816	1	0.007
28. Washington	6,549,224	4	0.006
29. New Mexico	1,984,356	1	0.005
30. California	36,756,666	13	0.004
31. Oregon	6,214,888	2	0.003
32. Connecticut	3,501,252	1	0.003
33. Pennsylvania	12,448,279	3	0.002
34. Colorado	4,939,456	1	0.002
35. New Hampshire	1,315,809	0	0.000
36. Kansas	2,802,134	0	0.000

Notes: Population based on U.S. Census Bureau 2008 Population Estimates. Executions: Total since reinstatement of the death penalty in 1976 through April 17, 2009.

SOURCE: "State Execution Rates," in *Executions in the United States*, Death Penalty Information Center, April 17, 2009, http://www.deathpenaltyinfo .org/state-execution-rates (accessed August 24, 2009)

per 10,000 population. It was followed by Texas (0.179 executions per 10,000 population), Delaware (0.160 executions per 10,000 population), Virginia (0.133 executions per 10,000 population), and Missouri (0.112 executions per 10,000 population). California, a state with a large death row population, had an execution rate of only 0.004 executions per 10,000 population.

Gender

The BJS does not provide state or yearly breakdowns of the number of women executed in the United States. However, Victor L. Streib of Ohio Northern University has been compiling information on female offenders and the death penalty in the United States since 1984. In *Death Penalty for Female Offenders: January 1, 1973, through June 30, 2009* (June 30, 2009, http://www.deathpenaltyinfo.org/files/Fem DeathJune2009.pdf), Streib notes that between 1632 and the time of his report, 568 documented executions of women had been reported. Of this number, 50 women were put to death between 1900 and 2005, the last execution of a female as of mid-2009. According to Fins in *Death Row U.S.A.: Winter 2009*, 11 women have been executed since the 1976 reinstatement of the death penalty.

Streib notes that the first female to be put to death since the reinstatement of capital punishment was Margie Velma Barfield, who was executed in 1984 in North Carolina for poisoning her boyfriend. The next, Karla Faye Tucker of Texas, was convicted of beating two people to death with a pickax. In 1998 Tucker became the first woman to be executed in Texas since the Civil War (1861–1865). (In 1863 Chipita Rodriguez, the last woman before Tucker to be executed in Texas, was put to death by hanging. She had been convicted of the ax murder of a horse trader.) In Florida Judias Buenoano was convicted of poisoning her husband with arsenic. She was also convicted of drowning her paraplegic son and of trying to kill her boyfriend. In 1998 Buenoano became the first woman to be executed in Florida since 1848, when a freed slave named Celia was hanged for killing her former owner.

In 2000 Betty Lou Beets was executed in Texas for killing her fifth husband. Christina Marie Riggs, convicted of killing her two children, was executed in Arkansas the same year. The last woman put to death in Arkansas before Riggs—Lavinia Burnett—was hanged in 1845 for being an accessory to murder.

In 2001 Oklahoma executed three female inmates: Wanda Jean Allen, Marilyn Kay Plantz, and Lois Nadean Smith. Allen was the first woman to be executed in Oklahoma since 1903. She was also the first African-American woman to be put to death in the United States since 1954. She was convicted of murdering her gay lover in 1988. Plantz was executed for the 1988 murder of her husband. She had hired two men to kill him. One of the men, William Bryson, was executed in June 2000 for the murder, and the other, Clinton McKimble, received a life sentence in exchange for his testimony against Plantz and Bryson. Smith was convicted of killing her son's girlfriend in 1982.

Lynda Lyon Block and her husband, George Sibley Jr., murdered a police officer in 1993. In 2002 Alabama executed Block, making her the first woman to be executed in the state in 45 years. Sibley was executed in 2005. Aileen Carol Wuornos, convicted of killing six men in Florida, was put to death by lethal injection in 2002. As of October 2009, the last woman executed in the United States was Frances Elaine Newton of Texas, executed in 2005 for murdering her husband and their two small children.

RACE AND ETHNICITY

Figure 6.8 shows the racial and ethnic makeup of prisoners executed between 1977 and 2008. The majority (57%) of

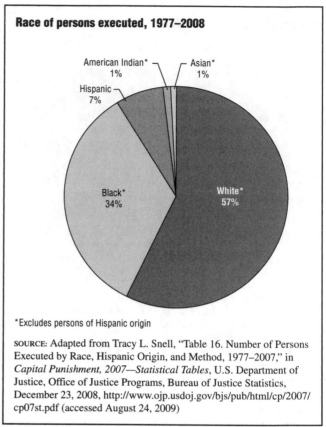

FIGURE 6.8

Race of persons executed, 1977–2008

American Indian* 1%
Asian* 1%
Hispanic 7%
Black* 34%
White* 57%

*Excludes persons of Hispanic origin

SOURCE: Adapted from Tracy L. Snell, "Table 16. Number of Persons Executed by Race, Hispanic Origin, and Method, 1977–2007," in *Capital Punishment, 2007—Statistical Tables*, U.S. Department of Justice, Office of Justice Programs, Bureau of Justice Statistics, December 23, 2008, http://www.ojp.usdoj.gov/bjs/pub/html/cp/2007/cp07st.pdf (accessed August 24, 2009)

those executed were white. Slightly more than a third (34%) were African-American, and a small portion (7%) were Hispanic, Native American (1%), and Asian (1%).

METHOD OF EXECUTION

As shown in Table 6.18, among the 1,136 prisoners executed between 1977 and 2008, 965 (85%) received lethal injection, followed by electrocution (155, or 14%). Eleven executions were carried out by lethal gas, three by hanging, and two by firing squad. Texas, the state with the largest number of prisoners executed, used lethal injection in all 423 cases. Virginia executed 74 inmates by lethal injection and 28 inmates by electrocution. Oklahoma put to death 88 prisoners, all by lethal injection. Table 6.19 provides a breakdown of executed inmates by method and racial and ethnic heritage between 1977 and 2008. Out of the 648 white inmates executed, the vast majority (553, or 85% of the total whites executed) were killed using lethal injection. Eighty-two of the white inmates, or 13% of the total whites executed, were put to death by electrocution. Among African-American inmates executed, 317, or 81%, were killed using lethal injection. Seventy of the African-American inmates (or 18% of the total African-Americans executed) went to the electric chair. Similar breakdowns are provided for other racial and ethnic backgrounds.

TABLE 6.18

Executions, by jurisdiction and method, 1977–2008

Jurisdiction	Number executed	Lethal injection	Electrocution	Lethal gas	Hanging	Firing squad
Federal	3	3	0	0	0	0
Alabama	38	14	24	0	0	0
Arizona	23	21	0	2	0	0
Arkansas	27	26	1	0	0	0
California	13	11	0	2	0	0
Colorado	1	1	0	0	0	0
Connecticut	1	1	0	0	0	0
Delaware	14	13	0	0	1	0
Florida	66	22	44	0	0	0
Georgia	43	20	23	0	0	0
Idaho	1	1	0	0	0	0
Illinois	12	12	0	0	0	0
Indiana	19	16	3	0	0	0
Kentucky	3	2	1	0	0	0
Louisiana	27	7	20	0	0	0
Maryland	5	5	0	0	0	0
Mississippi	10	6	0	4	0	0
Missouri	66	66	0	0	0	0
Montana	3	3	0	0	0	0
Nebraska	3	0	3	0	0	0
Nevada	12	11	0	1	0	0
New Mexico	1	1	0	0	0	0
North Carolina	43	41	0	2	0	0
Ohio	28	28	0	0	0	0
Oklahoma	88	88	0	0	0	0
Oregon	2	2	0	0	0	0
Pennsylvania	3	3	0	0	0	0
South Carolina	40	33	7	0	0	0
South Dakota	1	1				
Tennessee	4	3	1	0	0	0
Texas	423	423	0	0	0	0
Utah	6	4	0	0	0	2
Virginia	102	74	28	0	0	0
Washington	4	2	0	0	2	0
Wyoming	1	1	0	0	0	0
Total:	**1,136**	**965**	**155**	**11**	**3**	**2**

SOURCE: Adapted from Tracy L. Snell, "Appendix Table 5. Executions, by State and Method, 1977–2005," in *Capital Punishment, 2005*, U.S. Department of Justice, Office of Justice Programs, Bureau of Justice Statistics, December 2006, http://www.ojp.usdoj.gov/bjs/pub/pdf/cp05.pdf (accessed August 24, 2009); Tracy L. Snell, "Table 9. Number of Persons Executed, by Jurisdiction, 1930–2006," and "Advance Count of Executions, January 1, 2007–December 31, 2007," in *Capital Punishment, 2006—Statistical Tables*, U.S. Department of Justice, Office of Justice Programs, Bureau of Justice Statistics, December 2007, http://www.ojp.usdoj.gov/bjs/pub/html/cp/2006/cp06st.pdf (accessed August 24, 2009); and Tracy L. Snell, "Advance Count of Executions, January 1, 2008–December 31, 2008," in *Capital Punishment, 2007—Statistical Tables*, U.S. Department of Justice, Office of Justice Programs, Bureau of Justice Statistics, December 2008, http://www.ojp.usdoj.gov/bjs/pub/html/cp/2007/cp07st.pdf (accessed August 24, 2009)

TABLE 6.19

Number of persons executed, by race, Hispanic origin, and method, 1977–2008

	White*	Black*	Hispanic	American Indian*	Asian*
Total	**648**	**390**	**84**	**8**	**6**
Lethal injection	553	317	82	7	6
Electrocution	82	70	2	1	0
Lethal gas	8	3	0	0	0
Hanging	3	0	0	0	0
Firing squad	2	0	0	0	0

*Excludes persons of Hispanic origin

SOURCE: Adapted from Tracy L. Snell, "Table 16. Number of Persons Executed, by Race, Hispanic Origin, and Method, 1977–2007," in *Capital Punishment, 2007—Statistical Tables*, U.S. Department of Justice, Office of Justice Programs, Bureau of Justice Statistics, December 23, 2008, http://www.ojp.usdoj.gov/bjs/pub/html/cp/2007/cp07st.pdf (accessed August 24, 2009)

CHAPTER 7
ISSUES OF FAIRNESS: RACIAL BIAS AND QUALITY OF LEGAL REPRESENTATION

Capital punishment opponents frequently raise issues about the fairness with which the death penalty is applied in the United States. These challenges avoid emotionally charged arguments about the moral rightness or wrongness of capital punishment to focus on more legally definable issues, such as discrimination and the denial of legal rights. An enduring idea of U.S. jurisprudence (the philosophy of law) is that "justice is blind." In other words the merits of a criminal case should be decided without regard to the race, ethnicity, or economic status of the accused. Death penalty opponents argue that death sentences are unfairly administered because of racial bias, political motivations, and—in the case of impoverished defendants—poor legal representation. These factors, they say, prove that the U.S. capital punishment system is flawed and should be eliminated. Death penalty advocates counter that the judicial process contains adequate safeguards to ensure that defendants receive fair trials. They believe that if any discrepancies do exist in capital convictions and sentences, they should be remedied by applying the death penalty more often, not less often.

RACIAL BIAS IN THE DEATH PENALTY?

One of the most contentious issues within the death penalty debate is race. Capital punishment opponents argue that racial bias on the behalf of prosecutors, judges, and juries results in disproportionately high numbers of convictions and death penalties for African-American defendants.

Racial Makeup of Death Row

Table 7.1 shows racial and geographical information provided by the U.S. Department of Justice's Bureau of Justice Statistics (BJS) for death row inmates. The BJS reports that 3,220 prisoners were under sentence of death at yearend 2007. The black-to-white ratios of death row prisoners by region were as follows:

- Northeast—82 white inmates (36% of the regional total) and 138 African-American inmates (60% of total)

- Midwest—144 white inmates (53% of the regional total) and 126 African-American inmates (46% of total)

- South—952 white inmates (55% of the regional total) and 764 African-American inmates (44% of total)

- West—605 white inmates (65% of the regional total) and 291 African-American inmates (31% of total)

According to Deborah Fins, writing for the Criminal Justice Project of the NAACP Legal Defense and Educational Fund in *Death Row U.S.A.: Winter 2009* (http://www.naacpldf.org/content/pdf/pubs/drusa/DRUSA_Winter_2009.pdf), there were 3,297 inmates on death row at yearend 2008 (3,239 male and 58 female). (See Table 6.13 in Chapter 6.) Fins reports that 1,475 of the inmates (44.7% of the total) were white, whereas 1,371 of the inmates (41.6% of the total) were African-American. Another 374 inmates (11.3% of the total) were classified as Latino or Latina. Much smaller numbers were believed to be Asian or Native American.

Race of Executed Prisoners

Table 7.2 shows BJS statistics regarding the racial makeup of prisoners executed between 1977 and 2008. Of the 1,136 inmates executed over this period, 728 (or 64% of the total) were white and 393 (or 35% of the total) were African-American.

The BJS also publishes data on the number of death row prisoners that are executed or removed from a sentence of death for various reasons. As Table 7.3 shows, 7,547 people were under sentence of death between 1977 and 2007. Of these, 1,099 or 14.6% were executed, and 3,228 or 42.8% received other dispositions (i.e., they were removed from death row for reasons other than execution, including vacated sentences, pardons, and death by other means). As of yearend 2007 a slightly larger percentage of whites (17.1%; 631 out of 3,681 total) than African-Americans

TABLE 7.1

Prisoners on death row, by region, state, and race, December 31, 2007

Region and jurisdiction	Prisoners under sentence of death, 12/31/07		
	Total[a]	White[b]	Black[b]
U.S. total	3,220	1,804	1,345
Federal[c]	48	21	26
State	3,172	1,783	1,319
Northeast	230	82	138
Connecticut	9	4	5
New Hampshire	0	0	0
New Jersey	0	0	0
New York	0	0	0
Pennsylvania	221	78	133
Midwest	273	144	126
Illinois	13	8	5
Indiana	14	11	3
Kansas	7	3	4
Missouri	45	25	20
Nebraska	9	8	1
Ohio	182	86	93
South Dakota	3	3	0
South	1,739	952	764
Alabama	199	106	93
Arkansas	38	14	24
Delaware	19	10	9
Florida	389	255	134
Georgia	105	58	46
Kentucky	39	31	8
Louisiana	86	31	54
Maryland	5	1	4
Mississippi	65	32	32
North Carolina	167	69	89
Oklahoma	80	43	33
South Carolina	59	23	36
Tennessee	96	56	38
Texas	372	216	151
Virginia	20	7	13
West	930	605	291
Arizona	116	99	14
California	655	389	238
Colorado	1	0	1
Idaho	17	17	0
Montana	2	2	0
Nevada	83	51	31
New Mexico	2	2	0
Oregon	35	31	3
Utah	9	7	1
Washington	8	5	3
Wyoming	2	2	0

Note: Some figures shown for yearend 2006 are revised from those reported.
[a]Totals include persons of races other than white and black.
[b]In this table white and black inmates include Hispanics.
[c]Excludes persons held under armed forces jurisdiction with a military death sentence for murder.

SOURCE: Adapted from Tracy L. Snell, "Table 4. Prisoners under Sentence of Death, by Region, Jurisdiction, and Race, 2006 and 2007," in *Capital Punishment, 2007—Statistical Tables*, U.S. Department of Justice, Office of Justice Programs, Bureau of Justice Statistics, December 23, 2008, http://www.ojp.usdoj.gov/bjs/pub/html/cp/2007/cp07st.pdf (accessed August 24, 2009)

TABLE 7.2

Executions, by race, 1977–2008

Year of execution	Number executed		
	All races[a]	White[b]	Black[b]
Total	1,136	728	393
1977–83	11	9	2
1984	21	13	8
1985	18	11	7
1986	18	11	7
1987	25	13	12
1988	11	6	5
1989	16	8	8
1990	23	16	7
1991	14	7	7
1992	31	19	11
1993	38	23	14
1994	31	20	11
1995	56	33	22
1996	45	31	14
1997	74	45	27
1998	68	48	18
1999	98	61	33
2000	85	49	35
2001	66	48	17
2002	71	53	18
2003	65	44	20
2004	59	39	19
2005	60	41	19
2006	53	32	21
2007	42	28	14
2008	37	20	17

[a]Includes American Indians, Alaska Natives, Asians, Native Hawaiians, and other Pacific Islanders.
[b]Includes persons of Hispanic origin.

SOURCE: Adapted from Tracy L. Snell, "Table 11. Time under Sentence of Death and Execution, by Race, 1977–2007," in *Capital Punishment, 2007—Statistical Tables*, U.S. Department of Justice, Office of Justice Programs, Bureau of Justice Statistics, December 23, 2008, http://www.ojp.usdoj.gov/bjs/pub/html/cp/2007/cp07st.pdf (accessed August 24, 2009)

Race of Victims of Executed Prisoners

The BJS does not provide statistics on the racial makeup of the victims of executed prisoners. These data are very difficult to collect and verify and may not be available for all victims. However, some private organizations do provide estimates. Fins reports in *Death Row U.S.A.: Winter 2009* that from 1977 through 2008, 78.4% of the victims of executed inmates were white, and 12.5% were African-American. (See Table 7.4.) However, an additional 19 defendants were executed for murdering multiple victims of different races. Examination of the defendant-victim racial combinations reveals that in 53% of cases that ended with execution between 1977 and 2008, white defendants had murdered white victims; 20.8% of cases involved an African-American defendant and a white victim; 11% of executions involved both a black perpetrator and a black victim; and 1.32% involved a white perpetrator and a black victim.

Figure 7.1 contains data on victim race reported by the Death Penalty Information Center (DPIC) in *Facts about the Death Penalty* (August 14, 2009). According to the DPIC, 78% of victims in death penalty cases have

(12%; 373 out of 3,096) on death row had been executed. African-American inmates on death row were also slightly more likely to receive a disposition other than execution between 1977 and 2007; 44.9% of black death row inmates were removed without execution, compared with 43% of white inmates and 32% of Hispanic inmates.

TABLE 7.3

Executions and other dispositions of inmates sentenced to death, by race and Hispanic origin, 1977–2007

Race/Hispanic origin	Total under sentence of death 1977–2007[b]	Prisoners executed		Prisoners who received other dispositions[a]	
		Number	Percent of total	Number	Percent of total
Total	7,547	1,099	14.6%	3,228	42.8%
White[c]	3,681	631	17.1%	1,584	43.0%
Black[c]	3,096	373	12.0	1,389	44.9
Hispanic	652	81	12.4	209	32.1
All other races[c,d]	118	14	11.9	46	39.0

[a]Includes persons removed from a sentence of death because of statutes struck down on appeal, sentences or convictions vacated, commutations, or death by other than execution.
[b]Includes 6 persons sentenced to death prior to 1977 who were still under sentence of death on 12/31/07; 374 persons sentenced to death prior to 1977 whose death sentence was removed between 1977 and 12/31/07; and 7,167 persons sentenced to death between 1977 and 2007.
[c]Excludes persons of Hispanic origin.
[d]Includes American Indians, Alaska Natives, Asians, Native Hawaiians and other Pacific Islanders.

SOURCE: Tracy L. Snell, "Table 10. Executions and Other Dispositions of Inmates Sentenced to Death, by Race and Hispanic Origin, 1977–2007," in *Capital Punishment, 2007—Statistical Tables*, U.S. Department of Justice, Office of Justice Programs, Bureau of Justice Statistics, December 23, 2008, http://www.ojp.usdoj.gov/bjs/pub/html/cp/2007/cp07st.pdf (accessed August 24, 2009)

TABLE 7.4

Breakdown of defendant and victim racial combinations in execution cases, 1977–2008

	White victim	Black victim	Latino/a victim	Asian victim	Native American victim
White defendant	602 (52.99%)	15 (1.32%)	13 (1.14%)	4 (.35%)	0 (0%)
Black defendant	236 (20.77%)	125 (11.00%)	15 (1.32%)	10 (.88%)	0 (0%)
Latino/a	38 (3.35%)	2 (.18%)	33 (2.90%)	2 (.18%)	0 (0%)
Asian defendant	2 (.18%)	0 (0%)	0 (0%)	5 (.44%)	0 (0%)
Native American	13 (1.14%)	0 (0%)	0 (0%)	0 (0%)	2 (.18%)
Total:	891 (78.43%)	142 (12.50%)	61 (5.37%)	21 (1.85%)	2 (.18%)

Note: In addition, there were 19 defendants executed for the murders of multiple victims of different races. Of those, 11 defendants were white, 5 black and 3 Latino. (1.67%)

SOURCE: "Defendant-Victim Racial Combinations," in *Death Row U.S.A.: Winter 2009*, NAACP Legal Defense and Educational Fund, Inc., January 1, 2009, http://www.naacpldf.org/content/pdf/pubs/drusa/DRUSA_Winter_2009.pdf (accessed August 24, 2009)

FIGURE 7.1

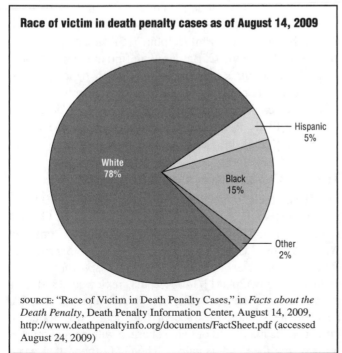

Race of victim in death penalty cases as of August 14, 2009

White 78%
Black 15%
Hispanic 5%
Other 2%

SOURCE: "Race of Victim in Death Penalty Cases," in *Facts about the Death Penalty*, Death Penalty Information Center, August 14, 2009, http://www.deathpenaltyinfo.org/documents/FactSheet.pdf (accessed August 24, 2009)

been white, 15% have been African-American, 5% have been Hispanic, and 2% were of other races.

These types of statistics have been used in court cases to decide the constitutionality of the death penalty. The courts have to consider whether whites who murdered African-Americans received lighter sentences than African-Americans who murdered whites and whether those sentences violated the equal protection rights of the Constitution.

Race and Homicide Statistics

According to James Alan Fox and Marianne W. Zawitz of the Bureau of Justice Statistics, in *Homicide Trends in the United States* (July 11, 2007, http://www.ojp.usdoj.gov/bjs/pub/pdf/htius.pdf), African-Americans are disproportionately represented among homicide offenders and victims. They examined the U.S. homicide rate per 100,000 population between 1976 and 2005 for African-American and white murderers. Fox and Zawitz note that more than half of the offenders (52.2%) were African-American, whereas 45.8% were white. Furthermore, they report that in 2005 the offending rate for African-Americans (26.5 per 100,000 population) was more than 7 times higher than the rate for whites (3.5). Their statistics also show that African-Americans make up a disproportionate percentage of homicide victims. Of all homicide victims between 1976 and 2005, 46.9% were African-American. White victims comprised 50.9% of the total. In 2005 the homicide victimization rate for African-Americans (20.6 per 100,000 population) was 6 times higher than the rate for whites (3.3).

Fox and Zawitz indicate that the vast majority of homicides committed between 1976 and 2005 were intraracial: 86% of white victims were murdered by whites, and 94% of African-American victims were murdered by African-Americans. Cases of "black on white" and "white on black" homicide are relatively uncommon.

Fox and Zawitz also investigated the circumstances of homicides committed by different races between 1976 and 2005. The data indicate that white murderers were most often involved in workplace (70.5%), sex-related (54.7%), and gang-related (54.3%) killings. African-American murderers were more frequently associated with drug-related killings (65%), felony murders (59.3%), and homicides resulting from arguments (51.1%).

Racial Bias in Jury Selection

In 2005 the U.S. Supreme Court issued a ruling in *Miller-El v. Dretke* (June 13, 2005, http://www.law.cornell.edu/supct/html/03-9659.ZO.html) regarding racial bias in jury selection for a capital case tried in Dallas County, Texas. The African-American defendant, Thomas Miller-El (1951?–), was convicted and sentenced to death in 1986 for killing Doug Walker and seriously wounding Donald Hall during an armed robbery the previous year. Miller-El's lawyers appealed, arguing that the prosecutor had improperly eliminated nearly all African-Americans in the venire (the pool of prospective jury members from which the actual jury members are selected). Only 1 of the 20 African-Americans in the venire actually served on the jury. Nine African-Americans in the pool were excused from jury duty for reasons considered legitimate. However, ten other African-Americans in the pool were "peremptorily struck" from the jury by the prosecutor. In a peremptory strike (or challenge) a potential juror is eliminated with no cause given for the removal. After reviewing the questions and procedures used by the prosecutor's office to screen African-American and white members of the venire the court concluded that the peremptory strikes had been racially motivated. The court also cited what it called historical evidence of racial bias in the county's jury selection process. Miller-El's conviction was overturned. In 2008 he pled guilty and agreed not to seek appeals in exchange for a life sentence.

In January 2009 the U.S. Court of Appeals for the Fifth Circuit cited similar racial bias in overturning the death sentence of another inmate convicted in Dallas County, Texas. Jonathan Reed (1951?–), who is white, received the death penalty for the 1978 murder of Wanda Wadle. His lawyers argued successfully that all five African-American members of the venire had been improperly struck from jury service. According to Steven McGonigle and Diane Jennings in the *Dallas Morning News* (January 13, 2009, http://www.dallasnews.com/sharedcontent/dws/dn/latestnews/stories/011308dntexconvictionreversed.1434cb1.html), during the early 1980s county prosecutors "routinely removed blacks from jury service out of a long-standing belief that they would empathize with defendants."

The Baldus Study

In 1986 lawyers appealing the case of Warren McCleskey (1947?–1991), a convicted murderer, brought before the U.S. Supreme Court the Baldus study, an analysis of 2,000 cases in Georgia in the 1970s by David C. Baldus, Charles A. Pulanski Jr., and George Woodworth. (The study actually consisted of two studies: "Comparative Review of Death Sentences: An Empirical Study of the Georgia Experience" [*Journal of Criminal Law and Criminology*, vol. 74, no. 3, 1983] and "Monitoring and Evaluating Contemporary Death Sentencing Systems: Lessons from Georgia" [*University of California Davis Law Review*, vol. 18, no. 1375, 1985].)

This study showed that African-American defendants who were convicted of killing whites were more likely to receive death sentences than white murderers or African-Americans who had killed African-Americans. The justices, in *McCleskey v. Kemp* (481 U.S. 279, 1987), rejected the study, declaring that "apparent disparities in sentencing are an inevitable part of our criminal justice system" and that there were enough safeguards built into the legal system to protect every defendant.

In "Racial Discrimination and the Death Penalty in the Post-*Furman* Era: An Empirical and Legal Analysis with Recent Findings from Philadelphia" (*Cornell Law Review*, vol. 83, 1998), David C. Baldus et al. find evidence of race-of-victim disparities in 26 out of 29 death penalty states. The researchers note that the race of the victim was related to whether capital punishment was imposed. A defendant was more likely to receive the death penalty if the victim was white than if the victim was African-American.

The U.S. General Accounting Office Study

These studies were consistent with a February 1990 U.S. government study of capital punishment. The U.S. General Accounting Office (GAO; now the U.S. Government Accountability Office), in *Death Penalty Sentencing: Research Indicates Pattern of Racial Disparities* (http://archive.gao.gov/t2pbat11/140845.pdf), reviewed 28 studies on race and the death penalty. The GAO reported that "in 82% of the studies, the race of the victim was found to influence the likelihood of being charged with capital murder or receiving the death penalty." The GAO found that when the victim was white, the defendant, whether white or African-American, was more likely to get the death sentence.

GAO added that in the small number of horrendous murders, death sentences were more likely to be imposed, regardless of race. Nevertheless, when the offender killed a person while robbing him or when the murderer had a previous record, the race of the victim played a role. The GAO also explained that for crimes of passion, the convicted person (regardless of race) rarely received the death penalty.

U.S. Department of Justice Study of Racial and Ethnic Bias, 2000

In July 2000 President Bill Clinton (1946–) ordered the U.S. Department of Justice (DOJ) to review the administration of the federal death penalty system. This order came in the aftermath of a request for clemency by Juan Raul Garza (1957?–2001), who was granted a stay by President Clinton, but who was ultimately executed in June 2001. Garza's lawyer contended that it was unfair to execute his client because the federal death penalty discriminated against members of minorities.

In September 2000 the Justice Department released *The Federal Death Penalty System: A Statistical Survey (1988–2000)* (September 12, 2000, http://www.usdoj.gov/dag/pubdoc/dpsurvey.html), which provided information on the federal death penalty since the passage of the first federal capital punishment law in 1988 (the Anti-Drug Abuse Act). From 1988 to 1994 prosecutors in the 94 federal districts were required to submit to the U.S. attorney general for review and approval only those cases that the attorney general deemed worthy for the death penalty. During this period the prosecutors sought the death penalty in 52 cases and received authorization from the attorney general in 47 cases.

In 1995 the Justice Department adopted a new protocol that required U.S. attorneys to submit for review all cases in which a defendant was charged with a crime subject to the death penalty, regardless of whether they intended to seek authorization to pursue the death penalty. These cases were first reviewed by the attorney general's Review Committee on Capital Cases, a committee of senior Justice Department lawyers.

The period 1995–2000, which provides a more extensive picture of the Justice Department's internal decision process as it pertains to the federal death penalty, showed that between January 27, 1995, and July 20, 2000, at every phase of the federal process, minority defendants were overrepresented. Of the 682 defendants whose cases were submitted for review by federal prosecutors, 47.5% were African-American, 28.6% were Hispanic, and 19.6% were white. The prosecutors recommended seeking the death penalty for 183 out of 682 cases submitted for review. Of these 183 cases, two-thirds (44.3% African-Americans and 21.3% Hispanics) were members of minorities. The attorney general reviewed 588 of the cases and authorized the U.S.

attorneys to seek the death penalty in 159 cases. Of the 159 defendants, 44.7% were African-American and 20.1% were Hispanic. Only about 27.7% were white.

Racial Disparity in Plea Bargaining?

It should be noted that the attorney general's decision to seek the death penalty may be changed up until the jury has returned a sentencing verdict. This change may be sought by the defense lawyer, the U.S. attorney, the Review Committee, or by the attorney general. A plea agreement is one avenue that may result in the withdrawal of the death penalty. This means that the defendant enters into an agreement with the U.S. attorney resulting in a guilty plea, saving him or her from the death penalty. From 1995 to 2000, after the attorney general sought the death penalty for 159 defendants, 51 defendants entered into plea agreements. Almost twice as many white defendants (48%, or 21 out of 44) as African-Americans (25%, or 18 out of 71) received a plea agreement. About 28% (9 out of 32) of Hispanics entered into a plea agreement.

GOVERNMENT DEFENDS DATA. The National Institute of Justice (NIJ) observes in *Research into the Investigation and Prosecution of Homicide: Examining the Federal Death Penalty System* (July 20, 2001, http://www.ncjrs.gov/pdffiles1/nij/sl000490.pdf) that, "generally speaking, once submitted for review [to obtain a death penalty authorization], minorities proceeded to the next stages in the death penalty process at lower rates than whites." The NIJ reports that the attorney general authorized the death penalty for 38% (44 out of 115) of whites being considered, compared with 25% (71 out of 287) of African-American defendants and 20% (32 out of 160) of Hispanic defendants.

Justice Department Supplemental Study of Racial and Ethnic Bias, 2001

On June 6, 2001, the Justice Department released a supplement to the September 2000 report—*The Federal Death Penalty System: Supplementary Data, Analysis, and Revised Protocols for Capital Case Review* (http://www.usdoj.gov/dag/pubdoc/deathpenaltystudy.htm). That same day U.S. attorney general John D. Ashcroft (1942–) told the Judiciary Committee of the U.S. House of Representatives that the report confirmed that the subsequent study of the administration of the federal death penalty showed no indication of racial or ethnic bias.

The follow-up study had been ordered by his predecessor, U.S. attorney general Janet Reno (1938–). Besides the 682 cases submitted by federal prosecutors for review in the first study of the federal death penalty, another 291 cases were analyzed, for a total of 973 cases. These included cases that should have been submitted for review for the first report but were not, those in which the defendant eventually entered into a plea agreement for a lesser sentence, and cases in which the death penalty could have been sought but was not. Among the 973 defendants, 408 (42%)

were African-American, 350 (36%) were Hispanic, and 166 (17%) were white.

According to the supplement, from 1995 to 2000, of the 973 defendants eligible for capital charges, federal prosecutors requested authorization to pursue the death penalty against 81% of whites, 79% of African-Americans, and 56% of Hispanics. The attorney general ultimately authorized seeking the death penalty for 27% of the white defendants, 17% of the African-American defendants, and 9% of the Hispanic defendants.

Critics of the supplementary report pointed out that the second federal review failed to address many issues. In "Analysis of June 6 Department of Justice Report on the Federal Death Penalty" (June 14, 2001, http://www.aclu.org/capital/general/10574pub20010614.html), the American Civil Liberties Union (ACLU) notes that, unlike the September 2000 Justice Department report, the June 2001 report did not include information on whether the supplemental 291 cases were from all or just some districts and, therefore, whether or not they represented all the death penalty–eligible cases between 1995 and 2000. The ACLU also pointed out that even though the report found that federal prosecutors were less likely to submit cases of African-American and Hispanic defendants to the attorney general for death penalty authorizations and that the attorney general authorized capital punishment for a higher proportion of whites than African-Americans and Hispanics, there was no information about the decision-making process behind prosecuting on the federal level and of offering plea agreements.

In June 2009 Josh Gerstein of CBS News reported in "Death Penalty Decisions Loom for Obama" that capital punishment opponents hope that Attorney General Eric Holder (1951–) will conduct a new study on possible racial disparities in the federal death penalty system. Holder was deputy attorney general in the Clinton administration when *The Federal Death Penalty System: A Statistical Survey (1988–2000)* was published. According to Gerstein, Holder has described the results of that study as "very disturbing." Gerstein also notes that a DOJ spokesperson has stated that Holder is "open to the idea of a new study" (June 22, 2009, http://www.cbsnews.com/stories/2009/06/21/politics/politico/main5101714.shtml). As of October 2009, however, no new federal study of the death penalty system had been published.

A North Carolina Study

On April 16, 2001, Isaac Unah and John Charles Boger of the University of North Carolina released the most comprehensive study of North Carolina's death penalty system in the state's history: *Race and the Death Penalty in North Carolina, an Empirical Analysis: 1993–1997* (http://www.common-sense.org/pdfs/NCDeathPenaltyReport2001.pdf). The researchers studied all 3,990 homicide cases between 1993 and 1997, including defendants who

received death sentences, as well as those sentenced to life imprisonment.

On first analysis of all homicide cases, Unah and Boger found that, overall, the death-sentencing rate for white victims (3.7%) was almost twice as high as the rate where the victims were nonwhite (1.9%). In addition, the death-sentencing rate for nonwhite defendants/white victims (6.4%) was over two times higher than the rate for white defendants/white victims (2.6%).

When Unah and Boger confined their investigation to death-eligible cases (those imposing the death penalty, such as a case involving the murder of a police officer), race determined whether the defendant received the death sentence. The death-sentencing rate in all death-eligible cases was much higher in white-victim cases (8%) than in cases in which the victims were nonwhite (4.7%). As with all cases, nonwhite defendants in white-victim homicides received the death sentence at a higher rate (11.6%) than white defendants who murdered whites (6.1%).

After the initial analysis, Unah and Boger performed a more comprehensive investigation involving 502 defendants, collecting 113 factors about each crime. These factors included the circumstances of the homicide, the evidence, the charges brought against the defendant, the character and background of the defendant and the victim, the presence or absence of aggravating or mitigating circumstances as specified under the law, as well as the presence or absence of aggravating or mitigating circumstances not specified under the law. The researchers also looked into other factors that might have influenced the imposition of the death penalty, such as the coming reelection of the district attorney prosecuting the crime. Unah and Boger found that race—specifically the race of the victim—played a role in the imposition of capital punishment in North Carolina from 1993 to 1997. On average, the odds of receiving the death penalty were increased by a factor of 3.5 times when the victim was white.

NORTH CAROLINA RACIAL JUSTICE ACT OF 2009. In August 2009 the state of North Carolina passed legislation allowing death row inmates the right to use county prosecutorial statistics to prove that bias was a factor in their death penalty convictions, thus gaining the right to have a sentence converted to life imprisonment. Simply put, if race was found to be a contributing factor in a death penalty case, then the conviction would not stand. Promoters of the bill saw it as a way to overcome racial disparities in death sentences. Opponents insisted it was a way to effectively end the death penalty in North Carolina and maintained that the argument from statistics was flawed: just because disproportionately more men than women were under a death sentence, they noted, it did not prove a prosecutorial bias against men. In addition, some observers expected all 163 death row inmates in North Carolina at the time to pursue an appeal based on the new statute, a caseload that would overtax the state's legal system and decimate the criminal justice budget.

A Maryland Study

In January 2003 Raymond Paternoster et al. released *An Empirical Analysis of Maryland's Death Sentencing System with Respect to the Influence of Race and Legal Jurisdiction* (http://www.newsdesk.umd.edu/pdf/finalrep.pdf), a state-commissioned study of the use of the death penalty in the state. The researchers reviewed 1,311 death-eligible cases out of 6,000 murder cases prosecuted between 1978 and 1999. Of the 1,311 death-eligible cases, state attorneys filed a formal notice to seek the death penalty in 353 (27%) cases. Of the 353 cases, state attorneys dropped the death penalty notice in 140 (40%) cases. The death penalty notice was retained in 213 (60%) cases, out of which 180 (84.5%) cases proceeded to the penalty phase.

Paternoster et al. examined the four decision stages in the death penalty sentencing system: the prosecutor's decision to seek the death penalty, the prosecutor's decision to drop or stick with the death penalty notice, the case's proceeding to a penalty trial, and the court's decision to impose the death sentence. The researchers "found no evidence that the race of the defendant matter[ed] in the processing of capital cases in the state." However, the race of the victim had an impact on whether the prosecutor sought the death penalty. Prosecutors were more likely to seek the death penalty for killers of white victims and were more likely to stick with their death penalty notification when the victims were white.

The study also revealed that jurisdictions affected whether state attorneys sought the death penalty. For example, a defendant in Baltimore County was 13 times more likely to face the death penalty and nearly 23 times more likely to receive a sentence of death than a defendant in a similar case in Baltimore City.

A California Study

Glenn Pierce and Michael Radelet, in "The Impact of Legally Inappropriate Factors on Death Sentencing for California Homicides, 1990–99" (*Santa Clara Law Review*, vol. 46, no. 1, 2005), reviewed data from all homicides committed in California from 1990 through 1999 and compared those that did and did not result in a death sentence. To examine any potential racial biases in conviction and sentencing, they excluded cases in which killers had multiple victims of different races.

Pierce and Radelet found that convicted murderers with non-Hispanic white victims were 4.7 times more likely to receive a death sentence than those who killed Latinos and 3.7 times more likely to receive a death sentence than those who killed African-Americans.

A 2004 National Study

In "Explaining Death Row's Population and Racial Composition" (*Journal of Empirical Legal Studies*, vol. 1, no. 1, March 2004), John Blume, Theodore Eisenberg, and Martin T. Wells compared 23 years of death row statistics to state murder rates. They found that between 1977 and 1999 the number of death row inmates in most states, including those with a reputation for sending a high number of defendants to death row, was nearly proportional to the number of murders in that state.

Overall, the number of inmates on death row in each state was between 0.4% (Colorado) and 6% (Nevada) of murders in that state, and the mean (average) "death sentencing rate" among all states was 2.2%. Despite having the highest number of executions per year, Texas came in below this average with a death row to murder ratio of 2%. Even though Texas juries sentenced 776 people to death row, a total of 37,879 murders had been committed during the study period. Florida, which had a total death row population of 735 inmates, had experienced 121,837 murders and a death sentencing rate of 3.4%. By contrast, Nevada had 124 death row inmates, but only 2,072 murders, giving the state a death sentencing rate 3 times that of Texas. California, Maryland, New Mexico, Virginia, and Washington all had death sentencing rates below 1.5%.

To explain the discrepancy between states, Blume, Eisenberg, and Wells looked at the states' statutes, politics, and other factors that might influence sentencing rates. They found that death sentencing rates were nearly twice as high in states where a judge handed out the sentence as opposed to a jury (4.1% versus 2.1%). State statutes also made a big difference. States with more open-ended statutes that allowed a jury to base their verdicts on subjective standards, such as the heinousness of the murder, had sentencing rates of 2.7%. Sentencing rates dropped to 1.9% in states where specific murders, such as the murder of a pregnant woman or police officer, warranted the death sentence.

Blume, Eisenberg, and Wells then compared the race of the death row inmates to the number of murders committed by race across the country. Nationwide, African-Americans committed 51.5% of murders between 1977 and 1999, but they only made up 41.3% of death row. The researchers analyzed data from seven states—Georgia, Indiana, Maryland, Nevada, Pennsylvania, South Carolina, and Virginia—to determine why these percentages did not match.

Generally, what Blume, Eisenberg, and Wells found was that juries give the death sentence to a far smaller percentage of African-American murderers when the victim was also African-American, rather than white. In South Carolina, for instance, only 0.3% of African-Americans who killed African-Americans received the death penalty, whereas 6.8% of African-Americans who murdered whites were sentenced to death. Because 94% of African-American homicide victims were killed by African-Americans, the percentage of African-Americans on death row tended to be lower than the percentage of African-American murderers. Even though the researchers speculated that racism may figure into these percentages, they also believed that African-American juries in communities with a great deal of African-American-on-African-American crime were less likely to hand out the death sentence.

An Ohio Study

The Ohio Associated Press (AP) published an extensive study on the Ohio death penalty system on May 7, 2005. The news organization reviewed 2,543 reported cases in which prisoners were brought up on capital charges between 1981 and 2002. This number was narrowed to 1,936 after analysts weeded out charges that were dismissed or erroneously reported. Roughly 270 of the indictments led to a death sentence. The AP analyzed the indictments to find any discrepancies in sentencing involving race, sex, or jurisdiction. The results were presented by Andrew Welsh-Huggins in the three-part series "Death Penalty Unequal" (*Cincinnati Enquirer*, May 7–9, 2005).

With respect to race, those indicted (formally accused) of capital murder in Ohio were much more likely to receive the death sentence if the victim was white. Some 17.9% of indictments led to a death sentence if the victim was white, as opposed to 8.5% if the victim was African-American. However, unlike the Baldus study, these percentages were not dependent on the race of the defendant. In cases where the offender and victim were both white, 18.3% of offenders received the death sentence. Roughly the same number of African-American offenders (17.9%) were sentenced to death if the victim was white. If the victim was African-American, 8.4% of African-American offenders were sentenced to death, compared with 8.7% for white offenders.

Jurisdiction had a bigger impact than race on who received the death sentence in Ohio. The AP looked at indictments by county and compared the numbers with those aspects of each county that might influence death penalty verdicts. The news organization found that the politics of a county played a significant role in determining the percentage of defendants who received the death penalty. Hamilton County (Cincinnati metropolitan area) and Cuyahoga County (Cleveland metropolitan area) are both large counties that paid their defense attorneys reasonably well. Yet only 8% of all capital cases ended with a death sentence in Democratic Cuyahoga County, as opposed to 43% in the largely Republican Hamilton County.

The Ohio report also found that compensation for lawyers who represent poor defendants varied drastically from county to county. The limits ranged from $3,000 maximum per death penalty case in rural Coshocton County (east-central Ohio) up to $75,000 in the more affluent Montgomery County (Dayton metropolitan area). Generally, death

penalty cases place an enormous strain on the resources of a small county court as opposed to a large county court. Rural judges reported having to dedicate all their resources for months on end when capital cases came through their courts.

Death Penalty Advocates Speak about the Race Issue

The Criminal Justice Legal Foundation (CJLF) is a California-based group that supports capital punishment. In March 2003 the CJLF collaborated with the California District Attorneys Association to publish *Prosecutors' Perspective on California's Death Penalty* (http://www.cdaa.org/WhitePapers/DPPaper.pdf). The report includes a section that attacks claims of racial bias in California's capital punishment system. The report notes that the racial makeup of the state's death row at the end of 2001 was 41.4% white, 34.6% African-American, 18.8% Hispanic, and 5.2% other races. However, the relatively large percentage of African-Americans among the condemned is attributed primarily to Los Angeles County gang activity: "It is well known that Los Angeles County is 'home territory' to many Black street gangs, such as Crips, Bloods, and the like. And, by their very nature, gang-member activities and prior criminal records frequently bring gang-related homicides within California's capital-sentencing scheme." The report claims that California's death row racial composition changes dramatically if condemned inmates in Los Angeles County are removed from the dataset. This results in a death row composition that is 49.6% white, 28.8% African-American, 17.1% Hispanic, and 4.5% other.

On February 1, 2006, the U.S. Senate Judiciary Subcommittee on the Constitution, Civil Rights, and Property Rights conducted the hearing "An Examination of the Death Penalty in the United States." One of the scholars who testified was John McAdams of Marquette University (http://judiciary.senate.gov/hearings/testimony.cfm?id=17 45&wit_id=4989). McAdams noted that death penalty opponents often "play the race card" in debates over capital punishment. He argued that statistical studies do not support the notion that African-American murderers suffer racial bias in capital punishment cases. However, he acknowledged that studies do show "a huge bias" against African-American victims of homicide. He testified, "This is clearly unjust, but it leaves open the question of whether the injustice should be remedied by executing nobody at all, or rather executing more offenders who have murdered black people."

LEGAL REPRESENTATION: QUESTIONS ABOUT QUALITY

The Sixth Amendment to the U.S. Constitution guarantees the "assistance of counsel for defense" in federal criminal prosecution. In *Gideon v. Wainwright* (372 U.S. 335, 1963), the U.S. Supreme Court extended the right to counsel to state criminal prosecution of indigent (poor) people charged with felonies. In *Argersinger v. Hamlin* (407 U.S. 25, 1972), the high court held that poor people charged with any crime that carries a sentence of imprisonment have the right to counsel.

The court later ruled in *Strickland v. Washington* (466 U.S. 688, 1984) that the lawyers provided for poor defendants must abide by certain professional standards in criminal cases. Some of these standards include demonstrating loyalty to the client, avoiding conflicts of interest, keeping the defendant informed of important developments in the trial, and conducting reasonable factual and legal investigations that may aid the client's case.

Ineffective Counsel?

Death penalty opponents claim that some lawyers who have defended capital cases were inexperienced, ill trained, or incompetent. They point to cases in which the defense lawyers fell asleep during trial, drank to excess the night before, or even showed up in the courtroom intoxicated. They also cite the well-publicized cases of inmates exonerated as a result of college students finding evidence that defense lawyers had failed to uncover.

In "In Pursuit of the Public Good: Lawyers Who Care" (April 9, 2001, http://www.supremecourtus.gov/publicinfo/speeches/sp_04-09-01a.html), Justice Ruth Bader Ginsburg (1933–) of the Supreme Court expressed her concerns about proper representation in capital cases. She states, "I have yet to see a death case, among the dozens coming to the Supreme Court on eve of execution petitions, in which the defendant was well represented at trial.... Public funding for the legal representation of poor people in the United States is hardly generous. In capital cases, state systems for affording representation to indigent defendants vary from adequate to meager."

The American Bar Association (ABA), in "*Gideon*'s Broken Promise: America's Continuing Quest for Equal Justice" (December 2004, http://www.abanet.org/legalservices/sclaid/defender/brokenpromise/fullreport.pdf), provides some insight into why poor defendants may receive inadequate counsel. The ABA analyzes the indigent defense system in 22 states and finds that lawyers who took on poor defendants received low pay and that judges tended to let legal protocols slide to clear overcrowded dockets. In noncapital cases involving lesser offenses, prosecutors and judges sometimes forced defendants to plead guilty before receiving counsel to move them through the system. In addition, the ABA notes that indigent defense systems lack the basic accountability and oversight needed to ensure decent legal representation or correct these problems.

States generally vary in fulfilling *Gideon*. Some states have undertaken the establishment and funding of an indigent defense system; others have passed the responsibility on to individual counties. Across the United States different jurisdictions use one or a combination of three systems to provide counsel to poor defendants. The first system used by some jurisdictions has public defenders that are usually government employees. Under the second system, the court-assigned counsel system, a judge appoints private lawyers to represent the poor. A third system involves contract lawyers who bid for the job of providing indigent defense.

Court-assigned lawyers belong to a list of private lawyers who accept clients on a case-by-case basis. In jurisdictions that employ these lawyers, judges appoint lawyers from a list of private bar members and determine their pay. In most cases the pay is low. Some states have no statewide public defender system and have taken few steps to put one in place. Other states have taken strides since the late 1990s to improve their systems. When New York brought back capital punishment in 1995, the death penalty statute required the establishment of a capital defender office. This office participated in the defense of nearly 200 defendants charged with capital crimes. In 2004 New York's death penalty was declared unconstitutional by the state's supreme court. In June 2001 Texas passed the Texas Fair Defense Act requiring state funding for indigent defense. The act required that counties adopt indigent defense systems meeting basic minimum standards specified in the statute (http://www.equaljusticecenter.org/new_page_2.htm).

To remedy some of the problems inherent in death penalty trials, Congress passed and President George W. Bush (1946–) signed the Innocence Protection Act of 2004. This act launched a program in which state governments receive grants from the federal government to improve the quality of legal representation for poor defendants in state capital cases. To receive such a grant, a state's capital defense system has to meet a number of requirements, which include establishing minimum standards for defense attorneys and monitoring the performance of these attorneys.

In 2005 Georgia legislation went into effect requiring defender offices within each judicial circuit to give representation in felony cases. Later that year a defendant named Brian Nichols (1971–) escaped from the Atlanta courthouse during his rape trial and killed four people before being recaptured. Nichols's death penalty trial in 2008 became the most expensive trial in Georgia history. Yet it ended with a deadlocked jury of eight African-Americans, three whites, and one Asian juror that could not unanimously vote to execute him. The trial judge imposed a sentence of life in prison without chance of parole. In July 2009 Rhonda Cook and Steve Visser reported in the *Atlanta Journal and Constitution* (July 21, 2009, http://www.ajc.com/news/atlanta/murderer-nichols-tab-3murderer-nichols-tab-3-97168.html) that at least $3 million had been spent on Nichols's defense costs. The tab included nearly $1.3 million for attorney's fees and almost $1 million to pay for mental health experts and other experts, investigators, and consultants used by the defense. Nichols offered to plead guilty before the trial started if prosecutors would not seek the death penalty; however, that offer was refused. Funding shortages forced Nichols's defense team to seek and receive several delays before the trial finally took place.

Counsel for Postconviction Review

Even though death row inmates have the right to seek review of their conviction and sentence, they do not have the right to counsel for postconviction proceedings per the Supreme Court ruling in *Murray v. Giarratano* (492 U.S. 1, 1989). Because most of those awaiting execution are poor, they must find lawyers willing to handle appeals for free. In 1995 Congress discontinued federal funding of private organizations (called resource centers) that represented death row inmates in postconviction proceedings. As a result, private organizations and law firms, both proponents and opponents of the death penalty, concerned with the increasing problems in capital cases, now volunteer their services. Some hold training seminars on the complex process of appellate review, whereas others provide research and investigation.

CHAPTER 8

EXONERATIONS, MORATORIUMS, AND REFORMS

Since the 1990s dozens of death row inmates have been exonerated, meaning that the original capital charges against them have been dropped. In some cases new evidence has come to light casting doubt on their guilt. In other cases legal challenges have changed the parameters used to determine who can be sentenced to capital punishment. Exonerations are heralded by death penalty opponents as proof that the U.S. capital punishment system is flawed and should be abandoned. Advocates of the death penalty argue that the importance of exonerations is exaggerated and their occurrence proves that the capital justice system protects the rights of defendants. Nevertheless, exonerations and other concerns about the capital punishment system have prompted reforms and spurred several states to temporarily cease conducting executions. These temporary moratoriums allow officials time to reexamine their capital punishment systems and determine if there are systematic problems in their administration.

EXONERATIONS

The Death Penalty Information Center (DPIC) is opposed to capital punishment. In "Innocence: List of Those Freed from Death Row" (September 19, 2009, http://www.deathpenaltyinfo.org/innocence-list-those-freed-death-row), the DPIC lists the names of 135 people that have been exonerated from death row since 1973. The so-called Innocence List is often touted by death penalty opponents as proof that the U.S. capital punishment system is flawed. Defendants are added to the DPIC list in one of two ways: when their conviction is overturned, and they are acquitted on retrial or all charges are dropped; or when they receive a governor's pardon because of new evidence of innocence.

Figure 8.1 shows the number of exonerations per year between 1974 and June 2009. Note that a single 1973 exoneration is not included in the figure. In addition, between June and September 2009, two additional inmates were added to the list, bringing the total to 135 exonerations.

As shown in Figure 8.2, Florida has had the most exonerations (23), followed by Illinois (20) and Texas (9). Arizona, Louisiana, North Carolina, and Oklahoma each had eight exonerations. The DPIC reports in "Innocence: List of Those Freed from Death Row" that 80 of the exonerated had their charges dismissed, 48 were acquitted, and 7 were pardoned. Seventeen defendants were exonerated based on deoxyribonucleic acid (DNA) evidence. The amount of time that elapsed between death sentence and exoneration ranged from 1 year to 33 years. Overall, the average amount of time that passed between death sentence and exoneration was 9.8 years.

Of the inmates exonerated, 69 were African-American and 52 were white. (See Table 8.1.) Twelve were Latino or Hispanic and two were classified as "other" races.

David Keaton—The First Exoneree

David Keaton (1952–), a Florida teenager who was wrongly convicted of murder in 1971, was the first person exonerated from death row in the modern era. His legal history is detailed by the Florida Commission on Capital Cases in *Case Histories: A Review of 24 Individuals Released from Death Row* (September 10, 2002, http://www.floridacapitalcases.state.fl.us/Publications/innocentsproject.pdf). Keaton was convicted of felony murder for the shooting of Thomas Revels during an armed robbery at a grocery store in Tallahassee in 1970. Keaton and four other men, known as the "Quincy Five," were indicted for the crime. Keaton was not accused of being the triggerman and initially confessed to being involved in the robbery, but later recanted. In 1971 Keaton was convicted and sentenced to death, based on his own confession and the testimony of eyewitnesses who placed him at the scene. The following year his sentence was converted to life in prison following the U.S. Supreme Court's finding in *Furman v. Georgia* that the death penalty, as then practiced, was unconstitutional. Meanwhile, three other men were arrested for the murder of

FIGURE 8.1

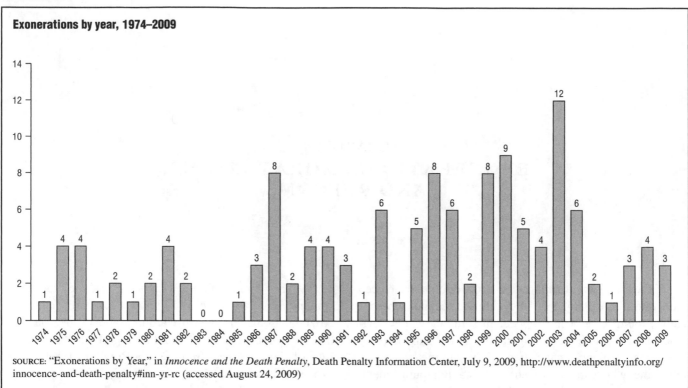

Exonerations by year, 1974–2009

SOURCE: "Exonerations by Year," in *Innocence and the Death Penalty*, Death Penalty Information Center, July 9, 2009, http://www.deathpenaltyinfo.org/innocence-and-death-penalty#inn-yr-rc (accessed August 24, 2009)

FIGURE 8.2

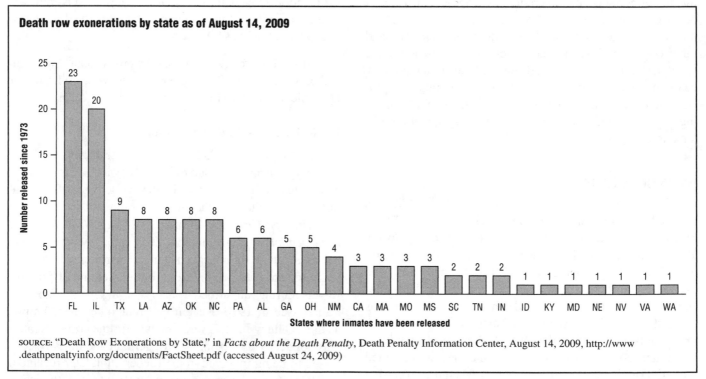

Death row exonerations by state as of August 14, 2009

SOURCE: "Death Row Exonerations by State," in *Facts about the Death Penalty*, Death Penalty Information Center, August 14, 2009, http://www.deathpenaltyinfo.org/documents/FactSheet.pdf (accessed August 24, 2009)

Revels based on fingerprint evidence and the testimony of an informant. In 1973 the Florida Supreme Court ordered a new trial for Keaton; however, the prosecutor decided not to retry the case. At the time, Keaton was serving a 20-year prison sentence for a separate robbery. He was released from prison at age 27 in 1979. In 2006 he told reporter Kathleen Allen in the *Arizona Daily Star* (January 5, 2006; http://www.azstarnet.com/allheadlines/109405), "I was a prayin' man, and I knew that somehow, someway, someone would prove I was innocent."

TABLE 8.1

Exonerations by race as of July 9, 2009

Race	Exonerations
Black	69
White	52
Latino	12
Other	2
Sum:	**135**

SOURCE: "Exonerations by Race," in *Innocence and the Death Penalty*, Death Penalty Information Center, July 9, 2009, http://www.deathpenaltyinfo.org/innocence-and-death-penalty#inn-yr-rc (accessed August 24, 2009)

Kirk Bloodsworth—The First Exoneree Freed by DNA Evidence

Kirk Bloodsworth (1960–) was the first person exonerated from death row based on DNA evidence that proved his innocence. He was convicted in 1984 of raping and murdering nine-year-old Dawn Hamilton in Maryland. Details about the Bloodsworth case can be found on the Web site of the Center on Wrongful Conviction (CWC) at the Northwestern University School of Law (http://www.law.northwestern.edu/wrongfulconvictions/exonerations/mdBloodsworthSummary.html). According to the CWC, five eyewitnesses identified Bloodsworth as being with the victim on the day of the murder or at the scene where the crime later occurred. In addition, the prosecution claimed that shoe prints on Hamilton's body corresponded with shoes owned by Bloodsworth. He was convicted and given a death sentence in March 1985. The following year his conviction was overturned by the Maryland Court of Appeals because the prosecution had withheld potentially exculpatory evidence from the defense. Bloodsworth was retried, again found guilty, and sentenced to two life terms in prison. In 1988 that sentence was upheld upon appeal. From his prison cell, Bloodsworth obtained court approval for DNA testing of crime scene evidence, and the DNA samples were found not to match Bloodsworth. The samples were retested by the Federal Bureau of Investigation, which also concluded that Bloodsworth's DNA did not match with crime scene evidence. Bloodsworth was released from prison in 1993, and the following year he was formally pardoned by Maryland Governor William Donald Schaefer (1921–). In 2003 further DNA testing identified a man named Kimberly Ruffner (1958–) as the perpetrator in Hamilton's murder. The following year Ruffner pleaded guilty to the murder and was sentenced to life in prison.

Since his release from prison Bloodsworth has become a vocal activist who speaks and writes about problems with the criminal justice system. In September 2008 Bloodsworth testified before the Maryland Commission on Capital Punishment saying, "I'm living proof that Maryland's capital punishment system is broken. And I'm living proof that

Maryland gets it wrong" (http://www.goccp.maryland.gov/capital-punishment/documents/transcript-sep-5.doc). In early 2009 Maryland legislators voted to limit capital cases to only those in which DNA evidence, videotaped confessions, or videotape linking the defendant to the murder are available. As of September 2009 Bloodsworth was affiliated with The Justice Project (http://www.thejusticeproject.org), a nonprofit organization based in Washington, DC. The State of Maryland paid $300,000 to Bloodsworth to compensate him for lost income during his years in prison.

Exonerations in 2009

According to the DPIC, five men had been exonerated from death row between January and September 2009:

- Nathson Fields (1953?–) was convicted in 1984 for murdering two rival gang members. The judge at his original trial was later imprisoned for accepting bribes on the bench. (He had found Fields guilty after accepting and then returning a $10,000 bribe for an acquittal.) Fields was released from prison on bond in 2003 to await his new trial and in April 2009 was acquitted on retrial.

- Ronald Kitchen (1966?–) was sentenced to death in 1988 for his involvement in the murder of two women and three children. He confessed to the crime and was linked to it by a friend's testimony. The trial witness later recanted, and Kitchen maintained his confession was the result of beatings and threats by police. In 2003 Kitchen's death sentence was commuted to life without parole when Governor George Ryan (1934–) issued a blanket clemency for all Illinois death row inmates. In July 2009 Kitchen was released from prison when the prosecutor's office declared it could not "sustain its burden of proof" in the midst of an investigation into widespread abuse of suspects by Chicago Police interrogators during the 1970s and 1980s.

- Paul House (1961?–) was convicted in 1986 for raping and murdering his neighbor Carolyn Muncey in Lutrell, Tennessee. Although some biological evidence tied House to the crime, more sophisticated DNA testing performed later linked Muncey's husband to the slaying. In 2006 the case reached the U.S. Supreme Court, which found in *House v. Bell* that the new evidence entitled him to a new trial. In 2008 he was released from prison to await his retrial. In May 2009 the prosecutor dropped the charges against House after newly acquired DNA evidence from hair found at the crime scene matched neither House nor Muncey's husband. As of September 2009 the murder remained under investigation.

- Daniel Wade Moore (1974–) was convicted of raping and murdering Karen Tipton in Decatur, Alabama, in 1999. The jury recommended a life sentence, but the judge imposed the death penalty. In 2003 a new trial was ordered when the judge learned that the prosecution had failed to turn over some evidence to the defense. In May 2009 Moore was acquitted at retrial.

- Herman Lindsey (1973?–) was convicted in 2006 for the murder of a store clerk in 1994. The conviction was overturned in July 2009 by the Florida Supreme Court after finding "that the evidence in the case was not sufficient to convict Lindsey." The prosecutor decided not to appeal the decision, and Moore was set free.

The Innocence List Disputed

Proponents of the death penalty are critical of the DPIC's Innocence List, claiming that it exaggerates the number of innocent people on death row. In 2000 the DPIC reported the 100th addition to the list, an event that was widely publicized in the media. In response, Ramesh Ponnuru attacked the list in "Bad List: A Suspect Roll of Death Row 'Innocents'" (*National Review*, September 16, 2002). Ponnuru claimed that most of the exonerations resulted from legal technicalities, rather than actual innocence. He recounted the violent criminal records of some of the exonerees and the formidable evidence introduced at trial against them. He described legal motions and maneuvers that ultimately resulted in the reversal of their sentences. He complained that "the list leads people to think that innocence has been proven when the most that can be said is that the legal system cannot establish guilt beyond a reasonable doubt."

Ponnuru argued that approximately 32 of the 102 exonerees on the list at that time could truly be regarded as innocent. He noted that more than 7,000 people have been on death row since 1973; thus, the percentage of actual innocence cases is extremely low.

In *Critique of DPIC List ("Innocence: Freed from Death Row")* (2002, http://www.prodeathpenalty.com/DPIC.htm), Ward A. Campbell, the supervising deputy attorney general in California, investigated the 102 cases of exonerated death row inmates on the DPIC list at that time. He concluded that at least 68 of the 102 inmates on the list should not have been included. Campbell found that "many defendants on the List were not 'actually innocent'"—that is, the prosecution found the defendant innocent of the crime. Some had pleaded guilty to lesser charges and had their sentences commuted. Campbell noted that "an acquittal because the prosecution has not proven guilt beyond a reasonable doubt does not mean that the defendant did not actually commit the crime."

On June 20, 2002, the Florida Commission on Capital Cases released *Case Histories: A Review of 24 Individuals Released from Death Row* (September 10, 2002, http://www.floridacapitalcases.state.fl.us/Publications/innocentsproject.pdf), which lists the results of its investigation into 24 cases on the DPIC list. The commission concluded:

Of these 24 inmates, none were found "innocent," even when acquitted, because no such verdict exists. A defendant is found guilty or not guilty, never innocent. The guilt of only four defendants, however, was subsequently doubted by the prosecuting office or the Governor and Cabinet members.... An analysis of the remaining 20 inmates can be divided into three categories that account for their releases: (1) seven cases were remanded due to evidence issues, (2) an additional seven were remanded in light of witness issues, and (3) the remaining six were remanded as a result of issues involving court officials.

QUESTIONS ABOUT LEGAL ERRORS IN DEATH PENALTY CASES
Liebman Study

James S. Liebman, Jeffrey Fagan, and Valerie West conducted the first study of its kind—a statistical study of modern U.S. capital appeals—for the U.S. Senate Judiciary Committee. The study, called *A Broken System: Error Rates in Capital Cases, 1973–1995* (June 12, 2000, http://www2.law.columbia.edu/instructionalservices/liebman/liebman_final.pdf), examined all death penalty sentences (5,760) imposed in the United States over a 23-year period.

On direct appeal, the state high courts reviewed 4,578 death sentences. Liebman, Fagan, and West found that 68% of the death sentences reviewed by courts across the country were found to have serious errors. For every 100 death sentences, 41 were returned to the courts during state appeal because of serious errors. Of the 59 death sentences that reached the second state appeal, another six went back to court because of errors. At the third level of appeal—with the federal courts—21 more cases were remanded to the lower courts because of errors found. In all, of the original 100 death penalty sentences, 68 had serious errors that required retrial. Of the 68 defendants who were retried, 82% (56) did not receive the death penalty at their retrial. Another five inmates were found not guilty of the capital crime for which they received the death sentence.

THE LIEBMAN STUDY IS ANALYZED. Critics challenged the results of the Liebman study. Appearing before the U.S. Senate Committee on the Judiciary hearing on "Reducing the Risk of Executing the Innocent: The Report of the Illinois Governor's Commission on Capital Punishment," Senator Strom Thurmond (R-SC, 1902–2003; June 12, 2002, http://judiciary.senate.gov/member_statement.cfm?id=256&wit_id&456) warned:

A Columbia University report known as the Liebman study is often cited as proof that capital punishment in this country is deeply flawed. This study... alleged that from 1973 to 1995, 70% of death penalty convictions were reversed on appeal. The implication is that 70% of the time, innocent people were sentenced to death. This study should be viewed carefully because during the time period addressed by this study, the Supreme Court issued a series of retroactive rules that nullified a number of verdicts. These reversals were not based on the actual innocence of defendants, but rather were based on procedural rules.

Latzer Study

In "Capital Appeals Revisited" (*Judicature*, vol. 84, no. 2, September–October 2000), Barry Latzer and James N. G. Cauthen noted that their reexamination of the Liebman study found that about one-fourth (27%)—and not two-thirds (68%)—of capital convictions were reversed between 1973 and 1995. Latzer and Cauthen stated that the Liebman study did not differentiate between reversals of convictions and reversals of death sentences.

Latzer and Cauthen conducted their own investigation, based on the theory that many of the appeals resulted in reversed sentences but not reversed convictions. The study covered the period 1990 to 1999, using reversal data in the same 26 states studied by Liebman and his colleagues. Latzer and Cauthen wanted more recent data of the death penalty system that would provide more complete reversal rate differences.

Latzer and Cauthen found that of the 837 death penalty reversals in state-level direct appeal or postconviction review, 61% were sentence reversals and 39% were conviction reversals (reversals addressing the guilt or innocence of the defendant). Using the Liebman study's conclusion that 5 out of 10 capital judgments were reversed at either the direct-appeal phase or postconviction review phase, Latzer and Cauthen applied this finding to their study and concluded that, of the five reversals, three were sentence reversals and two were conviction reversals.

Latzer and Cauthen also investigated reversals at the federal level—the third stage of death penalty judgment review—using data from the Ninth Circuit Court of Appeals, the largest of the circuit courts. Of the 29 capital cases reversed by the court during the 10-year period, 21 (72.4%) were sentence reversals and 8 (27.7%) were conviction reversals. This was consistent with their findings regarding direct-appeal and postconviction sentence reversals at the state level. Using the Liebman study's finding that 68 out of 100 capital judgments were reversed, Latzer and Cauthen concluded, "If 68 of 100 capital decisions are reversed after direct, post-conviction, and federal habeas corpus review, and 39 percent of these are conviction reversals, then convictions in 26.52 (39 percent of 68) of 100 capital decisions are reversed."

FORENSIC SCIENCE

Forensic science is the application of scientific knowledge to legal problems. In the modern era the criminal justice system relies heavily on forensic science to reveal the guilt (or innocence) of suspects. Examples include fingerprint analysis, firearms testing, DNA testing, autopsies, arson and explosives investigations, and analysis of bloodstains, handwriting, bite marks, etc. DNA testing, in particular, plays a major role in capital case investigations. DNA, which stores the genetic code of the human body, is found in saliva, skin tissue, bones, blood, semen, and the root of hair.

The science of DNA testing is improving rapidly. When DNA testing was first used in criminal trials starting in the mid-1980s, DNA samples had to be not only fresh but also contain thousands of cells. As DNA technology has become more sophisticated, scientists are able to test a single cell for DNA patterns that could link suspects to hair or semen found on a victim. In the 21st century a crime laboratory can identify unique DNA patterns in a tiny sample of fewer than 50 cells.

Postconviction DNA Testing

Before DNA testing became available as proof of identity, the U.S. Supreme Court held the view that U.S. appellate courts could not reverse a murder conviction based on newly discovered post-trial evidence. In *Herrera v. Collins* (506 U.S. 390, 1993), the Supreme Court ruled that newly discovered evidence does not constitute grounds for a federal habeas relief if there is no evidence of a constitutional violation occurring during state criminal proceedings. (In this case, Leonel Torres Herrera [1947–1993] alleged 10 years after his initial trial that he was innocent of a double murder, presenting evidence that his brother, who had since died, had committed the crime.) The commission, however, stated that with the availability of DNA testing, "the possibility of demonstrating actual innocence has moved from the realm of theory to the actual."

The federal Innocence Protection Act became law on October 30, 2004. The law established the conditions under which a federal prisoner who pleads not guilty can receive postconviction DNA testing. If a trial defendant is convicted, the act calls for the preservation of the defendant's biological evidence. A five-year, $25 million grant program was also established to help eligible states pay for postconviction testing. The DPIC reports in "Innocence: List of Those Freed from Death Row" that as of July 2009, 17 of the 135 inmates released from death row since 1973 were exonerated by DNA evidence.

Backlog of DNA Testing

Given the high price of analyzing DNA samples, DNA evidence from crime scenes often goes untested. Such testing, however, could exonerate death row inmates who have been falsely accused. In December 2000 Congress authorized the U.S. Department of Justice to provide state crime laboratories more than $30 million to analyze the backlog of DNA samples that had been collected but never tested. Under the DNA Analysis Backlog Reduction Act of 2000, states would receive funding to conduct tests on about half a million samples collected from criminals and crime scenes that had never been analyzed. In August 2001 the U.S. attorney general John Ashcroft (1942–) announced that, besides the state initiative, the Justice Department had authorized the collection of DNA samples from about 20,000 to 30,000 federal, military, and District of Columbia offenders.

In the *Report to the Attorney General on Delays in Forensic DNA Analysis* (March 2003, http://www.ncjrs .gov/pdffiles1/nij/199425.pdf), the National Institute of Justice (NIJ) reveals that a task force assembled by the NIJ found a continuing backlog in the testing of DNA samples collected at crime scenes. Even though an estimated 350,000 rape and homicide DNA samples needed testing at that time, just 10% of the samples were in forensic crime laboratories. Most of the evidence samples were in the custody of law enforcement agencies because most laboratories lacked the proper storage facilities for preventing damage to the evidence.

Even if the laboratories had the proper storage facilities, the analysis of DNA samples could not take place because of the shortage of trained forensic scientists. Newly hired scientists need on-the-job training that requires an experienced scientist to spend time working one-on-one with new hires. The task force found that even when these problems were confronted, public crime laboratories could not retain their staff because of their lower compensation, compared to that paid by private companies.

Questions about the Validity of Forensic Science

The *Science, State, Justice, Commerce, and Related Agencies Appropriations Act of 2006* authorized the National Academy of Sciences to create an independent Forensic Science Committee (FSC) to assess the conditions and needs of the nation's forensic science community, specifically state and local crime laboratories, medical examiners, and coroners. In 2009 the FSC issued a 352-page report, *Strengthening Forensic Science in the United States: A Path Forward* (February 18, 2009, http://www.nap.edu/catalog.php?record _id=12589).

The committee acknowledges the valuable role that forensic science has played in the U.S. justice system in recent decades in terms of convicting the guilty and exonerating the innocent. However, serious problems are described regarding the scientific basis of some procedures and general practices that characterize the forensic community. The report notes, "There is no uniformity in the certification of forensic practitioners, or in the accreditation of crime laboratories. Indeed, most jurisdictions do not require forensic practitioners to be certified, and most forensic science disciplines have no mandatory certification programs. Moreover, accreditation of crime laboratories is not required in most jurisdictions." The FSC also found that "in some cases, substantive information and testimony based on faulty forensic science analyses may have contributed to wrongful convictions of innocent people." Regarding scientific validity the FSC states, "The simple

reality is that the interpretation of forensic evidence is not always based on scientific studies to determine its validity. This is a serious problem. Although research has been done in some disciplines, there is a notable dearth of peer-reviewed, published studies establishing the scientific bases and validity of many forensic methods."

The FSC also recognizes as problems the significant backlogs at crime laboratories around the country and lack of educational and training requirements among medical examiners and coroners' offices. It notes that state and local forensic laboratories are "underresourced and understaffed." The committee calls for upgrades to systems and organizational structures, better training, and widespread adaptation of uniform training, certification, and accreditation procedures. Although the FSC supports national oversight of the forensic community, it recommends against assigning that responsibility to a unit of the U.S. Department of Justice or any entity principally devoted to law enforcement. The committee states that forensic science should be "equally available" to law enforcement officials and defendants in the criminal justice system.

Some of the problems identified by the FSC have already received public attention. In the January/February 2006 edition of the National Association of Defense Lawyers' journal *The Champion*, William C. Thompson describes problems uncovered at numerous crime laboratories around the country in "Tarnish on the 'Gold Standard': Recent Problems in Forensic DNA Testing" (http://www .nacdl.org/public.nsf/0/6285f6867724e1e685257124006 f9177). Thomson cites incidences of poor quality control procedures, mishandling of samples, testing errors, and dishonest analysts. He notes that in some cases postconviction DNA testing has brought laboratory problems to light when the postconviction test results do not match the pretrial results.

An Innocent Man Executed?

The validity of forensic science techniques, specifically arson investigations, has taken center stage in the debate over the possible innocence of a man executed in Texas in 2004. Cameron Todd Willingham (1968–2004) was executed for setting a house fire that killed his three young children in 1991. His conviction rested largely on expert testimony from the state fire marshal that the fire had been deliberately set. In "Man Executed on Disproved Forensics" (December 9, 2004, http://www.chicagotribune.com/news/nationworld/ chi-0412090169dec09,0,1173806.story), *Chicago Tribune* writers Steve Mills and Maurice Possley describe the findings of several arson investigators hired by the newspaper to review the trial evidence. All of the investigators disputed the original finding that the fire was definitely an arson.

In August 2009 a private company hired by the Texas Forensic Science Commission (http://www.fsc.state.tx.us/)

issued a scathing report criticizing the lack of scientific methods employed by the original fire investigators. A copy of the report, *Analysis of the Fire Investigation Methods and Procedures Used in the Criminal Arson Cases against Ernest Ray Willis and Cameron Todd Willingham* (August 17, 2009, http://www.deathpenaltyinfo.org/docum ents/BeylerArsonRpt082509.pdf) has been made public by the DPIC. The report details numerous shortcomings in the original investigation and describes subsequent development of fire science standards by the National Fire Protection Association (NFPA). The report concludes, "The investigators had poor understandings of fire science and failed to acknowledge or apply the contemporaneous understanding of the limitations of fire indicators. Their methodologies did not comport with the scientific method or the process of elimination. A finding of arson could not be sustained based upon the standard of care expressed by NFPA 921, or the standard of care expressed by fire investigation texts and papers in the period 1980–1992."

The controversial case continued to develop in late 2009 as Governor Rick Perry (1950–) replaced chairman Sam Bassett and three other members of the Texas Forensic Science Commission just days before a scheduled hearing on the Willingham case at which the commission planned to review the report. Perry's critics suggested that the commission appointments were politically motivated and were a preemptive move designed to stall inquiry into the Willingham execution. However, Perry defended his decision not to stay the execution in 2004, stating that Willingham's death sentence had been upheld at every level of the Texas court system and that reports challenging forensic testimony amounted to little more than opinions. Quoted in the *New York Times* (October 19, 2009, http://www.nytimes.com/2009/10/20/us/20texas.html), Perry said, "Willingham was a monster."... Here's a guy who murdered his three children.... Person after person has stood up and testified to the facts in this case."

Opponents of the death penalty in Texas, however, maintained that in executing Willingham the state had killed an innocent man. His story was featured at a march and rally at the Texas capitol in Austin in October 2009, where hundreds of protestors from throughout the state called for an end to the death penalty.

MORATORIUMS AND REFORMS

Since the turn of the 21st century a number of measures have been put in place in death penalty states in an attempt to remedy perceived problems in their capital punishment systems. These include reforms and moratoriums (suspensions) in executions. Moratoriums fall into two types—de jure and de facto. The term *de jure* means "by right." A de jure moratorium is a moratorium imposed by law. The term *de facto* means "in reality" or "actually." A de facto morato-

rium on executions means that some other factor besides a law has caused executions not to take place.

States with de Jure Moratoriums

As of September 2009, 14 states had no capital offenses in their statutes: Alaska, Hawaii, Iowa, Maine, Massachusetts, Michigan, Minnesota, New Jersey, New Mexico, North Dakota, Rhode Island, Vermont, West Virginia, and Wisconsin. The District of Columbia (DC) also did not have the death penalty. As described in Chapter 1 most of these states and DC outlawed capital punishment many years ago:

- 1853—Wisconsin
- 1887—Maine
- 1911—Minnesota
- 1957—Alaska and Hawaii (both then territories)
- 1963—Michigan
- 1965—Iowa, Vermont, and West Virginia
- 1975—North Dakota
- 1984—Massachusetts and Rhode Island
- 2007—New Jersey
- 2009—New Mexico

In reality, some of these states had not executed anyone for decades before capital punishment was officially ended; for example, Alaska, Hawaii, Maine, Michigan, Minnesota, and Rhode Island had not executed anyone since 1930. (See Table 8.2.) The District of Columbia and eight other states—Iowa, Kansas, Massachusetts, New Hampshire, New Jersey, New York, Vermont, and West Virginia—had not executed anyone since 1977. Kansas, New Hampshire, and New York ceased executions due to de facto moratoriums, discussed below.

NEW JERSEY. In 2006 the New Jersey legislature created the New Jersey Death Penalty Study Commission to assess the administration of capital punishment in the state. All death sentences were put on hold until at least 60 days after completion of the commission's report, *New Jersey Death Penalty Study Commission Report* (January 2007, http://www.njleg.state.nj.us/committees/dpsc_final .pdf). The report included eight major findings and recommendations:

- "No compelling evidence" was found to support the idea that the death penalty "serves a legitimate penological" purpose.
- The costs of capital punishment were found to be higher than the costs of life in prison without parole.
- Evidence indicated that the death penalty is "inconsistent with evolving standards of decency."

TABLE 8.2

States with no executions since 1930 and no executions since 1977

	No executions since 1930	No executions since 1977
New York		X
New Jersey		X
District of Columbia		X
West Virginia		X
Massachusetts		X
Iowa		X
Kansas		X
Vermont		X
New Hampshire		X
Alaska	X	X
Hawaii	X	X
Maine	X	X
Michigan	X	X
Minnesota	X	X
Rhode Island	X	X

SOURCE: Adapted from Tracy L. Snell, "Table 9. Number of Persons Executed, by Jurisdiction, 1930–2007," in *Capital Punishment, 2007—Statistical Tables*, U.S. Department of Justice, Office of Justice Programs, Bureau of Justice Statistics, December 23, 2008, http://www.ojp.usdoj.gov/bjs/pub/html/cp/2007/cp07st.pdf (accessed August 24, 2009)

- Data did not support the idea that racial biases affect the application of capital punishment in New Jersey.

- The abolishment of the death penalty would eliminate the "risk of disproportionality in capital sentencing."

- The penological benefit of capital punishment was deemed not worth the risk of possibly making an "irreversible mistake."

- Life sentences with no chance of parole were declared sufficient to ensure public safety and address other social and penological concerns.

- State funds should be allocated to provide needed services to the families of murder victims.

In December 2007 New Jersey officially abolished the death penalty. According to Keith B. Richburg in the *Washington Post* (December 14, 2007, http://www.washingtonpost.com/wp-dyn/content/article/2007/12/13/AR2007121301302.html), New Jersey law replaced the death penalty with a sentence of life in prison without the possibility of parole. As shown in Table 7.1 in Chapter 7 there were no inmates on death row at the time.

NEW MEXICO. In March 2009 New Mexico Governor Bill Richardson (1957–) signed into law a bill that repealed the state's death penalty and replaced it with a sentence of life in prison with no chance for parole. CNN reports in "New Mexico Governor Repeals Death Penalty in State" (March 18, 2009, http://www.cnn.com/2009/CRIME/03/18/new.mexico.death.penalty/?iref=hpmostpop) that Richardson described himself as a "firm believer in the death penalty as a just punishment—in very rare instances, and only for the most heinous crimes." However, the governor expressed

serious reservations about capital punishment, particularly noting the number of cases in which death row prisoners had been exonerated. He was also concerned that minorities are "over-represented" in the nation's death row population. However, the law change does not affect New Mexico's existing death row population. Writing for the Criminal Justice Project of the NAACP Legal Defense and Educational Fund in *Death Row U.S.A.: Winter 2009* (http://www.naacpldf.org/content/pdf/pubs/drusa/DRUSA_Winter_2009.pdf), Deborah Fins lists two inmates under sentence of death in the state as of January 1, 2009. The last execution in New Mexico was in 2001.

Death Penalty States with Long-Standing de Facto Moratoriums

As of September 2009, 36 states had death penalty statutes. However, three of these states—Kansas, New Hampshire, and New York—had not executed anyone since 1977.

KANSAS. The last executions in Kansas were in June 1965. It was not until 1994 that the state reinstated the death penalty following the nationwide moratorium triggered by the U.S. Supreme Court's decision in *Furman v. Georgia*. However, no inmate has been executed in Kansas under the new statute. For more than a decade the state's new death penalty law was subject to court challenges regarding its constitutionality. The issue was settled by the U.S. Supreme Court in 2006 in *Kansas v. Marsh* in which the new law was upheld. In *Death Row U.S.A.: Winter 2009*, Fins notes that Kansas had 10 inmates on death row as of January 1, 2009. In March 2009 a bill was introduced in the Kansas Senate to repeal the death penalty law. However, as of September 2009 that bill had not been subject to a vote.

NEW HAMPSHIRE. New Hampshire has not executed anyone since July 1939. Two death sentences handed out during the 1950s were later overturned by courts. In December 2008 a New Hampshire jury sentenced Michael Addison (1980–) to death for killing a police officer. According to Fins in *Death Row U.S.A.: Winter 2009*, Addison was the sole inmate on death row as of January 1, 2009. New Hampshire law limits the crimes for which a death sentence can be imposed to the following: murder for hire, murdering a police officer, and murder during the course of a kidnapping. However, another man convicted of capital murder during 2009 received life in prison from a jury. John J. Brooks was found guilty of paying three men to kill a man he believed had cheated him. Katie Zezima reports in the *New York Times* (December 19, 2008, http://www.nytimes.com/2008/12/19/us/19death.html) that the disparity in sentences between the two cases aroused controversy because Addison is black and not wealthy, while Brooks is white and a millionaire.

In March 2009 the New Hampshire House voted to repeal the state's death penalty law. As of September 2009, the state senate had not voted on the measure. However, in late July 2009 Governor John Lynch (1952–) established a commission to study the scope of New Hampshire's death penalty system, along with its strengths and weaknesses, associated costs, and such issues as discrimination and how best to serve the interests of crime victims. The commission included legislators as well as appointees representing prosecuting attorneys, defense lawyers, law enforcement officers, family members of murder victims, mental health professionals, and special interest organizations with objectives related to the capital punishment debate. A report analyzing the death penalty in New Hampshire was expected from the commission by December 1, 2010.

NEW YORK. Until 1998 New York's death penalty statute prohibited the imposition of a death sentence when a defendant entered a guilty plea. The maximum penalty in such a case would be life imprisonment without parole. However, a defendant who pleaded not guilty would have to stand trial and face the possibility of a death sentence. The law provided two levels of penalty for the same offense, imposing the death penalty only on those who claimed innocence.

Defendants in two capital cases challenged the plea provisions of New York's death penalty statute, claiming these provisions violated their Fifth Amendment right against self-incrimination and Sixth Amendment right to a jury trial. This was the first major constitutional challenge to New York's death penalty law. On December 22, 1998, the New York Court of Appeals (New York's highest court), in *Hynes v. Tomei* (including *Relin v. Mateo*, 92 N.Y. 2d. 613, 706 N.E. 2d. 1201, 684 N.Y.S. 2d. 177), unanimously agreed, thereby striking down these plea-bargaining provisions as unconstitutional. The court, relying on the U.S. Supreme Court decision in *United States v. Jackson* (390 U.S. 570, 1968), observed that "the Supreme Court in *Jackson* prohibited statutes that 'needlessly' encourage guilty pleas, which are not constitutionally protected, by impermissibly burdening constitutional rights." The ruling left the death penalty intact, but the court could no longer give preference to those who entered a guilty plea.

JURY DEADLOCK INSTRUCTIONS. In 2004 the New York Court of Appeals agreed to hear another challenge to the constitutionality of New York's death penalty. Stephen LaValle (1967–) was sentenced to death in 1999 by a New York jury for the murder and rape of Cynthia Quinn. Under New York law, a jury can sentence a defendant convicted of murder to life in prison without parole or to death. All jurors must vote unanimously. In the event of a hung jury, the court sentences a guilty defendant to life imprisonment with parole eligibility after serving a minimum of 20 to 25 years, leaving room for the convict to be released.

LaValle claimed that this "jury deadlock instruction" violated his constitutional rights because it would encourage members of the jury who do not favor the death penalty

to vote for the death penalty if they are in the minority. LaValle even presented a study showing that most jurors would choose the death penalty if given the choice of the death penalty or imprisonment with a chance of parole. In *People v. LaValle* (783 NYS 2d, 485, 2004), the New York Court of Appeals agreed with LaValle and vacated his sentence. The state high court stated that this jury instruction was a cruel and unusual punishment in violation of the 8th and 14th Amendments, citing the U.S. Supreme Court's decision in *Woodson v. North Carolina* (428 U.S. 280, 1976). The court held in *Woodson* that a mandatory death sentence for a capital offense was unconstitutional and forced jurors to charge the defendant with a lesser charge if they did not want to see the defendant sentenced to death.

This decision by the New York court in 2004 effectively put a de facto moratorium on the New York death penalty until the New York state legislature could change the death penalty statutes. Roughly a year later, the New York State Assembly Codes Committee (the state legislative committee in charge of changing death penalty statutes) defeated a bill to reinstate the death penalty, claiming that the system was riddled with flaws. In 2007 the state's last death row inmate was resentenced to life in prison without the chance of parole. As of September 2009, the de facto moratorium on the death penalty remained in effect in New York.

Death Penalty States with Recent de Facto Moratoriums

Since 2000 many death penalty states have put into place de facto moratoriums on executions for a number of reasons. As described in Chapter 3 the U.S. Supreme Court's decision in September 2007 to hear a case concerning the constitutionality of Kentucky's lethal injection protocol triggered a de facto moratorium on executions around the country. In *Baze v. Rees* (April 2008) the nation's highest court upheld that protocol. Some states resumed executions immediately; however, other states have been reexamining and sometimes adjusting their lethal injection protocols to ensure their constitutionality.

ILLINOIS. On January 31, 2000, Illinois became the first state in the modern death penalty era to declare a moratorium on the death penalty. Governor George Ryan, a death penalty supporter, suspended all executions because he believed the state's death penalty system was "fraught with errors." The *Chicago Tribune* had issued a report showing that 13 inmates in Illinois had been released from death row since 1976. The reasons for the exoneration of these inmates ranged from DNA evidence showing innocence, to false testimonies by jailhouse informants, to coercion of so-called witnesses by the prosecution and police.

Governor Ryan then established the Governor's Commission on Capital Punishment to investigate the 13 cases, as well as all capital cases in Illinois. In April 2002 the

Report of the Governor's Commission on Capital Punishment (http://www.idoc.state.il.us/ccp/ccp/reports/commission_report/summary_recommendations.pdf) was released. The commission issued 85 recommendations it thought would help reform the state's death penalty process. The recommended reforms included videotaping of capital suspects during interrogation at police facilities, banning the death penalty in cases where the conviction is based on a single eyewitness testimony, and thorough examination of a jailhouse-informant testimony at a pretrial hearing to determine whether to use that testimony during trial.

On January 10, 2003, the day before leaving office, Governor Ryan pardoned 4 inmates who had been on death row in Illinois at least 12 years. The governor claimed the men were innocent of the murders for which they had been convicted. He found that the police had tortured the men into making false confessions. Three of the men had been released. The fourth inmate remained in prison because of a separate conviction. The following day Governor Ryan commuted 167 death sentences to life imprisonment without the possibility of parole, emptying death row.

As of September 2009, the Illinois moratorium had not been lifted. However, the Illinois death row has not remained empty. According to Fins in *Death Row U.S.A.: Winter 2009*, there were 15 inmates on death row in Illinois as of January 1, 2009.

CALIFORNIA. In 2004 the California Commission on the Fair Administration of Justice (CCFAJ) was created by the state's legislators to examine California's criminal justice system and make recommendations to remedy any problems. The CCFAJ (http://www.ccfaj.org/reports.html) released eight reports containing its findings and recommendations:

- *Report and Recommendations Regarding Eye Witness Identification Procedures* (April 13, 2006)

- *Report and Recommendations Regarding False Confessions* (July 25, 2006)

- *Report and Recommendations Regarding Informant Testimony* (September 29, 2006)

- *Report and Recommendations Regarding Forensic Science Evidence* (May 8, 2007)

- *Emergency Report and Recommendations Regarding DNA Testing Backlogs* (February 20, 2007)

- *Report and Recommendations on Professional Responsibility and Accountability of Prosecutors and Defense Lawyers* (October 18, 2007)

- *Official Recommendations on the Fair Administration of the Death Penalty in California* (June 30, 2008)

- *Final Report* (June 30, 2008)

California legislators acted on the recommendations provided in the early reports by passing bills designed to reform the state's eyewitness identification procedures and require recording of suspect interrogations. In 2006 Governor Arnold Schwarzenegger (1947–) vetoed both bills citing procedural problems with them. Revamped versions of the bills passed the legislature in 2007 but were again vetoed by the governor.

In December 2006 a federal judge in California ruled in *Morales v. Tilton* (No. C 06 219 JF RS) the state's lethal injection protocol was unconstitutional after hearing arguments from the lawyers for the death row inmate Michael Morales (1959–). The judge complained that the protocol "lacks both reliability and transparency" and results in "undue and unnecessary risk of an Eighth Amendment violation." The state began construction of a new execution chamber and development of new lethal injection protocols. Fins notes in *Death Row U.S.A.: Winter 2009* that California's death row contained 678 inmates as of January 1, 2009, the largest number of any state. As of September 2009, a de facto moratorium remained in effect in California.

PHYSICIAN INVOLVEMENT. One issue that has triggered or prolonged temporary execution moratoriums in California, Missouri, and North Carolina has been the role of physicians in the execution process. Kevin O'Reilly reports on this issue on behalf of the American Medical Association (AMA) in "Controversial California Ruling Focuses on Physician Role in Execution," (March 13, 2006, http://www.ama-assn.org/amednews/2006/03/13/prl20313.htm). He notes that a federal judge in February 2006 ordered the state of California to have an anesthesiologist present during executions to ensure that the lethal injection procedure rendered the prisoner fully unconscious. California, like most other death penalty states, uses a three-part lethal injection protocol in which the first drug renders the prisoner unconscious, a second drug paralyzes the prisoner, and a third drug stops the heart beating. Questions have arisen about the effectiveness of the first drug at keeping prisoners fully unconscious during the remaining procedures.

The AMA and some state medical associations have warned doctors that actively participating in an execution would violate their ethical responsibilities. O'Reilly notes in "Physicians Resist Push for Execution Involvement," (May 14, 2007, http://www.ama-assn.org/amednews/2007/05/14/prl20514.htm) that AMA policy prohibits doctors from being present at executions "in a professional capacity," taking any part in the execution process, or offering "technical advice" regarding execution. The only role the organization allows is for doctors to certify that a prisoner is dead. However, recent court rulings in California, Missouri, and North Carolina have forced corrections officials in those states to use doctors actively in the execution process. O'Reilly reports that doctors have been reluctant to participate for fear of losing their medical licenses. In March 2007 corrections officials in North

Carolina sued that state's medical board after the board threatened disciplinary action against any doctor that actively participated in an execution. According to O'Reilly in "North Carolina Medical Board Can't Discipline Doctors for Execution Work," (October 22, 2007, http://www.ama-assn.org/amednews/2007/10/22/prsc1022.htm), in September 2007 a state court judge ruled that the medical board had "overstepped its authority" in making the threat.

As of September 2009 none of these states had resumed executions because of ongoing efforts to ensure that their lethal injection protocols were constitutional.

Death Penalty States That Rarely Impose the Death Penalty

As shown in Table 8.3, 16 states that had the death penalty in 2008 had executed 10 or fewer inmates between 1977 and 2008:

- Colorado (1)
- Connecticut (1)
- Idaho (1)
- Kentucky (3)
- Maryland (5)
- Mississippi (10)
- Montana (3)
- Nebraska (3)
- New Mexico (1)
- Oregon (2)
- Pennsylvania (3)
- South Dakota (1)
- Tennessee (4)
- Utah (6)
- Washington (4)
- Wyoming (1)

According to Fins in *Death Row U.S.A.*, 12 states had between 1 and 10 inmates on death row as of January 1, 2009—Colorado (3), Connecticut (10), Kansas (10), Maryland (5), Montana (2), Nebraska (10), New Hampshire (10), New Mexico (2), South Dakota (3), Utah (10), Washington (9), and Wyoming (1). With the exception of Connecticut, Maryland, and New Hampshire, all of these states are in the West. New Mexico abolished capital punishment in 2009; however, the new law was not retroactive in commuting existing death sentences. Kansas and New York have long-standing moratoriums in place, as described earlier. The DPIC reports (2009, http://www.deathpenaltyinfo.org/costs-death-penalty) that in 2009, legislation was introduced to repeal the death penalty in Colorado, Connecticut, Kansas, Maryland, Montana, Nebraska, and New Hampshire. In

TABLE 8.3

Number of persons executed, by jurisdiction, 1977–2008

Jurisdiction	Since 1977
U.S. total	**1,136**
Texas	423
Virginia	102
Oklahoma	88
Florida	66
Missouri	66
Georgia	43
North Carolina	43
South Carolina	40
Alabama	38
Ohio	28
Louisiana	27
Arkansas	27
Arizona	23
Indiana	19
Delaware	14
California	13
Illinois	12
Nevada	12
Mississippi	10
Utah	6
Maryland	5
Tennessee	4
Washington	4
Pennsylvania	3
Kentucky	3
Federal system	3
Montana	3
Nebraska	3
Oregon	2
Colorado	1
Connecticut	1
New Mexico	1
Wyoming	1
Idaho	1
South Dakota	1

SOURCE: Adapted from Tracy L. Snell, "Table 9. Number of Persons Executed, by Jurisdiction, 1930–2007," in *Capital Punishment, 2007—Statistical Tables*, U.S. Department of Justice, Office of Justice Programs, Bureau of Justice Statistics, December 23, 2008, http://www.ojp.usdoj.gov/bjs/pub/html/cp/2007/cp07st.pdf (accessed August 24, 2009)

Colorado, the House of Representatives approved a measure to end the death penalty and reappropriate its funding to solving cold-case homicides, but the bill failed to pass the state senate in May 2009. As of September 2009, no laws had been passed that abolished the death penalty in these states.

REFORMS TO DEATH PENALTY LAWS
Maryland

In July 2001 a de facto moratorium occurred in Maryland pending the resolution by the state's high court of an appeal by inmate Steven Oken (1962–2004) challenging the constitutionality of Maryland's capital punishment laws. Oken was sentenced to death in 1991 for the 1987 murder of Dawn Marie Garvin. He had also received life sentences for killing his sister-in-law and a motel desk clerk in Maine.

In May 2002 Governor Parris N. Glendening (1942–) imposed a moratorium to allow for the completion of a study on capital punishment in Maryland. Robert L. Ehrlich Jr. (1957–), the newly elected governor, lifted the ban on executions in January 2003.

Maryland again imposed a moratorium in February 2003 after the state's highest court stayed the execution of Oken, who was scheduled to die the following month. The Maryland Court of Appeals granted the temporary reprieve to hear Oken's case at a future date. On May 1, 2003, during his fourth review by the state's appellate court, Oken argued that the state's death penalty is unconstitutional in light of the Supreme Court ruling in *Apprendi v. New Jersey* (530 U.S. 466, 2000), which held that jurors must use the higher standard of "beyond a reasonable doubt" rather than "by a preponderance of evidence" in considering evidence during the sentencing phase of a trial.

In *Oken v. State* (No. 117, November 17, 2003), the Maryland Court of Appeals upheld Oken's death sentence. The court did not address Oken's *Apprendi* argument and ruled only on his claim that *Ring v. Arizona* (536 U.S. 584, 2002) implicated the state's death penalty law. The court rejected this claim. In 2003 Ehrlich signed Oken's death warrant, and Maryland's moratorium ended on June 17, 2004, with the execution of Oken by lethal injection.

In December 2006 another moratorium began after the Maryland Court of Appeals ordered a legislative review of the manual detailing lethal injection procedures for executions. In March 2008 the Urban Institute published *The Cost of the Death Penalty in Maryland* (John Roman et al., http://www.urban.org/UploadedPDF/411625_md_death_penalty.pdf). The report notes that an average case in Maryland in which a death sentence was not sought cost more than $1.1 million. An average case in which a death sentence was sought, but not imposed, cost $1.8 million. An average case in which a death sentence was sought and imposed cost just over $3 million. The breakdown for the latter was about $1.7 million for adjudication costs and about $1.3 million for incarceration costs. As noted earlier in this chapter, in March 2009 Maryland legislators voted to limit capital cases to only those in which DNA evidence, videotaped confessions, or videotape linking the defendant to the murder are available.

Nebraska

In May 1999 the Nebraska legislature became the first in the country to pass a bill proposing a two-year moratorium on executions. The bill also called for a study, during the moratorium, to determine the fairness of the administration of the death penalty. Governor Mike O. Johanns (1950–) vetoed the bill. The governor also vetoed the proposed study, but the legislature overrode his veto.

Prior to 2007, electrocution was the only method used to administer the death penalty in Nebraska. However, this method was ruled unconstitutional by the state's Supreme

Court in 2008. In 2009 Nebraska lawmakers authorized lethal injection as the state's only method of execution. As of September 2009 Nebraska was still developing lethal injection protocols to be in compliance with the U.S. Supreme Court's findings in *Baze v. Rees*.

Ohio Developing New Injection Protocols

After Ohio executioners tried and failed in 18 attempts over two hours to find a suitable vein in which to deliver lethal drugs to convicted murderer Romell Broom (1956–), his execution on September 15, 2009, was halted by order of Governor Ted Strickland (1941–). In response to the unprecedented event, Strickland imposed a temporary moratorium on further executions in Ohio, giving prison officials five months to develop alternative injection protocols that comply with state and federal law. A stay of execution was granted in Broom's case by the U.S. District Court for the Southern District of Ohio, which planned a hearing on the case in late November 2009. Similarly, the U.S. Court of Appeals for the Sixth Circuit issued a stay of execution for another Ohio inmate, Lawrence Reynolds (1966–), who was scheduled to be executed in early October 2009. Strickland also ordered a delay of Reynolds's case, postponing the execution to March 2010, and issued reprieves for other inmates facing imminent execution. Although stopping short of an outright moratorium on executions in the state, Strickland charged the Ohio Department of Rehabilitation and Correction with implementing appropriate procedures and training to ensure that such an occurrence as happened in the Broom case would not happen again.

North Carolina Creates Innocence
Inquiry Commission

In 2006 the North Carolina governor Mike F. Easley (1950–) signed a new law that created the North Carolina Innocence Inquiry Commission (NCIIC). The eight-member committee will review innocence claims and new evidence not previously presented at trial. After a majority recommendation by the committee, a disputed case will be reviewed by a panel of three North Carolina Superior Court judges. A unanimous decision by the panel can overturn a conviction. The NCIIC is the first commission of its type in the United States. In "North Carolina Becomes First State with an Innocence Commission" (TalkLeft.com, August 3, 2003), Jeralyn Merritt reports that after signing the bill the governor remarked, "As a state that exacts the ultimate punishment, we should continue to ensure that we have the ultimate fairness in the review of our cases."

As of May 2009 (http://www.innocencecommission-nc.gov/statistics.htm) the NCIIC reported that it had considered more than 500 cases of proclaimed innocence. The vast majority, 441, of the cases were rejected, with roughly another 70 cases in various stages of review, inquiry, or investigation.

Texas

In *Recommendations to Governor Rick Perry* (January 2006, http://www.governor.state.tx.us/divisions/general_counsel/files/CJAC-0106.doc), the Governor's Criminal Justice Advisory Council (CJAC) in Texas makes a number of recommendations to change the state's justice system to reduce the number of wrongful convictions. These include changes to allow greater postconviction DNA testing and grants for innocence projects at the state's law schools. In addition, the CJAC recommends greater funding for a public defenders office and increased compensation for prisoners who have been wrongfully convicted.

In June 2009 the Texas legislature passed legislation funding an office to manage postconviction appeals in death penalty cases. The Office of Capital Writs was established with funding of $1 million and a nine-member staff to oversee state habeas corpus proceedings for death row inmates. It was expected that the office would handle about 12 cases per year. At the same time, the legislature passed a companion act that outlined improved compensation for defendants wrongfully incarcerated. Commenting in *Time* magazine (September 19, 2009, http://www.time.com/time/nation/article/0,8599,1924278,00.html) on the perceived role of the Office of Capital Writs, Andrea March of the Texas Fair Defense Project said, "Since 2004, 2005, there has been documented some horrible lawyering.... But the hope [in Texas] is that we will stop seeing stories where the defendant never had a fair shot."

Virginia

An attempt in Virginia to expand the list of offenses that warrant the death penalty was vetoed by Governor Timothy Kaine (1958–) on March 27, 2009. The bill would have made killing a fire marshal or auxiliary police officer in the line of duty punishable by death and would have extended the death penalty to accomplices in a homicide case. It was the third time Kaine had vetoed legislation that sought to expand capital punishment in Virginia.

THE AMERICAN BAR ASSOCIATION ADVOCATES A NATIONWIDE MORATORIUM

The American Bar Association (ABA) is a voluntary professional association for people in the legal profession. In 2001 the ABA began the Death Penalty Moratorium Implementation Project (DPMIP), an effort to secure a nationwide moratorium on the death penalty.

In 2004 the DPMIP began assessing state death penalty systems to determine their level of agreement with "minimum standards of fairness and due process." The project relies on the ABA publication *Death without Justice: A Guide for Examining the Administration of the Death Penalty in the United States* (June 2001, http://www.abanet.org/irr/finaljune28.pdf) to provide protocols (codes for correct conduct) against which it assesses each state's capital punishment laws and processes. As of September 2009, eight state assessments had been published:

- *Evaluating Fairness and Accuracy in State Death Penalty Systems: The Georgia Death Penalty Assessment Report* (January 2006, http://www.abanet.org/moratorium/assessmentproject/georgia/report.pdf)

- *Evaluating Fairness and Accuracy in State Death Penalty Systems: The Alabama Death Penalty Assessment Report* (June 2006, http://www.abanet.org/moratorium/assessmentproject/alabama/report.pdf)

- *Evaluating Fairness and Accuracy in State Death Penalty Systems: The Arizona Death Penalty Assessment Report* (July 2006, http://www.abanet.org/moratorium/assessmentprojcct/arizona/Report.pdf)

- *Evaluating Fairness and Accuracy in State Death Penalty Systems: The Florida Death Penalty Assessment Report* (September 2006, http://www.abanet.org/moratorium/assessmentproject/florida/report.pdf)

- *Evaluating Fairness and Accuracy in State Death Penalty Systems: The Tennessee Death Penalty Assessment Report* (March 2007, http://www.abanet.org/moratorium/assessmentproject/tennessee/finalreport.pdf)

- *Evaluating Fairness and Accuracy in State Death Penalty Systems: The Indiana Death Penalty Assessment Report* (February 2007, http://www.abanet.org/moratorium/assessmentproject/indiana/report.pdf)

- *Evaluating Fairness and Accuracy in State Death Penalty Systems: The Ohio Death Penalty Assessment Report* (September 2007, http://www.abanet.org/moratorium/assessmcntproject/ohio/finalreport.pdf)

- *Evaluating Fairness and Accuracy in State Death Penalty Systems: The Pennsylvania Death Penalty Assessment Report* (October 2007, http://www.abanet.org/moratorium/assessmentproject/pennsylvania/finalreport.pdf)

Alabama

The DPMIP report for Alabama calls for reform of seven major problems it cites in the state's capital punishment system:

- Inadequate indigent defense services at trial and on direct appeal

- Lack of defense counsel for state postconviction proceedings

- Lack of a statute protecting people with mental retardation from execution

- Lack of a postconviction DNA testing statute

- Inadequate proportionality review by the Alabama Court of Criminal Appeals

- Lack of effective limitations on the interpretation of the "heinous, atrocious, or cruel" aggravating circumstance that could allow the circumstance to be used improperly as a "catchall provision"

- Capital juror confusion as evidenced by interviews with capital jurors indicating confusion about mitigating and aggravating factors and other legal issues arising during trial

Arizona

The DPMIP report for Arizona recommends reforms for four major problems identified in the state's capital punishment system:

- Decentralized defense services that lack adequate oversight and standards

- Insufficiently compensated appointed counsel

- Lack of a mechanism to ensure proportionality review to protect against arbitrariness in capital sentencing

- Lack of effective limitations on the "especially cruel, heinous, or depraved" aggravating circumstance to prevent ambiguity in its interpretation by capital juries

Florida

The DPMIP report for Florida identifies 11 major problems requiring reform in the state's capital punishment system:

- Florida leads the nation in death-row exonerations

- Inadequate compensation for conflict trial counsel in death penalty cases

- Lack of qualified and properly monitored capital collateral registry counsel ("private lawyers who are appointed from the statewide registry to represent death-sentenced inmates during post-conviction proceedings")

- Inadequate compensation for capital collateral registry attorneys

- Significant capital juror confusion as evidenced by interviews with capital jurors

- Lack of unanimity in jury's sentencing decision in capital cases

- The practice of judicial override of jury recommendations of life imprisonment

- Lack of transparency in the clemency process

- Racial disparities in Florida's capital sentencing that make African-American defendants more likely to receive the death penalty if the victim is white, than if the victim is African-American

- Geographic disparities in Florida's capital punishment system

- Death sentences imposed on people with severe mental disability

Georgia

The DPMIP report for Georgia highlights seven major problems within the state's capital sentencing process:

- Inadequate defense counsel at trial

- Lack of defense counsel for state habeas corpus proceedings

- Inadequate proportionality review by the Georgia Supreme Court

- Inadequate jury instructions on mitigating factors as evidenced by interviews with capital jurors

- Racial disparities in capital sentencing in which both the race of the defendant and the race of the victim predict who is sentenced to death

- Inappropriate burden of proof for mentally retarded defendants

- Death penalty for felony murder (a killing in the commission of a felony irrespective of malice, meaning that a conviction of felony murder does not require a finding of an intent to kill or of a reckless indifference to life)

Indiana

The DPMIP report for Indiana recommends reform of six problem areas identified in the state's capital punishment system:

- Inadequate qualification standards for defense counsel

- Lack of an independent appointing authority

- Lack of meaningful proportionality review of death sentences

- Significant capital juror confusion over roles and responsibilities when deciding whether to impose a death sentence

- Racial disparities that mean those convicted of killing white victims are sentenced more severely than those convicted of killing nonwhite victims.

- Death sentences imposed on people with severe mental disability

Ohio

The DPMIP report for Ohio notes 10 major problems in the state's capital punishment system:

- Inadequate procedures to protect the innocent, specifically failure to require preservation of biological evidence for as long as the defendant remains incarcerated, failure to require that crime laboratories and law enforcement agencies be certified by nationally recognized certification organizations, failure to require the audio or videotaping of all interrogations in potential capital cases, and failure to implement lineup procedures that protect against incorrect eyewitness identifications

- Inadequate access to experts and investigators

- Inadequate qualification standards for defense counsel

- Insufficient compensation for defense counsel representing indigent capital defendants and death row inmates

- Inadequate appellate review of claims of error

- Lack of meaningful proportionality review of death sentences

- Virtually nonexistent discovery provisions in state postconviction

- Racial disparities in capital sentencing wherein perpetrators are more likely to end up on death row if the homicide victim is white rather than African-American

- Geographic disparities in capital sentencing within the state

- Death sentences imposed and carried out on people with severe mental disability

Pennsylvania

The DPMIP report for Pennsylvania identifies eight major problems requiring reform in the state's capital punishment system:

- Inadequate procedures to protect the innocent, specifically failure to require preservation of biological evidence for as long as the defendant remains incarcerated, failure to require the audio or videotaping of all interrogations in potential capital cases, and failure to implement lineup procedures that protect against incorrect eyewitness identifications

- Inadequate safeguards against poor legal representation, specifically failure to guarantee the appointment of two attorneys at all stages of a capital case, inadequate compensation afforded capital attorneys, and lack of a statewide independent appointing authority responsible for training, selecting, and monitoring capital defense attorneys to ensure that competent representation is provided to each capital defendant

- No state funding of capital indigent defense services

- Inadequate access to experts and investigators

- Lack of data on death-eligible case means that Pennsylvania cannot ensure that its system ensures proportionality in charging or sentencing, or determine the extent of racial or geographic bias in its capital system

- Significant limitations on postconviction relief

- Significant capital juror confusion wherein capital jurors fail to understand their roles and responsibilities when deciding whether to impose a death sentence

- Racial and geographical disparities in the state's capital sentencing

Tennessee

The DPMIP report for Tennessee notes 10 major problem areas in the state's capital punishment system:

- Inadequate procedures to address innocence claims and ensure they receive adequate judicial review

- Excessive caseloads for defense counsel in public defender offices representing capital defendants

- Inadequate access to experts and investigators by capital defendants

- Inadequate qualification and performance standards for defense counsel

- Lack of meaningful proportionality review by the Tennessee Supreme Court and the Tennessee Court of Criminal Appeals

- Lack of transparency in the clemency process

- Significant capital juror confusion as evidenced by capital juror interviews

- Racial disparities in the state's capital sentencing that favor the "majority" race or ethnicity

- Geographical disparities in the state's capital punishment system

- Death sentences imposed on people with severe mental disability

CHAPTER 9

PUBLIC ATTITUDES TOWARD CAPITAL PUNISHMENT

Like all statistics, those contained in public opinion polls should be viewed cautiously. The way a question is phrased can influence the respondents' answers. Many other factors may also influence a response in ways that are often difficult to determine. Respondents might never have thought of the issue until asked, or they might be giving the pollster the answer they think the pollster wants to hear. Organizations that survey opinions do not claim absolute accuracy. Their findings are approximate snapshots of the attitudes of the nation at a given time.

THE MORALITY OF CAPITAL PUNISHMENT

Lydia Saad of the Gallup Organization, in "Americans Evenly Divided on Morality of Homosexuality" (June 18, 2008, http://www.gallup.com/poll/108115/Americans-Evenly-Divided-Morality-Homosexuality.aspx), reports on a May 2008 values and beliefs poll regarding Americans' views about various moral issues. Respondents were asked about 16 particular issues deemed important to society. As shown in Table 9.1 nearly two-thirds (62%) of those asked rated the death penalty as morally acceptable. It was the third most morally acceptable issue to Americans, after divorce (70% expressed moral acceptance) and gambling (63% moral acceptance). Capital punishment was considered more morally acceptable than many other controversial issues, including sex between an unmarried man and woman, having a baby outside of marriage, doctor-assisted suicide, and abortion.

SUPPORT FOR THE DEATH PENALTY
Gallup Poll

According to Gallup poll results from December 1936, about three out of five (59%) respondents favored the death penalty at that time. (See Figure 9.1.) This was the first time the Gallup Organization polled Americans regarding their attitudes toward the death penalty for murder. For the next three decades support for capital punishment fluctuated,

dropping to its lowest point in 1966 (42%). This was a period of civil rights and anti–Vietnam War marches and the peace movement. It was also the only time in the period of record that those who opposed capital punishment (47%) outnumbered those who favored it. Starting in early 1972 support for capital punishment steadily increased, peaking at 80% in 1994. (See Figure 9.1.) Between 1999 and 2008 support hovered at 60% to 70%. In October 2008 Gallup found that 64% of Americans favored the death penalty for people convicted of murder.

The results for 2008 are broken down by political party affiliation in Figure 9.2. Overall, 78% of Republicans supported the death penalty, whereas 18% opposed it. There was less support from respondents identifying themselves as independents. Two-thirds (66%) of them supported the death penalty, compared with 28% who were against. However, capital punishment received the least support from Democrats questioned by Gallup. As shown in Figure 9.2, only a slim majority (52%) of Democrats expressed support for the death penalty; 44% were opposed to it.

In previous Gallup surveys, pollsters have asked respondents to choose between the death penalty and life imprisonment with "absolutely" no possibility of parole as the "better penalty" for murder. As shown in Table 9.2 this question was last asked in 2006. At that time the breakdown was nearly equal, with 47% choosing the death penalty and 48% choosing the life imprisonment option. Another 5% had no opinion on the matter. Over the years the breakdown between the two choices has varied somewhat. Preference for the death penalty was highest in 1997, when 61% of respondents chose it over the life imprisonment option. Preference for life imprisonment with absolutely no chance of parole was highest in the 2006 poll.

In *Racial Disagreement over Death Penalty Has Varied Historically* (July 30, 2007, http://www.gallup.com/poll/28243/Racial-Disagreement-Over-Death-Penalty-Has-Varied-Historically.aspx), Saad discusses the results of

TABLE 9.1

Public opinion on the moral acceptability of various issues, May 2008

NEXT, I'M GOING TO READ YOU A LIST OF ISSUES. REGARDLESS OF WHETHER OR NOT YOU THINK IT SHOULD BE LEGAL, FOR EACH ONE, PLEASE TELL ME WHETHER YOU PERSONALLY BELIEVE THAT IN GENERAL IT IS MORALLY ACCEPTABLE OR MORALLY WRONG.

	Morally acceptable	Morally wrong
	%	%
Divorce	70	22
Gambling	63	32
The death penalty	62	30
Medical research using stem cells obtained from human embryos	62	30
Sex between an unmarried man and woman	61	36
Medical testing on animals	56	38
Having a baby outside of marriage	55	41
Buying and wearing clothing made of animal fur	54	39
Doctor assisted suicide	51	44
Homosexual relations	48	48
Abortion	40	48
Cloning animals	33	61
Suicide	15	78
Cloning humans	11	85
Polygamy, when one husband has more than one wife at the same time	8	90
Married men and women having an affair	7	91

SOURCE: Lydia Saad, "Next I'm Going to Read You a List of Issues. Regardless of Whether or Not You Think It Should Be Legal, for Each One, Please Tell Me Whether You Personally Believe That in General It Is Morally Acceptable or Morally Wrong," in *Americans Evenly Divided on Morality of Homosexuality*, The Gallup Organization, June 18, 2008, http://www.gallup.com/poll/108115/Americans-Evenly-Divided-Morality-Homosexuality.aspx (accessed August 24, 2009). Copyright © 2008 by the Gallup Organization. Reproduced by permission of The Gallup Organization.

a June 2007 poll that included a question about capital punishment. The results indicated that support for the death penalty for convicted murderers was voiced by 70% of whites, but only 40% of African-Americans. In fact, a majority (56%) of African-Americans were opposed to capital punishment. Saad notes that the difference of opinion between African-Americans and whites on this issue is evident in Gallup polls dating back to 1972. Historically, African-American respondents have expressed less support for the death penalty than have white respondents.

Opinion Research/CNN Poll

In an Opinion Research Corporation/CNN poll conducted in May 2009 (June 7, 2009, http://www.angus-reid.com/polls/view/americans_pick_death_penalty_for_murder_cases), respondents were asked to choose between two penalties for murder—the death penalty or life imprisonment with "absolutely" no possibility of parole. The results indicated that a slim majority (53%) preferred the death penalty, compared with 46% that chose the life imprisonment option. Another 2% were not sure of their preference. Pollsters also asked people if they considered the death penalty a "cruel and unusual punishment." Nearly three-quarters (73%)

answered "no," and 26% answered "yes." The remaining 1% were not sure of an answer.

The Harris Poll

The results from a February 2008 survey conducted by The Harris Poll are discussed in "Over Three in Five Americans Believe in Death Penalty" (March 18, 2008, http://www.harrisinteractive.com/harris_poll/index.asp?PID=882). Pollsters found that 63% of those asked supported the death penalty, whereas 30% were opposed to it. A slim majority (52%) of respondents believed that the death penalty has little deterrent effect. A lower percentage, 42%, thought that capital punishment deters people from committing murder. The article notes that belief in the deterrent capability of capital punishment has declined significantly since the 1970s. When the same question was asked in 1976 a majority (59%) thought that the death penalty was a deterrent, while 34% doubted it deterred others from murdering.

Another question in the 2008 poll involved the number of convicted criminals that are executed. The Harris Poll found that 36% of respondents believed there should be an increase in the number of convicted criminals that are executed. Just over one-fourth (26%) said the number should decrease. Another 31% felt there should be no change in the number executed. This breakdown of opinions is far different from that recorded by pollsters in 1997 when the same question was asked. In 1997 a majority (53%) of those asked said that executions should increase. Only 14% believed that the number of executions should decrease.

Pew Research Center Poll

According to the report *Trends in Political Values and Core Attitudes: 1987–2007* (March 22, 2007, http://people-press.org/reports/pdf/312.pdf), a poll performed between December 2006 and January 2007 for the Pew Research Center by Princeton Survey Research Associates revealed that 64% of Americans supported capital punishment for those convicted of murder. Comparison to results from previous years shows that support had gradually declined since 1996, when it was at 78%.

The Pew Research Center notes that levels of support for the death penalty differed by gender, race, and political affiliation. Sixty-eight percent of men expressed support, compared with 60% of women. White respondents favored the death penalty much more than people of other races. Sixty-nine percent of whites expressed support for capital punishment, compared with 45% of Hispanics and 44% of African-Americans. More than three-fourths (78%) of Republicans and slightly over half (56%) of Democrats supported the death penalty.

Higher Education Research Institute Poll

The Higher Education Research Institute (HERI) of California conducts annual surveys on the opinions of

FIGURE 9.1

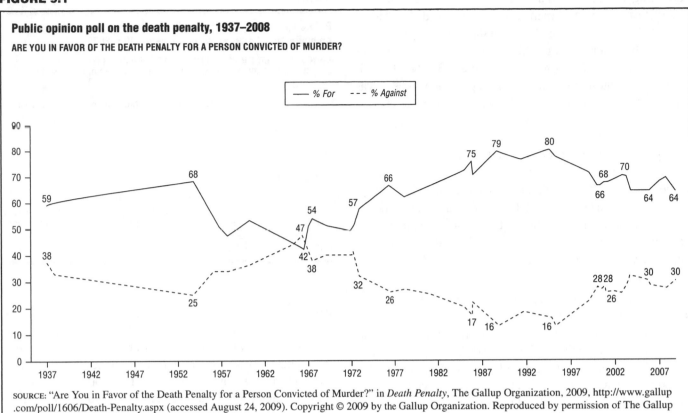

Public opinion poll on the death penalty, 1937–2008

ARE YOU IN FAVOR OF THE DEATH PENALTY FOR A PERSON CONVICTED OF MURDER?

— % For   - - - % Against

SOURCE: "Are You in Favor of the Death Penalty for a Person Convicted of Murder?" in *Death Penalty*, The Gallup Organization, 2009, http://www.gallup.com/poll/1606/Death-Penalty.aspx (accessed August 24, 2009). Copyright © 2009 by the Gallup Organization. Reproduced by permission of The Gallup Organization.

FIGURE 9.2

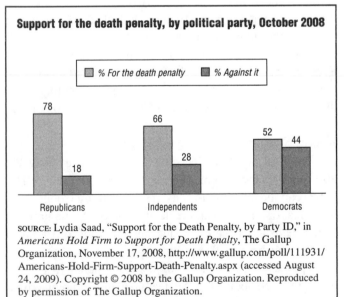

Support for the death penalty, by political party, October 2008

☐ % For the death penalty   ☐ % Against it

SOURCE: Lydia Saad, "Support for the Death Penalty, by Party ID," in *Americans Hold Firm to Support for Death Penalty*, The Gallup Organization, November 17, 2008, http://www.gallup.com/poll/111931/Americans-Hold-Firm-Support-Death-Penalty.aspx (accessed August 24, 2009). Copyright © 2008 by the Gallup Organization. Reproduced by permission of The Gallup Organization.

TABLE 9.2

Public preference for the death penalty versus life imprisonment, with absolutely no possibility of parole, selected years 1985–2006

IF YOU COULD CHOOSE BETWEEN THE FOLLOWING TWO APPROACHES, WHICH DO YOU THINK IS THE BETTER PENALTY FOR MURDER [ROTATED: THE DEATH PENALTY (OR) LIFE IMPRISONMENT, WITH ABSOLUTELY NO POSSIBILITY OF PAROLE]?

	The death penalty	Life imprisonment	No opinion
	%	%	%
2006 May 5–7*	47	48	5
2001 Feb 19–21*	54	42	4
2000 Aug 29–Sep 5*	49	47	4
2000 Feb 20–21	52	37	11
1999 Feb 8–9*	56	38	6
1997 Aug 12–13*	61	29	10
1993 Oct 13–18	59	29	12
1992 Mar 30–Apr 5	50	37	13
1991 Jun 13–16	53	35	11
1986 Jan 10–13	55	35	10
1985 Jan 11–14	56	34	10

*Asked of a half sample

SOURCE: "If You Could Choose between the Following Two Approaches, Which Do You Think Is the Better Penalty for Murder—[ROTATED: the Death Penalty (or) Life Imprisonment, with Absolutely No Possibility of Parole]?" in *Death Penalty*, The Gallup Organization, 2009, http://www.gallup.com/poll/1606/Death-Penalty.aspx (accessed August 24, 2009). Copyright © 2009 by the Gallup Organization. Reproduced by permission of The Gallup Organization.

college freshmen around the country. In *The American Freshman: Forty Year Trends* (2007, http://www.gseis.ucla.edu/heri/40yrtrends.php), HERI reports the opinions of college freshmen in surveys conducted between 1969 and 1971 and between 1978 and 2006. Among other topics in the poll, participants were asked to express their level of support for abolishing the death penalty. In 2006 more than one-third (34.5%) of college freshmen surveyed indicated they "agree strongly" or "agree somewhat" that the death penalty should be abolished. Support for abolishment was slightly stronger among women (37.6%) than among men (30.7%). Historically, the greatest discontent with capital punishment was reported between 1969 and 1971, when an average of 58% of respondents favored its abolishment. In 1978 support for abolishment was dramatically lower at 33.6%. It increased through the end of the decade and then began to decline, reaching a low of 21.2% in 1994. By 2008 support for an end to the death penalty had rebounded somewhat, with 34.9% of college freshmen (31.2% of male and 38% of female respondents) favoring abolishing the death penalty. A summary of polling data from 1969 through 2006 is available online at http://www.albany.edu/sourcebook/pdf/t2932006.pdf.

REASONS FOR SUPPORTING AND OPPOSING THE DEATH PENALTY

As of October 2009, the most recent nationwide Gallup poll (http://www.gallup.com/poll/1606/death-penalty.aspx) in which respondents were asked to give their reasons for supporting or opposing the death penalty was conducted in May 2003. At that time, 64% of respondents believed that the death penalty was the appropriate punishment for murder. These capital punishment supporters were asked why they favor the death penalty for convicted murderers. Most of the responses reflect a philosophical, moral, or religious basis of reasoning. Thirty-seven percent gave their reason as "an eye for an eye/they took a life/fits the crime." Another 13% said "they deserve it," whereas 5% cited biblical beliefs. Four percent stated that the death penalty would "serve justice," and 3% considered it a "fair punishment." Together, these morality-based responses comprise 62% of all responses.

A minority of people who supported capital punishment in 2003 did so because of practical considerations. Eleven percent said the death penalty saves taxpayers' money. Another 11% thought that putting a murderer to death would set an example so that others would not commit similar crimes; 7% responded that the death penalty prevents murderers from killing again; 2% each said that capital punishment helps the victims' families or believed that prisoners could not be rehabilitated. One percent each noted that prisoners given life sentences do not always spend life in prison or said that capital punishment relieves prison overcrowding. In total, just over a third (35%) of the reasons given for supporting the death penalty appear to be based on issues of practicality, rather than on morality.

Interestingly enough, death penalty opponents also rely heavily on moral reasoning to support their position. In 2003 just 32% of respondents in the Gallup poll expressed opposition to capital punishment. Nearly half of opponents (46%) said that it is "wrong to take a life." A quarter feared that some innocent suspects may be "wrongly convicted."

TABLE 9.3

Public opinion poll on the death penalty as a deterrent to the commitment of murder, selected year 1985–2006

DO YOU FEEL THAT THE DEATH PENALTY ACTS AS A DETERRENT TO THE COMMITMENT OF MURDER, THAT IT LOWERS THE MURDER RATE, OR NOT?

	Yes, does	No, does not	No opinion
	%	%	%
2006 May 8–11	34	64	2
2004 May 2–4	35	62	3
1991 Jun 13–16	51	41	8
1986 Jan 10–13	61	32	7
1985 Jan 11–14	62	31	7

SOURCE: "Do You Feel That the Death Penalty Acts As a Deterrent to the Commitment of Murder, That It Lowers the Murder Rate, or Not?" in *Death Penalty*, The Gallup Organization, 2009, http://www.gallup.com/poll/1606/Death-Penalty.aspx (accessed August 24, 2009). Copyright © 2009 by the Gallup Organization. Reproduced by permission of The Gallup Organization.

Another 13% cited their religious beliefs or noted that "punishment should be left to God"; 5% said that murderers "need to pay/suffer longer/think about their crime" (presumably by serving long prison sentences). By contrast, 5% said that there is a possibility of rehabilitation, and 4% opposed the death penalty because of "unfair application."

In another series of Gallup polls, respondents were asked about the deterrent value of the death penalty. As shown in Table 9.3 just over one-third (34%) of those asked in 2006 thought that capital punishment "acts as a deterrent to the commitment of murder." Nearly two-thirds (64%) believed that it was not a deterrent. Another 2% had no opinion on the matter. Belief in the deterrent value of the death penalty has declined dramatically since 1985 when Gallup first raised the issue in a poll. In 1985, 62% of respondents said that capital punishment deterred others from committing murder, 31% thought it was not a deterrent, and 7% expressed no opinion.

Recent State Polls

The Quinnipiac University Polling Institute (May 28, 2009, http://www.quinnipiac.edu/x1296.xml?ReleaseID= 1303) conducted a poll in May 2009 regarding Connecticut residents' opinions about the death penalty. At the time the state's legislators were considering legislation to abolish capital punishment. The polling results revealed that 61% of respondents favored keeping the death penalty, whereas 34% preferred abolishing the death penalty and replacing it with a sentence of lifetime imprisonment with no chance of parole. Support for keeping the death penalty was stronger among men (68% in favor) than it was among women (55% in favor). Republican support for maintaining capital punishment was 77%, compared with 50% among Democrats and 31% among independents.

The press release "New Poll by UCSC Professor Reveals Declining Support for the Death Penalty" (September 2009, http://www.ucsc.edu/news_events/press_releases/text.asp?pid=3168) from the University of California, Santa Cruz (UCSC), discusses the results of polling performed in California in February and March 2009. The poll, designed by UCSC psychology professor Craig Haney, was nearly identical to a similar survey Haney had conducted 20 years earlier in 1989. The results indicate a decline in support for the death penalty in California from 79% in 1989 to 66% in 2009. The percentage of respondents describing themselves as "strong" supporters of capital punishment also declined from 50% in 1989 to 38% in 2009. Haney believes that declining support is due to concerns among Californians about problems in the death penalty system, rather than the morality of the punishment. In the 2009 poll 44% of those asked said they were concerned that innocent people had been executed. In 1989 that percentage was only 23%.

IS THE DEATH PENALTY IMPOSED TOO OFTEN?

In October 2008 Gallup pollsters also asked people whether they believed the death penalty was imposed "too often," "about the right amount," or "not often enough." As shown in Table 9.4 only 21% of respondents thought capital punishment was imposed too often. Almost one-quarter (23%) believed the death penalty was imposed about the right amount. Nearly half (48%) said the death penalty was not imposed enough. Another 8% had no opinion on the matter. This breakdown differs little from that obtained in previous Gallup polls between 2001 and 2007.

FAIRNESS OF THE DEATH PENALTY

Figure 9.3 shows public opinion gauged by Gallup regarding the fairness of the death penalty. In 2008 a majority

TABLE 9.4

Public opinion poll on the appropriate use of the death penalty, 2001–08

IN YOUR OPINION, IS THE DEATH PENALTY IMPOSED [ROTATED: TOO OFTEN, ABOUT THE RIGHT AMOUNT, OR NOT OFTEN ENOUGH]?

	Too often	About the right amount	Not enough	No opinion
	%	%	%	%
2008 Oct 3–5	21	23	48	8
2007 Oct 4–7	21	26	49	4
2006 May 8–11	21	25	51	3
2005 May 2–5	20	24	53	3
2004 May 2–4	23	25	48	4
2003 May 5–7	23	26	48	3
2002 May 6–9	22	24	47	7
2001 May 10–14	21	34	38	7

SOURCE: "In Your Opinion, Is the Death Penalty Imposed—[ROTATED: Too Often, about the Right Amount, or Not Often Enough]?" in *Death Penalty*, The Gallup Organization, 2009, http://www.gallup.com/poll/1606/Death-Penalty.aspx (accessed August 24, 2009). Copyright © 2009 by the Gallup Organization. Reproduced by permission of The Gallup Organization.

FIGURE 9.3

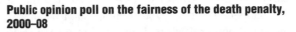

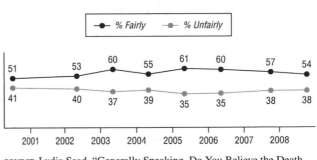

Public opinion poll on the fairness of the death penalty, 2000–08

GENERALLY SPEAKING, DO YOU BELIEVE THE DEATH PENALTY IS APPLIED FAIRLY OR UNFAIRLY IN THIS COUNTRY TODAY?

SOURCE: Lydia Saad, "Generally Speaking, Do You Believe the Death Penalty Is Applied Fairly or Unfairly in This Country Today?" in *Americans Hold Firm to Support for Death Penalty*, The Gallup Organization, November 17, 2008, http://www.gallup.com/poll/111931/Americans-Hold-Firm-Support-Death-Penalty.aspx (accessed August 24, 2009). Copyright © 2008 by the Gallup Organization. Reproduced by permission of The Gallup Organization.

(54%) of those asked said the death penalty is applied fairly in the United States. More than a third (38%) said it is not applied fairly. These percentages are very similar to those found by Gallup in polls dating back to 2001.

THE DEATH PENALTY AND INNOCENCE

In "Over Three in Five Americans Believe in Death Penalty" Harris Interactive notes that its February 2008 poll revealed that nearly all Americans (95%) believe that innocent people are "sometimes" convicted of murder. These respondents indicated that, on average, for every 100 people convicted of murder, approximately 12% are innocent. Women guessed that this occurred more often (estimated 14%) than men did (10%). African-Americans estimated that 25% of people convicted of murder were innocent, which was a higher estimate than those offered by Hispanics (12%) or by white respondents (9%). Democrats and those with a high school diploma or less were more likely to believe that a higher proportion of innocent people (15% and 14%, respectively) were convicted of murder, as opposed to Republicans and those with postgraduate degrees (6% and 8%, respectively).

Though 95% of respondents indicated they believe that at least some of those charged with murder are innocent, the 12% error rate in executions did not seem to qualify as "substantial." When asked if they would still support the death penalty if a "substantial" number of innocent people were convicted of murder, only 35% said they would still support the death penalty. Over half (58%) would oppose it under these conditions.

In 2003, 2005, and 2006 Gallup pollsters found that a majority of people believed that an innocent person had been executed within the previous five years. (See Table 9.5.) In 2006 nearly two-thirds (63%) of those asked said that this had likely happened, while 27% thought such a thing had not happened. Another 10% had no opinion on the matter. The percentage of respondents expressing belief that an innocent person has been executed decreased over time from a high of 73% recorded in 2003.

TABLE 9.5

Opinions regarding the innocence of the executed, 2003, 2005, and 2006

HOW OFTEN DO YOU THINK THAT A PERSON HAS BEEN EXECUTED UNDER THE DEATH PENALTY WHO WAS, IN FACT, INNOCENT OF THE CRIME HE OR SHE WAS CHARGED WITH—DO YOU THINK THIS HAS HAPPENED IN THE PAST FIVE YEARS, OR NOT?

	Yes, in past five years	No, not	No opinion
2006 May 8–11	63%	27	10
2005 May 2–5	59%	33	8
2003 May 5–7	73%	22	5

SOURCE: "How Often Do You Think That a Person Has Been Executed under the Death Penalty Who Was, in Fact, Innocent of the Crime He or She Was Charged with—Do You Think This Has Happened in the Past Five Years, or Not?" in *Death Penalty*, The Gallup Organization, 2009, http://www.gallup.com/poll/1606/Death-Penalty.aspx (accessed August 24, 2009). Copyright © 2009 by the Gallup Organization. Reproduced by permission of The Gallup Organization.

CHAPTER 10

CAPITAL PUNISHMENT AROUND
THE WORLD

UNITED NATIONS RESOLUTIONS

Capital punishment is controversial not only in the United States but also in many other countries. The ethical arguments that fuel the debate in the United States also characterize the discussions around the world. The United Nations' (UN) position on capital punishment is a compromise among those countries that want it completely abolished, those that want it limited to serious offenses, and those that want it left up to each country to decide. In 1946, just after the end of World War II (1939–1945), the UN General Assembly gathered to draft a bill of human rights for all UN member nations to follow. From the beginning, the death penalty was a topic of contention, and in 1948, when the assembly released the International Bill of Human Rights, there was no mention of the death penalty. After nine years of debate, the General Assembly included a statement on the death penalty in the International Covenant on Civil and Political Rights, which was later added to the International Bill of Human Rights. On December 16, 1966, the General Assembly adopted the covenant in Resolution 2200 (http://www.un-documents.net/iccpr.htm). Article 6 of the covenant states:

1. Every human being has the inherent right to life. This right shall be protected by law. No one shall be arbitrarily deprived of his life.

2. In countries which have not abolished the death penalty, sentence of death may be imposed only for the most serious crimes in accordance with the law in force at the time of the commission of the crime and not contrary to the provisions of the present Covenant and to the Convention on the Prevention and Punishment of the Crime of Genocide [systematic killing of a racial, political, or cultural group]. This penalty can only be carried out pursuant to a final judgment rendered by a competent court.

3. When deprivation of life constitutes the crime of genocide, it is understood that nothing in this article shall authorize any State Party to the present Covenant to derogate [turn away] in any way from any obligation assumed under the provisions of the Convention on the Prevention and Punishment of the Crime of Genocide.

4. Anyone sentenced to death shall have the right to seek pardon or commutation of the sentence [replacement of the death sentence with a lesser sentence]. Amnesty, pardon or commutation of the sentence of death may be granted in all cases.

5. Sentence of death shall not be imposed for crimes committed by persons below 18 years of age and shall not be carried out on pregnant women.

6. Nothing in this article shall be invoked to delay or to prevent the abolition of capital punishment by any State Party to the present Covenant.

The General Assembly has dealt with the death penalty in several other documents and meetings. Among them is Resolution 2393 (November 26, 1968, http://untreaty.un .org/cod/UNJuridicalYearbook/pdfs/english/ByChapter/ chpIII/1968/chpIII.pdf), which specifies the following legal safeguards that should be offered to condemned prisoners by countries with capital punishment:

1. A person condemned to death shall not be deprived of the right to appeal to a higher judicial authority or, as the case may be, to petition for pardon or reprieve;

2. A death sentence shall not be carried out until the procedures of appeal or, as the case may be, of petition for pardon or reprieve have been terminated;

3. Special attention shall be given in the case of indigent [poor] persons by the provision of adequate legal assistance at all stages of the proceedings.

Since that time the General Assembly has more explicitly appealed for an end to capital punishment throughout the world. Resolution 2857 (December 20, 1971, http://www.un .org/documents/ga/res/26/ares26.htm) observes that "in order fully to guarantee the right to life, provided for in article 3 of the Universal Declaration of Human Rights [a section of the International Bill of Human Rights], the main objective to be pursued is that of progressively restricting the number of offences for which capital punishment may be imposed, with a view to the desirability of abolishing this punishment in all countries."

The UN Economic and Social Council Resolution 1574 of May 20, 1971, made a similar declaration. In 1984 the Economic and Social Council then adopted the *Safeguards Guaranteeing Protection of the Rights of Those Facing the Death Penalty*, including those of people younger than age 18 at the time the crime was committed. Over the succeeding years, resolutions emanating from the General Assembly and Economic and Social Council have continued to call for the abolition of the death penalty.

On December 15, 1989, the General Assembly, under Resolution 44/128, adopted the Second Optional Protocol to the International Covenant on Civil and Political Rights, aimed at abolishing the death penalty. This international treaty allows countries to retain the death penalty in wartime as long as they reserve the right to do so at the time they become party to the treaty. As of September 22, 2009, 35 countries had signed the treaty (http://treaties.un.org/Pages/ViewDetails.aspx?src=TREATY&mtdsg_no=IV-12&chapter=4&lang=en), which indicated their intention to become parties to it at a later date. Signatories are not legally bound by the treaty but are obliged to avoid acts that would go against the treaty. Seventy-one countries had become parties to the protocol by ratification or accession, which means that they are legally bound by the terms of the treaty. Accession is similar to ratification, except that it occurs after the treaty has entered into force. In 1992 the United States ratified the International Covenant on Civil and Political Rights, but as of September 22, 2009, it had not signed the Second Optional Protocol to this treaty.

Push for a Moratorium

On December 18, 2000, the UN secretary general Kofi Annan (1938–; http://www.unhchr.ch/huricane/huricane.nsf/view01/0CFC538C82EBB17FC12569BA002BE9A6?opendocument) announced that he received a petition signed by more than 3 million people from 130 countries appealing for an end to executions. Subsequently, the secretary general called for a worldwide moratorium on the death penalty, noting that the taking of life as punishment for crime is "too absolute [and] too irreversible."

Since April 1997 the UN Human Rights Council (formerly the UN Commission on Human Rights) has adopted resolutions calling for a moratorium on executions and an eventual abolition of the death penalty. The United States has consistently voted against these resolutions. In a 2004 statement the U.S. delegation to the UN Commission on Human Rights (http://geneva.usmission.gov/humanrights/2004/statements/0421L-94.htm) noted "International law does not pro-

hibit the death penalty when due process safeguards are respected and when capital punishment is applied only to the most serious crimes."

During its 2002 session the Human Rights Council, in Resolution 2002/77 (http://www.unhchr.ch/Huridocda/Huridoca.nsf/0/e93443efabf7a6c4c1256bab00500ef6?Opendocument), asked countries with the death penalty "to ensure that . . . the death penalty is not imposed for non-violent acts such as financial crimes, non-violent religious practice or expression of conscience and sexual relations between consenting adults." The part of the resolution referring to sexual relations between consenting adults resulted from the potential execution of a Nigerian woman who became pregnant while divorced. She was convicted of adultery and, in March 2002, was sentenced to die by stoning. The man who fathered the child claimed innocence, brought in three men to corroborate his claim as required by law, and was released. The woman was acquitted on September 25, 2003.

The Commission on Human Rights adopted Resolution 2003/67 on April 24, 2003. For the first time, the commission asked countries that retained capital punishment not to extend the application of the death penalty to offenses to which it does not currently apply. It also admonished those countries to inform the public of any scheduled execution and to abstain from holding public executions and inhuman forms of executions, such as stoning. The UN also called on death penalty countries not to impose the death sentence on mothers with dependent children.

On December 18, 2007, the UN General Assembly adopted resolution 62/149 by a vote of 104 to 54 with 29 abstentions calling for a worldwide moratorium on the use of the death penalty (http://www.un.org/News/Press/docs/2007/ga10678.doc.htm). The United States was among the nations that voted against the resolution. On December 18, 2008, the General Assembly reaffirmed its call for the moratorium through passage of resolution 63/168 by a vote of 106 to 46 with 34 abstentions (http://www.un.org/News/Press/docs/2008/ga10801.doc.htm). The United States also voted against this resolution. Both resolutions are nonbinding (i.e., they are not issuances of international law).

RETENTIONIST COUNTRIES

Amnesty International is a private human rights organization that calls the death penalty "the ultimate denial of human rights" (http://www.amnesty.org/en/death-penalty). Amnesty International maintains information on capital punishment throughout the world. The organization refers to countries that retain and use the death penalty as retentionist countries; those that no longer use the death penalty are called abolitionist countries.

As of September 2009, 58 countries and territories retained and used the death penalty as a possible punishment

TABLE 10.1

Countries and territories that retain the death penalty for ordinary crimes

Afghanistan	Lebanon
Antigua and Barbuda	Lesotho
Bahamas	Libya
Bahrain	Malaysia
Bangladesh	Mongolia
Barbados	Nigeria
Belarus	North Korea
Belize	Oman
Botswana	Pakistan
Chad	Palestinian Authority
China	Qatar
Comoros	Saint Kitts and Nevis
Democratic Republic of Congo	Saint Lucia
Cuba	Saint Vincent and the Grenadines
Dominica	Saudi Arabia
Egypt	Sierra Leone
Equatorial Guinea	Singapore
Ethiopia	Somalia
Guatemala	Sudan
Guinea	Syria
Guyana	Taiwan
India	Thailand
Indonesia	Trinidad and Tobago
Iran	Uganda
Iraq	United Arab Emirates
Jamaica	United States of America
Japan	Viet Nam
Jordan	Yemen
Kuwait	Zimbabwe

SOURCE: "Countries and Territories that Retain the Death Penalty for Ordinary Crimes," in *Abolitionist and Retentionist Countries*, Amnesty International, 2009, http://www.amnesty.org/en/death-penalty/abolitionist-and-retentionist-countries#allcrimes (accessed August 24, 2009)

TABLE 10.2

Reported foreign nationals under sentence of death in the United States, by foreign nationality, June 19, 2009

[By foreign nationality: total nationalities: 34]

Active death sentences		Inactive death sentences	
Mexico	56	Mexico (reversed on appeal)	1
Cuba	7	Jamaica (awaiting resentencing)	1
Jamaica	3	Germany (awaiting resentencing)	1
El Salvador	8	Lebanon (reversed on appeal)	1
Colombia	4		
Cambodia	5		
Viet Nam	6		
Honduras	4		
Germany	2		
Philippines	2		
Lithuania	2		
Croatia	1		
Iran	2		
Peru	1		
Canada	1		
St. Kitts and Nevis	1		
Bahamas	2		
Spain	1		
Tonga	1		
Trinidad	1		
Costa Rica	1		
Nicaragua	1		
Laos	1		
Estonia	1		
Egypt	1		
Bangladesh	1		
Haiti	1		
Unknown nationality*	4		
Jordan	1		
Russia	1		
Guatemala	1		
France	1		
Argentina	1		
China	1		

*Inmates with INS (U.S. Immigration Services) or USCIS (U.S. Citizenship and Immigration Services) registration numbers (indicating foreign nationality), but for whom no specific nationality information is currently available.
Notes: Totals include all reported foreign nationals under sentence of death, including those awaiting new sentencing hearings and cases where the individual's immigration status is uncertain or their nationality is disputed. Confirmed cases of dual citizenship (individuals possessing both U.S. citizenship and that of another country) are not listed.

SOURCE: "Reported Foreign Nationals under Sentence of Death in the U.S. by Foreign Nationality," in *Foreign Nationals and the Death Penalty in the U.S.*, Death Penalty Information Center, June 19, 2009, http://www.deathpenaltyinfo.org/foreign-nationals-and-death-penalty-us#Reported-DROW (accessed August 24, 2009)

for ordinary crimes. (See Table 10.1.) Ordinary crimes are crimes committed during peacetime. Ordinary crimes that could lead to the death penalty include murder, rape, and, in some countries, robbery or embezzlement of large sums of money. Exceptional crimes are military crimes committed during exceptional times, mainly wartime. Examples are treason, spying, or desertion (leaving the armed services without permission).

Amnesty International notes in "Figures on the Death Penalty" (2009, http://www.amnesty.org/en/death-penalty/numbers) that only 25 of the retentionist countries were known to have carried out executions in 2008. The organization estimates that at least 2,390 people were executed in 2008. It estimates that 93% of these executions took place in only five countries—China (1,718), Iran (346), Saudi Arabia (102), the United States (37), and Pakistan (36). Amnesty International reports that 52 countries imposed a total of 8,864 death sentences in 2008.

United States

The United States remains the only major Western country that practices capital punishment. (As of September 2009, the federal government, the U.S. military, and 35 states had death penalty laws.)

FOREIGN NATIONALS. The Death Penalty Information Center reports that as of June 19, 2009, 130 foreign nationals were on death row in the United States. (See Table 10.2.) The largest number (56) were Mexican. As shown in Table 10.3 the vast majority of foreign nationals under the sentence of death were in California (55), Texas (26), and Florida (20).

Under Article 36 of the Vienna Convention on Consular Relations (VCCR) local U.S. law enforcement officials are required to notify detained foreigners "without delay" of their right to consult with the consulate of their home country. The United States ratified (formally approved and sanctioned) this international agreement and an Optional Protocol to the VCCR in 1969. The Optional Protocol provided that the International Court of Justice (ICJ; the UN's highest

TABLE 10.3

Reported foreign nationals under sentence of death in the United States, by state of confinement, June 19, 2009

[By state of confinement: totals by jurisdiction]

California (55)	Alabama (2)
Texas (26)	Virginia (1)
Florida (20)	Oregon (1)
Arizona (3)	Montana (1)
Ohio (3)	Georgia (1)
Nevada (4)	Mississippi (1)
Pennsylvania (4)	Nebraska (1)
Louisiana (3)	Federal (4)

Notes: Totals include all reported foreign nationals under sentence of death, including those awaiting new sentencing hearings and cases where the individual's immigration status is uncertain or their nationality is disputed. Confirmed cases of dual citizenship (individuals possessing both U.S. citizenship and that of another country) are not listed.

SOURCE: "Reported Foreign Nationals under Sentence of Death in the U.S. by State of Confinement," in *Foreign Nationals and the Death Penalty in the U.S.*, Death Penalty Information Center, J une 19, 2009, http://www.deathpenaltyinfo.org/foreign-nationals-and-death-penalty-us#Reported-DROW (accessed August 24, 2009)

court) would have the authority to decide when VCCR rights have been violated. Capital punishment opponents claim that the United States has a poor record of informing foreign nationals under arrest of their rights under the VCCR.

During the 1990s Paraguay and Germany brought suits against the United States before the ICJ regarding pending executions in Virginia and Arizona, respectively. In both cases the ICJ ruled that the executions should be stayed (postponed) pending further analysis. However, both condemned men—Angel Francisco Breard (1966–1998) of Paraguay and Walter LaGrand (1962–1999) of Germany—were executed for murder. The U.S. Supreme Court refused to intervene in Breard's case, noting in *Breard v. Greene* that because he had failed to exercise his Vienna Convention rights at the state level, he could not raise a claim of violation on federal habeas review.

MEXICO SUES THE UNITED STATES. In 2003 the ICJ was asked to settle another case involving the United States and consular notification. Mexico sued the United States for allegedly violating the VCCR with respect to 54 Mexican nationals on death row in U.S. prisons. The ICJ ordered that the pending executions of three of the inmates be stayed until it could make a final ruling in the case. In 2004 the ICJ found that the United States had violated sections of the Vienna Convention by not informing the 54 Mexicans on death row of their right to notify their government about their detention. The court did not annul the convictions and sentences as Mexico had requested, but it did rule that the United States must review and reconsider the Mexican nationals' convictions and sentences.

José Medellin (1975–2008) was one of the 54 Mexicans on death row. Texas jurors sentenced him to death for participating in the rape and murder of two teenage girls in

1993. The Mexican consular did not learn of or have the opportunity to help Medellin with his legal defense until 1997, after Medellin had exhausted most of his appeals. When the ICJ decision regarding Mexican nationals was handed down, Medellin appealed once again to the U.S. Court of Appeals for the Fifth Circuit, claiming that he did not receive adequate counsel and that he was not allowed to contact the Mexican consulate after his indictment. The federal appellate court ruled against Medellin. The court cited *Breard v. Greene*, which stated that the issues addressed by the Vienna Convention had to be considered in the state courts before they could be addressed in federal court. Because Medellin had already gone through his appeals on the state level, he had no recourse. Medellin appealed to the U.S. Supreme Court, and on December 10, 2004, the court agreed to hear his case and to reassess its position on the Vienna Convention and ICJ rulings.

Just before the oral arguments in the Medellin case, President George W. Bush (1946–) signed an executive order on February 28, 2005, demanding that the appropriate U.S. state courts review the sentences and convictions of the 54 Mexicans on death row without applying the procedural default rule discussed in *Breard v. Greene*. By issuing this order, the president in essence tried to force the courts to comply with the ICJ ruling regarding the Mexicans. In light of the executive order, the U.S. Supreme Court dismissed Medellin's case, and it was sent back to the state courts for review.

According to Linda Greenhouse, in "Supreme Court to Hear Appeal of Mexican Death Row Inmate" (*New York Times*, May 1, 2007), the Texas Court of Criminal Appeals subsequently accused Bush of "intrusive" meddling in the state's court system and refused to comply with the president's order. In response, the Bush administration urged the U.S. Supreme Court to overturn the Texas court's decision. In March 2008 the U.S. Supreme Court ruled in *Medellin v. Texas* that the Vienna Convention was not binding upon state courts because it had not been enacted into law by Congress. In August 2008 Medellin was executed by the state of Texas.

THE U.S. WITHDRAWS FROM THE OPTIONAL PROTOCOL TO THE VCCR. On March 9, 2005, President Bush pulled the United States out of the Optional Protocol to the VCCR, which had been in place for 30 years. Charles Lane indicates in "U.S. Quits Pact Used in Capital Cases" (*Washington Post*, March 10, 2005) that the administration no longer wanted the U.S. court system to be influenced by the ICJ with regard to executing foreign nationals.

EXTRADITION AND CAPITAL PUNISHMENT. An increasing number of countries refuse to extradite (surrender for trial) criminals to the United States who might face the death penalty. In 2005 the German government refused to extradite Mohammed Ali Hamadi (1964–) to the United States out of fear that Hamadi would face the death penalty for his role in killing a U.S. Navy diver during a 1985 airplane hijacking. Hamadi served 19 years of a life sentence in Germany for the hijacking before being paroled and deported to his native Lebanon. The Lebanese government has refused to turn him over to U.S. authorities. As of 2009, Hamadi was on the Federal Bureau of Investigation's "Most Wanted Terrorists" list, and a $5 million reward was offered for information leading to his capture.

In 2007 U.S. authorities filed an extradition request for the accused drug-cartel leader Benjamin Arellano-Félix (1952–), who has been in custody in Mexico since 2002. His brother Francisco Javier Arellano-Félix (1969–) was captured by the U.S. Coast Guard while in international waters in 2006. Both men are accused of operating a violent drug smuggling ring and committing multiple capital crimes subject to the death penalty under U.S. law. In November 2007 Francisco Javier Arellano-Félix received a life sentence without parole after a plea bargain deal was reached that eliminated the death penalty as an option in exchange for his guilty plea. It is considered unlikely that Mexico will extradite Benjamin Arellano-Félix without similar assurances that he will not face capital punishment.

China

Human rights groups claim that China executes more people each year than all the other death penalty nations combined. The Chinese government does not publish statistics on death sentences or executions. In *Report 2009* (http://www.amnesty.org/en/region/china/report-2009) Amnesty International estimates that at least 1,700 executions took place in China in 2008 and at least 7,000 death sentences were handed out. The organization notes that the numbers could be higher.

In July 2009 Tania Branigan reported in the *Guardian* (July 29, 2009, http://www.guardian.co.uk/world/2009/jul/29/china-death-penalty-executions/print) that a member of the Chinese supreme people's court had announced that restrictions will be tightened on the use of capital punishment so that fewer people will be executed. The announcement was greeted with cautious optimism by human rights activists. However, Amnesty International spokesperson Si-si Liu told Branigan that it will be difficult for outside observers to track any decrease, because the number of executions conducted each year is a "state secret." According to Branigan, more than 60 crimes are punishable by the death penalty in China, including nonviolent offenses and economic crimes.

Joseph Kahn reports in "China Quick to Execute Drug Official" (*New York Times*, July 11, 2007) that in July 2007 Zheng Xiaoyu (1944–2007), the nation's former head of food and drug safety, was executed for taking bribes to approve medicines that had not been properly tested. He was sentenced in May 2007 and lost a subsequent appeal to China's Supreme Court. Zheng's execution was believed by many observers to be a political move to bolster international confidence in the quality of Chinese food and drugs after well-publicized problems surfaced with some products, including pet foods and toothpaste sold in the United States.

Japan

In *Report 2009* (http://www.amnesty.org/en/region/japan/report-2009) Amnesty International notes that 15 executions took place in Japan in 2008, the highest annual total since 1975. Amnesty International claims that one of the men executed was mentally ill. The organization also reports that 100 prisoners remained on Japan's death row. Amnesty International complains that conditions on death row in Japan were particularly bleak: "Death row inmates continued to be confined to single cells, day and night, with limited opportunity to exercise or socialize. They were typically notified of their execution only on the morning of their execution, and their families were informed only after the execution had taken place."

In September 2009 Japan's newly elected prime minister appointed a death penalty opponent to head the nation's justice department. Abolitionists are hopeful that the appointment will bring about reforms and possibly even a moratorium to Japan's capital punishment system.

ABOLITIONISM IN PRACTICE

Table 10.4 is a list of 36 countries that Amnesty International considers abolitionist in practice. These countries have death penalty laws for such crimes as murder but have not carried out an execution for several years. Some of these nations have not executed anyone for the past 50 years or more. Others have made an international commitment not to impose the death sentence.

ABOLITIONIST COUNTRIES

Amnesty International reports that 93 countries around the world are abolitionist for all crimes. (See Table 10.5.) Since 1976, when the United States reinstated the death penalty after a nine-year moratorium, many countries have stopped imposing capital punishment. Belgium, the United Kingdom, and Greece, the last three west European democracies to have the death sentence, abolished it for all crimes in 1996, 1998, and 2004, respectively. In reality, Belgium has not executed any prisoner since 1950. The last two executions in the United Kingdom occurred in 1964. In 2002 Yugoslavia (now Serbia and Montenegro) and Cyprus abolished the death penalty for all crimes. Armenia shut down its death penalty system in 2003. The governments of Bhutan, Samoa, Senegal, and Turkey all announced that they abolished the death penalty for all crimes in 2004, and Mexico abolished the death penalty for all crimes in 2005. They were followed by the Philippines in 2006,

TABLE 10.4

Countries that are abolitionist in practice

[Countries that retain the death penalty for ordinary crimes such as murder but can be considered abolitionist in practice in that they have not executed anyone during the past 10 years and are believed to have a policy or established practice of not carrying out executions. The list also includes countries which have made an international commitment not to use the death penalty.]

Abbreviations: Date (last ex.)=date of last execution; K=date of last known execution; Ind.=no executions since independence

The Russian Federation introduced a moratorium on executions in August 1996. However, executions were carried out between 1996 and 1999 in the Chechen Republic.

Country	Date (last ex.)
Algeria	1993
Benin	1987
Brunei	1957K
Burkina Faso	1988
Cameroon	1997
Central African Republic	1981
Congo (Republic of)	1982
Eritrea	1989
Gabon	1981
Gambia	1981
Ghana	1993
Grenada	1978
Kenya	1987
Laos	1989
Liberia	2000
Madagascar	1958K
Malawi	1992
Maldives	1952K
Mali	1980
Mauritania	1987
Morocco	1993
Myanmar	1980s
Nauru	Ind.
Niger	1976K
Papua New Guinea	1950
Russian Federation	1999
South Korea	1997
Sri Lanka	1976
Suriname	1982
Swaziland	1983
Tajikistan	2004
Tanzania	1995
Togo	1978
Tonga	1982
Tunisia	1991
Zambia	1997

SOURCE: Death Penalty: Countries Abolitionist in Practice, in *Abolitionist and Retentionist Countries*, Amnesty International, 2009, http://www.amnesty.org/en/death-penalty/countries-abolitionist-in-practice (accessed August 24, 2009)

Albania and Rwanda in 2007, Argentina and Uzbekistan in 2008, and Burundi in early 2009.

Abolitionist Countries for Ordinary Crimes Only

According to the Amnesty International ten countries did not impose the death penalty for ordinary crimes committed during peacetime, although they may impose it for exceptional crimes. (See Table 10.6.) Since 2000 three countries—Chile (2001), Kyrgyzstan (2007), and Kazakhstan (2007)—have joined this group.

A list of all countries that have abolished the death penalty for ordinary crimes or for all crimes since 1976 is provided by year in Table 10.7.

TABLE 10.5

Countries that are abolitionist for all crimes

[Countries whose laws do not provide for the death penalty for any crime]

Abbreviations: Date (A)=date of abolition for all crimes; Date (AO)=date of abolition for ordinary crimes; Date (last ex.)=date of last execution; K=date of last known execution; Ind.=no executions since independence

Country	Date (A)	Date (AO)	Date (last ex.)
Albania	2007	2000	
Andorra	1990		1943
Angola	1992		
Argentina	2008	1984	
Armenia	2003		
Australia	1985	1984	1967
Austria	1968	1950	1950
Azerbaijan	1998		1993
Belgium	1996		1950
Bhutan	2004		1964K
Bosnia-Herzegovina	2001	1997	
Bulgaria	1998		1989
Burundi	2009		
Cambodia	1989		
Canada	1998	1976	1962
Cape Verde	1981		1835
Colombia	1910		1909
Cook Islands	2007		
Costa Rica	1877		
Cote D'ivoire	2000		
Croatia	1990		1987
Cyprus	2002	1983	1962
Czech Republic	1990		
Denmark	1978	1933	1950
Djibouti	1995		Ind.
Dominican Republic	1966		
Ecuador	1906		
Estonia	1998		1991
Finland	1972	1949	1944
France	1981		1977
Georgia	1997		1994K
Germany	1987		
Greece	2004	1993	1972
Guinea-Bissau	1993		1986K
Haiti	1987		1972K
Honduras	1956		1940
Hungary	1990		1988
Iceland	1928		1830
Ireland	1990		1954
Italy	1994	1947	1947
Kiribati			Ind.
Liechtenstein	1987		1785
Lithuania	1998		1995
Luxembourg	1979		1949
Macedonia	1991		
Malta	2000	1971	1943
Marshall Islands			Ind.
Mauritius	1995		1987
Mexico	2005		1961
Micronesia			Ind.
Moldova	1995		
Monaco	1962		1847
Montenegro	2002		
Mozambique	1990		1986
Namibia	1990		1988K
Nepal	1997	1990	1979
Netherlands	1982	1870	1952
New Zealand	1989	1961	1957
Nicaragua	1979		1930
Niue			
Norway	1979	1905	1948
Palau			
Panama	1922		1903K

INTERNATIONAL PUBLIC OPINION

The Associated Press and Ipsos Public Affairs conducted a survey on the death penalty in 2007 in Canada,

TABLE 10.5

Countries that are abolitionist for all crimes [CONTINUED]

[Countries whose laws do not provide for the death penalty for any crime]

Abbreviations: Date (A)=date of abolition for all crimes; Date (AO)=date of abolition for ordinary crimes; Date (last ex.)=date of last execution; K=date of last known execution; Ind.=no executions since independence

Country	Date (A)	Date (AO)	Date (last ex.)
Paraguay	1992		1928
Philippines	2006 (1987)		2000
Poland	1997		1988
Portugal	1976	1867	1849K
Romania	1989		1989
Rwanda	2007		1998
Samoa	2004		Ind.
San Marino	1865	1848	1468K
Sao Tome and Principe	1990		Ind.
Senegal	2004		1967
Serbia (Incl. Kosovo)	2002		1992
Seychelles	1993		Ind.
Slovakia	1990		
Slovenia	1989		
Solomon Islands		1966	Ind.
South Africa	1997	1995	1991
Spain	1995	1978	1975
Sweden	1972	1921	1910
Switzerland	1992	1942	1944
Timor-Leste	1999		
Turkey	2004	2002	1984
Turkmenistan	1999		
Tuvalu			Ind.
Ukraine	1999		
United Kingdom	1998	1973	1964
Uruguay	1907		
Uzbekistan	2008		2005
Vanuatu			Ind.
Holy See	1969		
Venezuela	1863		

SOURCE: "Death Penalty: Countries Abolitionist for All Crimes," in *Abolitionist and Retentionist Countries*, Amnesty International, 2009, http://www.amnesty.org/en/death-penalty/countries-abolitionist-for-all-crimes (accessed August 24, 2009)

TABLE 10.6

Countries that are abolitionist for ordinary crimes only

[Countries whose laws provide for the death penalty only for exceptional crimes such as crimes under military law or crimes committed in exceptional circumstances, such as wartime crimes.]

Abbreviations: Date (AO)=date of abolition for ordinary crimes; Date (last ex.)=date of last execution; K=date of last known execution

Country	Date (AO)	Date (last ex.)
Bolivia	1997	1974
Brazil	1979	1855
Chile	2001	1985
El Salvador	1983	1973K
Fiji	1979	1964
Israel	1954	1962
Kazakstan	2007	
Kyrgyzstan	2007	
Latvia	1999	1996
Peru	1979	1979

SOURCE: "Death Penalty: Countries Abolitionist for Ordinary Crimes Only," in *Abolitionist and Retentionist Countries*, Amnesty International, 2009, http://www.amnesty.org/en/death-penalty/countries-abolitionist-for-ordinary-crimes-only (accessed August 24, 2009)

France, Germany, Great Britain, Italy, Mexico, South Korea, Spain, and the United States (http://surveys.ap.org/data/Ipsos/international/2007-04%20AP%20Globus%20topline_042507.pdf). When asked whether they favored or opposed the death penalty for convicted murderers, 50% of British respondents, 45% of French respondents, 31% of Italian respondents, 28% of Spanish respondents, and 69% of American respondents voiced their support for capital punishment. However, only 34% in Great Britain, 21% in France, 16% in Italy, 12% in Spain, and 52% in the United States preferred the death penalty over prison when given a choice of sentences.

The results were much different in the non-European countries included in the survey. In Mexico 71% of those asked favored the death penalty for convicted murderers, and 46% preferred capital punishment over imprisonment. Nearly three-quarters (72%) of South Koreans expressed support for the death penalty for convicted murderers. When given a choice of sentences, only half as many favored capital punishment over imprisonment.

TABLE 10.7

Countries that have abolished the death penalty since 1976

Year	Description
1976	Portugal abolished the death penalty for all crimes.
1978	Denmark abolished the death penalty for all crimes.
1979	Luxembourg, Nicaragua and Norway abolished the death penalty for all crimes. Brazil, Fiji and Peru abolished the death penalty for ordinary crimes.
1981	France and Cape Verde abolished the death penalty for all crimes.
1982	The Netherlands abolished the death penalty for all crimes.
1983	Cyprus and El Salvador abolished the death penalty for ordinary crimes.
1984	Argentina abolished the death penalty for ordinary crimes.
1985	Australia abolished the death penalty for all crimes.
1987	Haiti, Liechtenstein and the German Democratic Republic[a] abolished the death penalty for all crimes.
1989	Cambodia, New Zealand, Romania and Slovenia[b] abolished the death penalty for all crimes.
1990	Andorra, Croatia[b], the Czech and Slovak Federal Republic[c], Hungary, Ireland, Mozambique, Namibia and Sao Tomé and Príncipe abolished the death penalty for all crimes.
1992	Angola, Paraguay and Switzerland abolished the death penalty for all crimes.
1993	Guninea-Bissau, Hong Kong[d] and Seychelles abolished the death penalty for all crimes.
1994	Italy abolished the death penalty for all crimes.
1995	Djibouti, Mauritius, Moldova and Spain abolished the death penalty for all crimes.
1996	Belgium abolished the death penalty for all crimes.
1997	Georgia, Nepal, Poland and South Africa abolished the death penalty for all crimes. Bolivia abolished the death penalty for ordinary crimes.
1998	Azerbaijan, Bulgaria, Canada, Estonia, Lithuania and the United Kingdom abolished the death penalty for all crimes.
1999	East Timor, Turkmenistan and Ukraine abolished the death penalty for all crimes. Latvia[e] abolished the death penalty for ordinary crimes.
2000	Cote D'Ivoire and Malta abolished the death penalty for all crimes. Albania[f] abolished the death penalty for ordinary crimes.
2001	Bosnia-Herzegovina[g] abolished the death penalty for all crimes. Chile abolished the death penalty for ordinary crimes.
2002	Cyprus and Yugoslavia (now two states Serbia and Montenegro[i]) abolished the death penalty for all crimes.
2003	Armenia abolished the death penalty for all crimes.
2004	Bhutan, Greece, Samoa, Senegal and Turkey abolished the death penalty for all crimes.
2005	Liberia[h] and Mexico abolished the death penalty for all crimes.
2006	Philippines abolished the death penalty for all crimes.
2007	Albania[f], Cook Islands and Rwanda abolished the death penalty for all crimes. Kyrgyzstan and Kazakhstan abolished the death penalty for ordinary crimes.
2008	Uzbekistan and Argentina abolish the death penalty for all crimes.
2009	Burundi and Togo abolished the death penalty for all crimes.

Notes:

[a]In 1990 the German Democratic Republic became unified with the Federal Republic of Germany, where the death penalty had been abolished in 1949.

[b]Slovenia and Croatia abolished the death penalty while they were still republics of the Socialist Federal Republic of Yugoslavia. The two republics became independent in 1991.

[c]In 1993 the Czech and Slovak Federal Republic divided into two states, the Czech Republic and Slovakia.

[d]In 1997 Hong Kong was returned to Chinese rule as a special administrative region of China. Since then Hong Kong has remained abolitionist.

[e]In 1999 the Latvian parliament voted to ratify Protocol No. 6 to the European Convention on Human Rights, abolishing the death penalty for peacetime offences.

[f]In 2007 Albania ratified Protocol No. 13 to the European Convention on Human Rights, abolishing the death penalty in all circumstances. In 2000 it had ratified Protocol No. 6 to the European Convention on Human Rights, abolishing the death penalty for peacetime offences.

[g]In 2001 Bosnia-Herzegovina ratified the Second Optional Protocol to the International Covenant on Civil and Political Rights, abolishing the death penalty for all crimes.

[h]In 2005 Liberia ratified the Second Optional Protocol to the International Covenant on Civil and Political Rights, abolishing the death penalty for all crimes.

[i]Montenegro had already abolished the death penalty in 2002 when it was part of a state union with Serbia. It became an independent member state of the United Nations on 28 June 2006. Its ratification of Protocol No. 13 to the European Convention on Human Rights, abolishing the death penalty in all circumstances, came into effect on 6 June 2006.

SOURCE: "Countries That Have Abolished the Death Penalty since 1976," in *Abolitionist and Retentionist Countries*, Amnesty International, 2009, http://www.amnesty.org/en/death-penalty/abolitionist-and-retentionist-countries#allcrimes (accessed August 24, 2009)

CHAPTER 11
THE DEBATE: CAPITAL PUNISHMENT SHOULD BE MAINTAINED

JOINT STATEMENT BY PERCEL ODEL ALSTON JR., RETIRED PRINCE GEORGE'S COUNTY POLICE OFFICER, REPRESENTING THE FRATERNAL ORDER OF POLICE; HONORABLE WILLIAM FRANK, MARYLAND STATE DELEGATE BALTIMORE COUNTY; RICK PROTHERO, FAMILY MEMBER OF A MURDER VICTIM; OLIVER SMITH, FAMILY MEMBER OF A MURDER VICTIM; HONORABLE JAMES N. ROBEY, MARYLAND STATE SENATE HOWARD COUNTY DISTRICT 13; HONORABLE WILLIAM SPELLBRING, RETIRED PRINCE GEORGE'S COUNTY CIRCUIT COURT JUDGE REPRESENTING THE MARYLAND JUDICIARY; SCOTT D. SHELLENBERGER, STATE'S ATTORNEY FOR BALTIMORE COUNTY; BERNADETTE DIPINO, POLICE CHIEF OCEAN CITY POLICE DEPARTMENT, REPRESENTING THE MARYLAND CHIEFS OF POLICE IN *MARYLAND COMMISSION ON CAPITAL PUNISHMENT: MINORITY REPORT,* **DECEMBER 12, 2008**

The death penalty in Maryland must be viewed in its proper historical and jurisprudential context. For hundreds of years, Maryland and every State in this Union have recognized the fundamental human right of self-defense.

The taking of a life is always to be avoided, but we in society accept it under certain circumstances where it is legally justified:

- Police are allowed to use deadly force to protect themselves or others

- Citizens are allowed to use deadly force in their homes to defend themselves or their families

The law recognizes that these split-second decisions are justified and no one contests the sound basis of those laws. When a terrible crime is committed against our community, we ask the community not to seek vigilante justice.

We ask them to allow a neutral body of 12, constrained by an elaborate system embodying due process and the law to mete out justice. We ask the community not to take justice into their own hands, but to allow a system, not motivated by revenge or passion, but guided by the dispassionate hand of the law to impose a sentence justified by the crime. We involve in the quest for justice a judge, a jury, highly qualified counsel, a specialized verdict sheet, direct appeals, collateral attacks, and due process at every single stage to provide for our community the same basic right of self-defense that is afforded each of its individual members. The death penalty is the State exercising its right to defend itself and her citizens against the worst of the worst.

We received information by way of several studies as to the deterrent affect of the death penalty. Some of the studies find the death penalty is a deterrent and others say it is not. There is no question it is a deterrence of one. [John Thanos, Steven Oken, Tyrone Gilliam, Wesley Baker and Flint Hunt], the five murderers executed since 1978 under Maryland law, will never murder again. Those who work in our correctional system can take some solace in that fact.

Indeed, the death penalty is a valid means of protecting the lives of those charged with the responsibility of guarding these criminals. The correctional officer, the nurse, and the warden can breathe just a little easier knowing this is so. There should be no murders in Maryland that go unpunished, particularly with regard to our correctional officers and police officers. What deterrent can there possibly be, what punishment can there possibly be, for a murderer serving a sentence of life or life without parole? You can only serve one life sentence....

There will not be millions to spend on victim services if the death penalty is repealed. Each State's Attorney's Office is funded by their respective county. Getting rid of the death penalty will not free up a large amount of funds for the State to direct to other services or programs. We applaud the Victim Witness Subcommittee and fully adopt their recommendations for expanding services to those who have lost a loved one. We believe this a laudable endeavor that should be supported. But extensive victim and witness services can be provided concurrently with the availability of the death penalty. It is simply a choice each jurisdiction makes based on its own budgetary considerations and on the will of the electorate.

While death penalty prosecutions do cost more, the actual costs are justified and are not substantial, and do not warrant a repeal of the death penalty....

There is no question that the delays between conviction and execution are difficult for victims' families. Ms. Bricker, whose parents, the Bronsteins, were the victims of John Booth, told us of 25 years of anguish. [*Editor's note*: Booth murdered the elderly Irvin and Rose Bronstein in 1983 and was sentenced to death in three separate trials; each sentence was later overturned.] She lost her parents to a brutal murder, has withstood three jury trials, countless appeals and delays, and yet she still seeks justice. Time cannot diminish her entitlement to justice!

Should not a victim's family have the right, after full disclosure of the facts, to say yes, I am willing to endure this process? Must the State tell victims because this lawful and constitutional punishment will only be achieved after a long and arduous process, that we are going to limit the justice that can be sought for their loved one? The answer to concerns about the length of the process is a meaningful reform of the time during which a defendant can appeal his sentence, or more rigid enforcement of the time-limiting provisions that are already in place.

The majority of the people of Maryland still believe in capital punishment. Victims should have the right to choose to endure whatever delay is reasonably necessary to achieve justice for them and for their community. A certain amount of delay is important to make sure justice has been achieved, but delay alone is no reason to abandon a just, legal sentence. This is especially so when those who cite delays in the death penalty process and subsequent added hardship for the victim's family as a reason for its repeal, are the very people who are responsible for the delay.

We recommend that every prosecutor, before making a decision concerning the death penalty, give a fair and reasoned accounting to the survivors so that they know what their future will hold and take their feelings into account when making their decision. The prolonged nature of death penalty proceedings is difficult and arduous, but is not a reason to repeal a lawful and just sentence....

When a crime is committed that would make a defendant eligible for the death penalty, there are enormous costs—the loss of victims, the loss of a feeling of personal safety, and a loss of the community's belief in its own safety. There is also a cost to the community to support the best defense possible for a defendant facing the death penalty. Even if the death penalty is rarely used over the forthcoming years, history has shown that man will again perform an act against his fellow man that demands the ultimate punishment. Any lesser penalty only diminishes the tools the State, and therefore the people, have in carrying out a just punishment.

If the death penalty is abolished, what deterrent is there to someone serving a sentence of life without parole who then kills in prison? Would the economists who testified before us then argue that this killer should not be charged or put on trial since there could be no further punishment? What would they tell the family of the correctional officer, or the nurse who was murdered by a prisoner serving a life sentence?

Unless our community says the costs of justice and safety are too high to bear, we must shoulder the burden and continue to seek justice as demanded by our community.

FROM SEPARATE STATEMENT OF COMMISSIONER WILLIAM J. BRATTON, CHIEF OF POLICE, LOS ANGELES, CALIFORNIA, IN *CALIFORNIA COMMISSION ON THE FAIR ADMINISTRATION OF JUSTICE: FINAL REPORT*, JULY 2008

I believe that the imposition of the death penalty is an appropriate remedy. I further believe that the imposition of the penalty should be imposed within a reasonable time and not unduly delayed. There must be an assurance that those convicted of murder and sentenced to death have received adequate representation, a full review of the legal issues involved and that they are in fact guilty of the crimes charged. The improvements in technology and its increased use in the determination of these cases has given me confidence that those who will be convicted and sentenced to death will be guilty of the crimes charged. I have supported the previous recommendations of the commission regarding eyewitness identification, use of jail-house informants, confessions, scientific evidence, the professional responsibility and accountability of prosecutors and defense lawyers to further ensure that this occurs.

I support the position that California has a dysfunctional system. A lapse of time of over two decades between sentence and imposition of sentence is unacceptable. To require the family of the victims to have to wait over 20 years to have the promised punishment imposed only adds to their pain and suffering and renders it an illusory punishment. The legislature and the people of California should undertake a meaningful debate to determine how to correct this problem. I realize correcting the problem will require a large expenditure of funds at a time when we are facing a budget crisis and may only result in the implementation of the penalty within 10 years rather than 20 years. However, if we are to impose the penalty, we should do it as expeditiously as possible, while ensuring that each defendant has received a fair trial and full review of all legal and factual issues.

I do not join in any proposal to limit the ultimate punishment to life without the possibility of parole or in narrowing the list of special circumstances.

FROM THE STATEMENT OF JUSTICE ANTONIN SCALIA, CONCURRING, IN *BAZE V. REES* (553 U.S. ___), U.S. SUPREME COURT, APRIL 16, 2008

According to JUSTICE STEVENS, the death penalty promotes none of the purposes of criminal punishment because it neither prevents more crimes than alternative measures nor serves a retributive purpose. Ante, at 9. He argues that "the recent rise in statutes providing for life imprisonment without the possibility of parole" means that states have a ready alternative to the death penalty. Ibid. Moreover, "[d]espite 30 years of empirical research in the area, there remains no reliable statistical evidence that capital punishment in fact deters potential offenders." Ante, at 10. Taking the points together, JUSTICE STEVENS concludes that the availability of alternatives, and what he describes as the unavailability of "reliable statistical evidence," renders capital punishment unconstitutional. In his view, the benefits of capital punishment—as compared to other forms of punishment such as life imprisonment—are outweighed by the costs.

These conclusions are not supported by the available data. JUSTICE STEVENS' analysis barely acknowledges the "significant body of recent evidence that capital punishment may well have a deterrent effect, possibly a quite powerful one." Sunstein & Vermeule, "Is Capital Punishment Morally Required? Acts, Omissions, and Life-Life Tradeoffs," 58 *Stan. L. Rev.* 703, 706 (2006); see also id., at 706, n. 9 (listing the approximately half a dozen studies supporting this conclusion). According to a "leading national study," "each execution prevents some 18 murders, on average." Id., at 706. "If the current evidence is even roughly correct . . . then a refusal to impose capital punishment will effectively condemn numerous innocent people to death." Ibid.

Of course, it may well be that the empirical studies establishing that the death penalty has a powerful deterrent effect are incorrect, and some scholars have disputed its deterrent value. See ante, at 10, n. 13. But that is not the point. It is simply not our place to choose one set of responsible empirical studies over another in interpreting the Constitution. Nor is it our place to demand that state legislatures support their criminal sanctions with foolproof empirical studies, rather than commonsense predictions about human behavior. "The value of capital punishment as a deterrent of crime is a complex factual issue the resolution of which properly rests with the legislatures, which can evaluate the results of statistical studies in terms of their own local conditions and with a flexibility of approach that is not available to the courts." *Gregg, supra,* at 186 (joint opinion of Stewart, Powell, and STEVENS, JJ.). Were JUSTICE STEVENS' current view the constitutional test, even his own preferred criminal sanction—life imprisonment without the possibility of parole—may fail constitutional scrutiny, because it is entirely unclear that enough empirical evidence supports that sanction as compared to alternatives such as life with the possibility of parole.

But even if JUSTICE STEVENS' assertion about the deterrent value of the death penalty were correct, the death penalty would yet be constitutional (as he concedes) if it served the appropriate purpose of retribution. I would think it difficult indeed to prove that a criminal sanction fails to serve a retributive purpose—a judgment that strikes me as inherently subjective and insusceptible of judicial review. JUSTICE STEVENS, however, concludes that, because the Eighth Amendment "protect[s] the inmate from enduring any punishment that is comparable to the suffering inflicted on his victim," capital punishment serves no retributive purpose at all. *Ante,* at 11. The infliction of any pain, according to JUSTICE STEVENS, violates the Eighth Amendment's prohibition against cruel and unusual punishments, but so too does the imposition of capital punishment without pain because a criminal penalty lacks a retributive purpose unless it inflicts pain commensurate with the pain that the criminal has caused. In other words, if a punishment is not retributive enough, it is not retributive at all. To state this proposition is to refute it, as JUSTICE STEVENS once understood. "[T]he decision that capital punishment may be the appropriate sanction in extreme cases is an expression of the community's belief that certain crimes are themselves so grievous an affront to humanity that the only adequate response may be the penalty of death." *Gregg,* 428 U.S., at 184 (joint opinion of Stewart, Powell, and STEVENS, JJ.).

JUSTICE STEVENS' final refuge in his cost-benefit analysis is a familiar one: There is a risk that an innocent person might be convicted and sentenced to death—though not a risk that JUSTICE STEVENS can quantify, because he lacks a single example of a person executed for a crime he did not commit in the current American system. See ante, at 15–17. His analysis of this risk is thus a series of sweeping condemnations that, if taken seriously, would prevent any punishment under any criminal justice system. According to him, "[t]he prosecutorial concern that death verdicts would rarely be returned by 12 randomly selected jurors should be viewed as objective evidence supporting the conclusion that the penalty is excessive." Ante, at 15. But prosecutors undoubtedly have a similar concern that any unanimous conviction would rarely be returned by 12 randomly selected jurors. That is why they, like defense counsel, are permitted to use the challenges for cause and peremptory challenges that JUSTICE STEVENS finds so troubling, in order to arrive at a jury that both sides believe will be more likely to do justice in a particular case.

JUSTICE STEVENS' concern that prosecutors will be inclined to challenge jurors who will not find a person guilty supports not his conclusion, but the separate (and equally erroneous) conclusion that peremptory challenges and challenges for cause are unconstitutional. According to JUSTICE STEVENS, "the risk of error in capital cases may be greater than in other cases because the facts are often so disturbing that the interest in making sure the crime does not go unpunished may overcome residual doubt concerning the identity of the offender." Ibid. That rationale, however, supports not JUSTICE STEVENS' conclusion that the death penalty is unconstitutional, but the more sweeping proposition that any conviction in a case in which facts are disturbing is suspect—including, of course, convictions resulting in life without parole in those states that do not have capital punishment. The same is true of JUSTICE STEVENS' claim that there is a risk of "discriminatory application of the death penalty." Ante, at 16. The same could be said of any criminal penalty, including life without parole; there is no proof that in this regard the death penalty is distinctive.

But of all JUSTICE STEVENS' criticisms of the death penalty, the hardest to take is his bemoaning of "the enormous costs that death penalty litigation imposes on society," including the "burden on the courts and the lack of finality for victim's families." Ante, at 12, and n. 17. Those costs, those burdens, and that lack of finality are in large measure the creation of JUSTICE STEVENS and other Justices opposed to the death penalty, who have "encumber[ed] [it] . . . with unwarranted restrictions neither contained in the text of the Constitution nor reflected in two centuries of practice under it"—the product of their policy views "not shared by the vast majority of the American people." *Kansas v. Marsh*, 548 U. S. 163, 186 (2006) (SCALIA, J., concurring).

FROM TESTIMONY OF JOHN MCADAMS, PROFESSOR OF POLITICAL SCIENCE, MARQUETTE UNIVERSITY, MILWAUKEE, WISCONSIN, BEFORE THE U.S. SENATE COMMITTEE ON THE JUDICIARY, SUBCOMMITTEE ON THE CONSTITUTION, CIVIL RIGHTS, AND PROPERTY RIGHTS, HEARING ON "AN EXAMINATION OF THE DEATH PENALTY IN THE UNITED STATES," FEBRUARY 1, 2006

One of the most compelling arguments against the death penalty, at least if one accepts the claims of the death penalty opponents at face value, is the claim that a great many innocent people have been convicted of murder and put on death row. Liberal Supreme Court Justice John Paul Stevens, just to pick one case out of hundreds, told the American Bar Association's Thurgood Marshall Award

dinner that "That evidence is profoundly significant, not only because of its relevance to the debate about the wisdom of continuing to administer capital punishment, but also because it indicates that there must be serious flaws in our administration of criminal justice."

The most widely publicized list of "innocents" is that of the Death Penalty Information Center (DPIC). As of January, 2003, it listed 122 people. That sounds like an appallingly large number, but even a casual examination of the list shows that many of the people on it got off for reasons entirely unrelated to being innocent. Back in 2001, I analyzed the list when it had 95 people on it. By the admission of the Death Penalty Information Center, 35 inmates on their list got off on procedural grounds. Another 14 got off because a higher court believed the evidence against them was insufficient. If the higher court was right, this would be an excellent reason to release them, but it's far from proof of innocence.

Interestingly, prosecutors retried 32 of the inmates designated as "innocent." Apparently prosecutors believed these 32 were guilty. But many whom prosecutors felt to be guilty were not tried again for a variety of reasons, including the fact that key evidence had been suppressed, witnesses had died, a plea bargain was thought to be a better use of scarce resources, or the person in question had been convicted and imprisoned under another charge.

More detailed assessments of the "Innocents List" have shown that it radically overstates the number of innocent people who have been on death row. For example, the state of Florida had put on death row 24 inmates claimed, as of August 5, 2002, to be innocent by the DPIC. The resulting publicity led to a thorough examination of the 24 cases by the Florida Commission on Capital Crimes, which concluded that in only 4 of the 24 cases was the factual guilt of these inmates in doubt.

Examinations of the entire list have been no more favorable. For example, a liberal federal district judge in New York ruled, in *United States v. Quinones*, that the federal death penalty is unconstitutional. In this case, the court admitted that the DPIC list "may be over-inclusive" and, following its own analysis, asserted that for 32 of the people on the list there was evidence of "factual innocence." This hardly represents a ringing endorsement of the work of the Death Penalty Information Center. In academia, being right about a third of the time will seldom result in a passing grade.

Other assessments have been equally negative. Ward A. Campbell, Supervising Deputy Attorney General of the State of California, reviewed the list in detail, and concluded that: "[I]t is arguable that at least 68 of the 102 defendants on the List should not be on the list at all—leaving only 34 released defendants with claims of actual innocence—less than ½ of 1% of the 6,930 defendants sentenced to death between 1973 and 2000."...

At this point, death penalty opponents will argue that it doesn't matter if their numbers are inflated. Even if only 20 or 30 innocent people have been put on death row, they will say, that is "too many" and calls for the abolition of the death penalty. If even one innocent person is executed, they claim, that would make the death penalty morally unacceptable.

This kind of rhetoric allows the speaker to feel very self-righteous, but it's not the sort of thinking that underlies sound policy analysis. Most policies have some negative consequences, and indeed often these involve the death of innocent people—something that can't be shown to have happened with the death penalty in the modern era. Just wars kill a certain number of innocent noncombatants. When the FDA approves a new drug, some people will quite likely be killed by arcane and infrequent reactions. Indeed, the FDA kills people with its laggard drug approval process. The magnitude of these consequences matters.

Death penalty opponents usually implicitly assume (but don't say so, since it would be patently absurd) that we have a choice between a flawed death penalty and a perfect system of punishment where other sanctions are concerned.

Death penalty opponents might be asked why it's acceptable to imprison people, when innocent people most certainly have been imprisoned. They will often respond that wrongfully imprisoned people can be released, but wrongfully executed people cannot be brought back to life. Unfortunately, wrongfully imprisoned people cannot be given back the years of their life that were taken from them, even though they may walk out of prison.

Perhaps more importantly, its cold comfort to say that wrongfully imprisoned people can be released, when there isn't much likelihood that that will happen. Wrongful imprisonment receives vastly less attention than wrongful death sentences, but Barry Scheck's book *Actual Innocence* lists ten supposedly innocent defendants, of whom only three were sent to death row.

Currently, the Innocence Project Web site lists 174 persons who have been exonerated on the basis of hard DNA evidence. But the vast majority was not sentenced to death. In fact, only 15 death row inmates have been exonerated due to DNA evidence.

There is every reason to believe that the rate of error is much lower for the death penalty than for imprisonment. There is much more extensive review by higher courts, much more intensive media scrutiny, cadres of activists trying to prove innocence, and better quality counsel at the appeals level (and increasingly at the trial level) if a case might result in execution....

Death penalty opponents tend to inhabit sectors of society where claiming "racial disparity" is an effective tactic for getting what you want. In academia, the media, the ranks of activist organizations, etc. claiming "racial disparity" is an excellent strategy for getting anybody who has qualms about what you are proposing to shut up, cave in, and get out of the way.

Unfortunately, this has created a hot-house culture where arguments thrive that carry little weight elsewhere in society, and carry little weight for good reasons.

Consider the notion that, because there is racial disparity in the administration of the death penalty, it must be abolished. Applying this principle in a consistent way would be unthinkable. Suppose we find that black robbers are treated more harshly than white robbers?

Does it follow that we want to stop punishing robbers? Or does it follow that we want to properly punish white robbers also? Nobody would argue that racial inequity in punishing robbers means we have to stop punishing robbers. Nobody would claim that, if we find that white neighborhoods have better police protection than black neighborhoods that we address the inequity by withdrawing police protection from all neighborhoods. Or that racial disparity in mortgage lending requires that mortgage lending be ended. Yet people make arguments exactly like this where capital punishment is concerned....

It cannot be stressed too strongly that we do not face the choice of a defective system on capital punishment and a pristine system of imprisonment. Rather, nothing about the criminal justice system works perfectly. Death penalty opponents give the impression that the death penalty is uniquely flawed by the simple expedient of dwelling on the defects of capital punishment (real and imagined) and largely ignoring the defects in the way lesser punishments are meted out.

The death penalty meets the expectations we can reasonably place on any public policy. But it can't meet the absurdly inflated standards imposed by those who are culturally hostile to it. But then, no other policy can either.

FROM TESTIMONY OF ANN SCOTT, TULSA, OKLAHOMA, BEFORE THE U.S. SENATE COMMITTEE ON THE JUDICIARY, SUBCOMMITTEE ON THE CONSTITUTION, CIVIL RIGHTS, AND PROPERTY RIGHTS, HEARING ON "AN EXAMINATION OF THE DEATH PENALTY IN THE UNITED STATES," FEBRUARY 1, 2006

Our daughter, Elaine Marie Scott, age 21, a fourth-year junior studying elementary education at the University of Oklahoma, was brutally beaten, tortured, sexually assaulted, and beaten to death by Alfred Brian Mitchell at the Pilot Recreation Center in Oklahoma City on January 7, 1991.

Mitchell had just been released on his 18th birthday from Lloyd Rader Juvenile Detention Center in Sand Springs, Oklahoma....

He had been locked up there for three years for raping a little 12-year-old girl that he dragged off from her bus stop early one morning. The Department of Human Services, DHS, could have kept him for another year, but chose not to because they couldn't help him. They needed his bed for someone that they thought that they could help, and so he came home.

Seventeen days after his release from Lloyd Rader, he beat, tortured, sexually assaulted, and beat our beautiful daughter to death using his fists and a golf club until it broke. He stabbed her in the neck five times with a compass that you would use to make circles with. And finally, he used a wooden coat tree that crushed her skull and sent shards of wood completely through her brain. She never had a chance....

In June 1992, the trial finally started after preliminary hearings, many delays because of a lack of funds for expert defense witnesses, and several different dates for motion hearings. Again, and all through the trial, Mitchell smiled and laughed at the news reporters. Even when he was on the witness stand, he never admitted that he and he alone had murdered Elaine. It took the jury one-and-a-half hours to find him guilty of murder, and two hours to give him the death penalty.

In 1999, there was an evidentiary hearing at the Federal court, where it was determined that the forensic chemist from the Oklahoma City Police Department had lied on the witness stand. Even though Judge Thompson from the Federal court threw out the rape charges, he upheld the death penalty because the murder itself was so heinous, atrocious, and cruel.

In July of 2000, at the Tenth Circuit Court, the judges overturned the sentence because it was felt by them that the jury might have given Mitchell a lesser punishment if the rape charge had never been presented, and so back to court we went in October of 2002 to redo the sentencing phase of the trial. After two weeks of listening to evidence, the case was given to the jury. It took them five hours, but they came back with a unanimous verdict and once again gave Mitchell the death penalty. Mitchell, true to form, stood at the elevator waiting to be taken back to prison, turned and gave our oldest son an ear-to-ear grin. He then got on the elevator and was once again taken away.

On October 11, 2005, we finally started the appeals process again with the State Court of Criminal Appeals. We have not as of this date had a decision from them, nor do we know when we will. But we will be ready to continue on and see this through to the end when it comes....

Through all of this, Mitchell has never shown any remorse for his actions. If you ask if we seek retribution, yes, we do. Alfred Brian Mitchell was found guilty by two different juries of his peers. He was given the death penalty because of his crime and because it was felt that he would commit more crimes if he were ever, under any circumstances, released. I, me, I want this bully gone. I want him to disappear off the face of this earth. I want him to rot in hell for all of eternity. He is a bad seed that never should have been born. He is an animal, and when you have animals that attack people, you take them to the pound and you have them put away. What this animal has taken from us can never be returned. It has taken a lot of the love and the laughter from our home.

I have had my husband break down and sob in my arms, and I have watched his health, both mental and physical, deteriorate over the years. I have seen Elaine's two brothers struggle with life. David, the oldest, has gone through panic attacks and at times thought that he should be dead because he has outlived his sister and that is not the way it should be. I have watched Elaine's little brother clam up. To this day, Robert still cannot talk about his most favorite person in the whole wide world. His big sister is gone, taken violently from him, and he still can't deal with it. The rest of us, my husband and I, have closed ranks with our children. Even though they have grown and David is married now, we still have become more protective and we are frightened every time that they are out of sight or we don't hear from them.

Will we ever get over the murder of our daughter? Will there ever be any closure for us? I don't think so. Even after Mitchell has been executed, we will still be left with all of our wonderful memories of Elaine and all of the horror that was done to her. But perhaps once he is gone, we will be able to spend more time on the happy memories and less on thinking how her life ended. We will be at Alfred Brian Mitchell's execution. We will not rejoice, because it won't bring Elaine back. But we don't expect that it will. However, the process will finally be over and we will no longer have to spend any time or effort on pursuing justice for our daughter. Perhaps we will finally hear the remorse that so far has not been expressed. But for certain, what it will do is to ensure that he will never be able to hurt anyone ever again, and I hope and pray that you will never have to walk in our shoes.

[*Editor's note*: Mitchell's second death sentence was overturned on appeal in May 2006; he was retried and sentenced to death for a third time in January 2008.]

CHAPTER 12

THE DEBATE: CAPITAL PUNISHMENT SHOULD BE ABOLISHED

FROM THE STATEMENT OF JUSTICE JOHN PAUL STEVENS, CONCURRING, IN *BAZE V. REES* (553 U.S. ___), U.S. SUPREME COURT, APRIL 16, 2008

In *Gregg v. Georgia*, 428 U.S. 153 (1976), we explained that unless a criminal sanction serves a legitimate penological function, it constitutes "gratuitous infliction of suffering" in violation of the Eighth Amendment. We then identified three societal purposes for death as a sanction: incapacitation, deterrence, and retribution. See id., at 183, and n. 28 (joint opinion of Stewart, Powell, and STEVENS, JJ.). In the past three decades, however, each of these rationales has been called into question.

While incapacitation may have been a legitimate rationale in 1976, the recent rise in statutes providing for life imprisonment without the possibility of parole demonstrates that incapacitation is neither a necessary nor a sufficient justification for the death penalty. Moreover, a recent poll indicates that support for the death penalty drops significantly when life without the possibility of parole is presented as an alternative option. And the available sociological evidence suggests that juries are less likely to impose the death penalty when life without parole is available as a sentence.

The legitimacy of deterrence as an acceptable justification for the death penalty is also questionable, at best. Despite 30 years of empirical research in the area, there remains no reliable statistical evidence that capital punishment in fact deters potential offenders. In the absence of such evidence, deterrence cannot serve as a sufficient penological justification for this uniquely severe and irrevocable punishment.

We are left, then, with retribution as the primary rationale for imposing the death penalty. And indeed, it is the retribution rationale that animates much of the remaining enthusiasm for the death penalty. As Lord Justice Denning argued in 1950, "'some crimes are so outrageous that society insists on adequate punishment, because the wrong-doer deserves it, irrespective of whether it is a deterrent or not.'" See Gregg, 428 U.S., at 184, n. 30. Our Eighth Amendment jurisprudence has narrowed the class of offenders eligible for the death penalty to include only those who have committed outrageous crimes defined by specific aggravating factors. It is the cruel treatment of victims that provides the most persuasive arguments for prosecutors seeking the death penalty. A natural response to such heinous crimes is a thirst for vengeance.

At the same time, however, as the thoughtful opinions by THE CHIEF JUSTICE and JUSTICE GINSBURG make pellucidly clear, our society has moved away from public and painful retribution towards ever more humane forms of punishment. State-sanctioned killing is therefore becoming more and more anachronistic. In an attempt to bring executions in line with our evolving standards of decency, we have adopted increasingly less painful methods of execution, and then declared previous methods barbaric and archaic. But by requiring that an execution be relatively painless, we necessarily protect the inmate from enduring any punishment that is comparable to the suffering inflicted on his victim. This trend, while appropriate and required by the Eighth Amendment's prohibition on cruel and unusual punishment, actually undermines the very premise on which public approval of the retribution rationale is based. See, e.g., Kaufman-Osborn, "Regulating Death: Capital Punishment and the Late Liberal State," 111 *Yale L. J.* 681, 704 (2001) (explaining that there is "a tension between our desire to realize the claims of retribution by killing those who kill, and . . . a method [of execution] that, because it seems to do no harm other than killing, cannot satisfy the intuitive sense of equivalence that informs this conception of justice"); A. Sarat, *When the State Kills: Capital Punishment and the American Condition* 60–84 (2001).

Full recognition of the diminishing force of the principal rationales for retaining the death penalty should lead this court and legislatures to reexamine the question recently posed by Professor Salinas, a former Texas prosecutor and judge: "Is It Time to Kill the Death Penalty?" See Salinas, 34 *Am. J. Crim. L.* 39 (2006). The time for a dispassionate, impartial comparison of the enormous costs that death penalty litigation imposes on society with the benefits that it produces has surely arrived....

Our decisions in 1976 upholding the constitutionality of the death penalty relied heavily on our belief that adequate procedures were in place that would avoid the danger of discriminatory application identified by Justice Douglas' opinion in *Furman*, id., at 240–257 (concurring opinion), of arbitrary application identified by Justice Stewart, id., at 306 (same), and of excessiveness identified by Justices Brennan and Marshall. In subsequent years a number of our decisions relied on the premise that "death is different" from every other form of punishment to justify rules minimizing the risk of error in capital cases. See, e.g., *Gardner v. Florida*, 430 U.S. 349, 357–358 (1977) (plurality opinion). Ironically, however, more recent cases have endorsed procedures that provide less protections to capital defendants than to ordinary offenders....

Of special concern to me are rules that deprive the defendant of a trial by jurors representing a fair cross section of the community. Litigation involving both challenges for cause and peremptory challenges has persuaded me that the process of obtaining a "death qualified jury" is really a procedure that has the purpose and effect of obtaining a jury that is biased in favor of conviction. The prosecutorial concern that death verdicts would rarely be returned by 12 randomly selected jurors should be viewed as objective evidence supporting the conclusion that the penalty is excessive....

Another serious concern is that the risk of error in capital cases may be greater than in other cases because the facts are often so disturbing that the interest in making sure the crime does not go unpunished may overcome residual doubt concerning the identity of the offender. Our former emphasis on the importance of ensuring that decisions in death cases be adequately supported by reason rather than emotion, *Gardner*, 430 U.S. 349, has been undercut by more recent decisions placing a thumb on the prosecutor's side of the scales. Thus, in *Kansas v. Marsh*, 548 U.S. 163 (2006), the court upheld a state statute that requires imposition of the death penalty when the jury finds that the aggravating and mitigating factors are in equipoise. And in *Payne v. Tennessee*, 501 U.S. 808 (1991), the court overruled earlier cases and held that "victim impact" evidence relating to the personal characteristics of the victim and the emotional impact of the crime on the victim's family is admissible despite the fact that it sheds no light on the question of guilt or innocence or on the moral culpability of the defendant, and thus serves no purpose

other than to encourage jurors to make life or death decisions on the basis of emotion rather than reason.

A third significant concern is the risk of discriminatory application of the death penalty. While that risk has been dramatically reduced, the court has allowed it to continue to play an unacceptable role in capital cases. Thus, in *McCleskey v. Kemp*, 481 U.S. 279 (1987), the court upheld a death sentence despite the "strong probability that [the defendant's] sentencing jury ... was influenced by the fact that [he was] black and his victim was white." Id., at 366 (STEVENS, J., dissenting); see also *Evans v. State*, 396 Md. 256, 323, 914 A. 2d 25, 64 (2006), cert. denied, 552 U.S. ___ (2007) (affirming a death sentence despite the existence of a study showing that "the death penalty is statistically more likely to be pursued against a black person who murders a white victim than against a defendant in any other racial combination").

Finally, given the real risk of error in this class of cases, the irrevocable nature of the consequences is of decisive importance to me. Whether or not any innocent defendants have actually been executed, abundant evidence accumulated in recent years has resulted in the exoneration of an unacceptable number of defendants found guilty of capital offenses. See Garrett, "Judging Innocence," 108 *Colum. L. Rev.* 55 (2008); Risinger, "Innocents Convicted: An Empirically Justified Factual Wrongful Conviction Rate," 97 *J. Crim. L. & C.* 761 (2007). The risk of executing innocent defendants can be entirely eliminated by treating any penalty more severe than life imprisonment without the possibility of parole as constitutionally excessive.

In sum, just as Justice White ultimately based his conclusion in *Furman* on his extensive exposure to countless cases for which death is the authorized penalty, I have relied on my own experience in reaching the conclusion that the imposition of the death penalty represents "the pointless and needless extinction of life with only marginal contributions to any discernible social or public purposes. A penalty with such negligible returns to the State [is] patently excessive and cruel and unusual punishment violative of the Eighth Amendment." *Furman*, 408 U.S., at 312 (White, J., concurring).

FROM TESTIMONY OF SENATOR EDWARD KENNEDY BEFORE THE U.S. SENATE COMMITTEE ON THE JUDICIARY, SUBCOMMITTEE ON THE CONSTITUTION, HEARING ON "THE ADEQUACY OF REPRESENTATION IN CAPITAL CASES," APRIL 8, 2008

The death penalty brings out the worst in the American criminal justice system. It has proven ineffective as a deterrent and cannot be carried out in a humane way. The validity of the verdicts on which it is based are often left in doubt, leaving real fears that innocent people have been put to death.

In many states, the responsibility of representing defendants in capital cases is often left in the hands of lawyers least prepared for the task. Death penalty cases raise the most complex issues faced by criminal defense attorneys. The procedures alone are intricate and require experience to understand. Many states lack capital defense units or public defenders dedicated to this complex litigation, and instead rely on appointed attorneys, whose compensation is at levels more consistent with minor offenses than death penalty cases.

The situation is even worse at the post-conviction level. States must provide some form of representation at trial, but no such obligation exists when a defendant complains after trial that his attorney was deficient or erred in some way. Some states provide attorneys for this important stage, but others leave it to defendants with little or no education, training, or assistance. Yet to defend their innocence and protect their lives, they have to navigate a legal system that even many lawyers are hard-pressed to understand.

The passage of the Antiterrorism and Effective Death Penalty Act [1996] exacerbated this problem by reducing funds for organizations that assist death row inmates and imposing new limitations on access to federal courts.

The death penalty is an issue that invokes strong passions. Many strongly support it, and just as many vehemently oppose it. But surely, when it is clear that defendants who face the death penalty are not receiving even the basic protection of competent counsel, we should be able to agree that this problem must be fixed. If the death penalty itself is to continue, it can only do so in a system that ensures it is not imposed unfairly or by mistake, and that has the basic protections that the rule of law demands.

If our country is to continue to be a beacon of freedom and democracy, we have to get our own house in order. If criminal defendants facing death sentences are not adequately represented in our own country, how can we criticize other nations for the same thing?

FROM TESTIMONY OF BRYAN A. STEVENSON, EQUAL JUSTICE INITIATIVE OF ALABAMA, EXECUTIVE DIRECTOR AND NYU SCHOOL OF LAW, PROFESSOR OF CLINICAL LAW BEFORE THE U.S. SENATE COMMITTEE ON THE JUDICIARY, SUBCOMMITTEE ON THE CONSTITUTION, HEARING ON "THE ADEQUACY OF REPRESENTATION IN CAPITAL CASES," APRIL 8, 2008

There remains considerable doubt about America's system of capital punishment. Although we have now executed 1,100 people in this country during the last 30 years there are fundamental problems with the fairness, reliability, and propriety of the death penalty in state and federal courts. In the last few years, we have uncovered a shocking rate of error in death penalty cases. Nearly 130 death row prisoners have been released from death row after being proved innocent or exonerated. Hundreds of other death row prisoners have had their convictions and death sentences overturned after it was established that they were illegally convicted or sentenced. Most disturbingly, there has been evidence that innocent people may have been executed. These problems with capital punishment have led to a decline in the rate of executions and a decrease in the death sentencing rate in recent years. A few months ago, New Jersey became the first state since the 1960s to completely abolish capital punishment. However, capital punishment remains a costly and dominant feature of the state and federal criminal justice system.

Many jurisdictions have implemented no reforms or review of their death penalty schemes and the practice of executing prisoners and imposing death sentences goes on without much reflection or review. Perhaps the single most significant problem with the administration of capital punishment is the inadequacy of indigent defense for capital defendants. Without competent and skilled counsel in death penalty cases, there can be no reliability or fairness in the outcomes of these proceedings.

Last month, I testified as an expert in a death penalty case in Oklahoma where a court was examining whether James Fisher had received adequate legal assistance at his capital trial. It was my second trip to Oklahoma on this case. Ten years ago, a federal appeals court reversed Mr. Fisher's capital murder conviction and death sentence because his appointed counsel maintained a trial schedule "so heavy he sometimes would finish one case in the morning and begin trying a new case in the afternoon while the jury was still deliberating." He was completely unfamiliar with the State's evidence and witnesses, conducted no investigation for Mr. Fisher, and called no witnesses. At the penalty phase, counsel called no witnesses and waived opening and closing arguments. Not surprisingly, Mr. Fisher was sentenced to death.

At his new trial in 2005, Mr. Fisher was represented by counsel who was abusing alcohol and suffering from drug addiction. This attorney was suspended from the practice of law and entered a rehab facility three months after Mr. Fisher's trial. At trial, the lawyer presented none of the available evidence or witnesses who could have assisted Mr. Fisher. Prior to trial, the lawyer got angry at Mr. Fisher, called him derogatory names and asked the guards to remove Mr. Fisher's handcuffs so he could "kick his ass." When Mr. Fisher complained to the court and insisted he would rather represent himself than be represented by his new counsel, he was barred from court during the trial. Mr. Fisher was therefore not present during his trial, when his impaired lawyer presented almost none of the available evidence, and he was found guilty and sentenced to death. [*Editor's note*: In April 2009 the Oklahoma Court of Criminal Appeals granted Fisher a new trial based on the inadequacy of his former legal representation.]

Unfortunately, examples of inadequate representation are not exceptional. Alabama has no state public defender offices, and trial judges appoint counsel, many of whom have little training or experience in capital litigation. Of the 203 people currently on Alabama's death row, more than half (59%) were represented by appointed lawyers whose compensation for preparing the case was capped at $1,000 by state statute. There are very few mitigation experts or investigative services available, and even though compensation has improved in recent years, compliance with the ABA Guidelines on Adequate Representation in Capital Cases is almost never accomplished.

There are people on death row in Texas who were defended by attorneys who had investigative and expert expenses capped at $500. In some rural areas in Texas, lawyers have received no more than $800 to handle a capital case. People still on Virginia's death row were provided lawyers who were effectively paid an hourly rate of less than $20 an hour. In Pennsylvania, there are currently death row prisoners who were sentenced to death in Philadelphia in the 1980s and 1990s when 80% of the capital cases were handled by appointed lawyers who received a flat fee of $1,700 plus $400 for each day in court. Similar restrictions can be found in many states, especially in states where the death penalty is frequently imposed.

Underfunded indigent defense has predictably caused flawed representation in many cases with corresponding doubts about the reliability and fairness of the verdict and sentence. Indigent accused facing execution have been represented by sleeping attorneys, 15 drunk attorneys, attorneys who are almost completely unfamiliar with trial advocacy, criminal defense generally, or death penalty law and procedure in particular, and attorneys who otherwise cannot provide the assurance of reliability or fairness in the client's conviction and death sentence.

Even in states where there are public defender systems, funding and compensation for attorneys remains low and resources for investigation and experts is scarce. Lawyers who are appointed to capital cases often do not have the resources, training and experience necessary to defend such a case. Capital cases involve different and complex investigative, preparation, and trial methods than other criminal cases. Lawyers who are not aware of these differences cannot be as effective. This becomes especially important during the penalty phase when defense counsel should present mitigating evidence. Lawyers with insufficient time, resources, or training will not know the best way to proceed in the penalty phase, denying indigent capital defendants an effective and compelling mitigation presentation.

The states with the most active death rows are those that have historically poor records of providing competent counsel to people accused of capital crimes. In such a system, the risk of wrongful convictions and error is unacceptably high.

FROM TESTIMONY OF HILARY O. SHELTON, DIRECTOR OF THE NATIONAL ASSOCIATION FOR THE ADVANCEMENT OF COLORED PEOPLE (NAACP), WASHINGTON BUREAU, WASHINGTON, D.C., BEFORE THE U.S. SENATE COMMITTEE ON THE JUDICIARY, SUBCOMMITTEE ON THE CONSTITUTION, CIVIL RIGHTS, AND PROPERTY RIGHTS, HEARING ON "OVERSIGHT OF THE FEDERAL DEATH PENALTY," JUNE 27, 2007

The NAACP remains resolutely opposed to the death penalty....

From the days of slavery, through years of lynchings and Jim Crow laws, and even today capital punishment has always been deeply affected by race. This is true among the states as well as at the federal level. Despite the fact that African-Americans make up only 13% of our nation's population, almost 50% of those who currently sit on the federal death row are African-American.

Furthermore, across the nation about 80% of the victims in the underlying murder in death penalty cases are white, while less than 50% of murder victims overall are white. This statistic implies that white lives are valued more than those of racial or ethnic minorities in our criminal justice system.

Finally, the NAACP is very concerned about the number of people who have been exonerated since being placed on death row. Since 1973, over 120 people have been released from death row with evidence of their innocence. The death penalty is the ultimate punishment, one that is impossible to reverse in light of new evidence.

The American criminal justice system has been historically, and remains today, deeply and disparately impacted by race. It is difficult for African-Americans to have confidence in or be willing to work with an institution that is fraught with racism. And the fact that African-Americans are so overrepresented on death row is alarming and disturbing, and certainly a critical element that leads to the distrust that exists in the African-American community of our nation's criminal justice system.

It bears repeating that 49% of all the people, or almost half of all those currently sitting on the federal death row, are African-American. Perhaps more disturbing is the fact that nobody at the Department of Justice [DOJ] can conclusively say that race is not a factor in determining which defendants are to be tried in federal death penalty cases.

According to the DOJ's own figures, 48% of the defendants in federal cases in which the death penalty was sought between 2001 and 2006 were African-Americans.

What we don't know, unfortunately, is whether or not this number is representative of the number of criminal defendants who are accused of crimes in which the death penalty may be sought. And, since there are several layers that must be examined to even begin to assess this number, including whether a crime is tried at the local or federal level, it is not an easy number to attain.

What is clear, though, is that at several different points in the process of determining who is tried in a federal death penalty case and who is not, a judgment is made by human beings in a process in which not everyone has similar views. And in a world in which 98% of the chief district attorneys in death penalty states are white and only 1% are black, it is this differential that gives us the most problem.

In addition to the factor of the race of the defendants, the NAACP is also deeply troubled by the role played in the race of the victim. Although at the federal level the weight of the victim's race appears to have changed over the last few years, at the state level the race of the victim still appears to play a big role. According to the Death Penalty Information Center, 79% of the murder victims in cases resulting in an execution were white, even though nationally only 50% of murder victims overall were white. A recent study in California found that those who killed whites were over three times more likely to be sentenced to death than those who killed African-Americans and more than four times more likely than those who killed Latinos. Another study in North Carolina found that the odds of receiving a death sentence rose by 3.5 times among defendants whose victims were white.

These studies, along with the fluctuations we see in all death penalty jurisdictions including the federal government, speak again to the varying factors involved in determining who is eligible for the death penalty and who is not. The overwhelming evidence that a defendant is more likely to be executed if the victim is white is also incredibly problematic; it sends a message that in our criminal justice system, white lives are more valuable than those of racial or ethnic minorities.

Obviously with race being so problematic and such an overwhelming factor in the application of the death penalty, the NAACP is also concerned that there be no room for error. Yet errors do occur, even today. Nationally, more than 120 people have been exonerated and freed from death row before they could be executed. Given the finality of the death sentence under which these people were living, they may in fact be considered the "lucky ones." Furthermore, considering the disparities in the number of African-Americans on death row, it is likely that more African-Americans are falsely executed, a fact that once again contributes to the mistrust that is endemic among the African-American community of the American criminal justice system.

FROM TESTIMONY OF VICKI A. SCHIEBER, CHEVY CHASE, MARYLAND, BEFORE THE U.S. SENATE COMMITTEE ON THE JUDICIARY, SUBCOMMITTEE ON THE CONSTITUTION, CIVIL RIGHTS, AND PROPERTY RIGHTS, HEARING ON "AN EXAMINATION OF THE DEATH PENALTY IN THE UNITED STATES," FEBRUARY 1, 2006

I am the mother of a murder victim, and I serve on the board of directors of Murder Victims' Families for Human Rights (MVFHR), a national nonprofit organization of people who have lost a family member to murder or state execution and who oppose the death penalty in all cases. There are MVFHR members in every state. [*Editor's note*: Schieber's daughter, Shannon, a doctoral student at Wharton School in Philadelphia, was raped and murdered in her home in May 1998 by Troy Graves (1972–), a serial rapist who later confessed to a dozen attacks on women and was sentenced to life terms without parole in both Colorado and Pennsylvania.]

Discussions of the death penalty typically focus on the offender, the person convicted of murder. My focus, and the focus of those whom I am representing through this testimony, is on the victims of murder and their surviving families.

Losing a beloved family member to murder is a tragedy of unimaginable proportions. The effects on the family and even on the wider community extend well beyond the initial shock and trauma. The common assumption in this country is that families who have suffered this kind of loss will support the death penalty. That assumption is so widespread and so unquestioned that a prosecutor will say to a grieving family, "We will seek the death penalty in order to seek justice for your family." A lawmaker introduces a bill to expand the application of the death penalty and announces that he is doing this "to honor victims." A politician believes that she must run on a pro–death penalty platform or risk being labeled soft on crime and thus unconcerned about victims.

As a victim's family member who opposes the death penalty, I represent a growing and for the most part underserved segment of the crime victim population. Along with the other members of MVFHR, I have come to believe that the death penalty is not what will help me heal. Responding to one killing with another killing does not honor my daughter, nor does it help create the kind of society I want to live in, where human life and human rights are valued. I know that an execution creates another grieving family, and causing pain to another family does not lessen my own pain. . . .

My husband and I were both raised in homes with a deep-seated religious faith. We were both raised in households where hatred was never condoned and where the ultimate form of hate was thought to be the deliberate taking of another person's life. The death penalty involves the deliberate, premeditated killing of another human being. In carrying forward the principles with which my husband and I were raised, and with which we raised our daughter, we cannot in good conscience support the killing of anyone, even the murderer of our own daughter, if such a person could be imprisoned without parole and thereby no longer a danger to society.

No one should infer from our opposition to the death penalty that we did not want Shannon's murderer caught, prosecuted, and put away for the remainder of his life. We believe he is where he belongs today, as he serves his prison sentence, and we rest assured that he will never again perpetrate his sort of crime on any other young women. But killing this man would not bring our daughter back. And it was very clear to us that killing him would have been partly dependent on our complicity in having it done. Had we bent to this natural inclination, however, it would have put us on essentially the same footing as the murderer himself: willing to take someone else's life to satisfy our own ends. That was a posture we were not willing to assume.

In my work with Murder Victims' Families for Human Rights, I have come to know several survivors of people who have been put to death by execution. Seeing the effects of an execution in the family, particularly the effects on children, raises questions for me about the short- and long-term social costs of the death penalty. What kind of message do we convey to young people when we tell them that killing another human being is wrong but then impose the death penalty on someone with whom they have some direct or indirect relationship? Isn't there the possibility that the imposition of the death penalty sends a conflicted message about our society's respect for life? Isn't it possible that the potentially biased application of the death penalty in certain racial contexts distorts the fundamental principles on which this nation was founded? Isn't it possible that the bitterness that arises out of this causes more social problems than it solves?

I remember when, back in 2001, then Attorney General John Ashcroft decided that family members of the Oklahoma City bombing victims should be allowed to witness the execution of Timothy McVeigh on closed-circuit television. His argument was that the experience would "meet their need for closure." The word closure is invoked so frequently in discussions of victims and the death penalty that victims' family members jokingly refer to it as "the c word." But I can tell you with all seriousness that there is no such thing as closure when a violent crime rips away the life of someone dear to you. As my husband and I wander through the normal things that we all do in our daily lives, we see constant reminders of Shannon and what we have lost. Killing Shannon's murderer would not stop the unfolding of the world around us with its constant reminders of unfulfilled hopes and dreams.

Indeed, linking closure for victims' families with the execution of the offender is problematic for two additional reasons: first, the death penalty is currently applied to only about 1% of convicted murderers in this country. If imposition of that penalty is really necessary for victims' families, then what of the 99% who are not offered it? Second, and even more critical from a policy perspective, a vague focus on executions as the potential source of closure for families too often shifts the focus away from other steps that could be taken to honor victims and to help victims' families in the aftermath of murder.

We have chosen to honor our daughter by setting up several memorials in her name—a scholarship at Duke University, and an endowment fund to replace roofs on inner city homes through the Rebuilding Together program in poor sections of our community, to name two. We also believe that we honor her by working to abolish the death penalty, because, for my husband and for me, working to oppose the death penalty is a way of working to create a world in which life is valued and in which our chief goal is to reduce violence rather than to perpetuate it.

IMPORTANT NAMES
AND ADDRESSES

American Bar Association
Criminal Justice Section
740 15th St. NW, 10th Fl.
Washington, DC 20005-1009
(202) 662-1000
URL: http://www.abanet.org/crimjust/
home.html

American Civil Liberties Union
125 Broad St., 18th Fl.
New York, NY 10004
URL: http://www.aclu.org/

Amnesty International U.S.A.
5 Penn Plaza
New York, NY 10001
(212) 807-8400
FAX: (212) 627-1451
E-mail: aimember@aiusa.org
URL: http://www.amnestyusa.org/

Bureau of Justice Statistics
U.S. Department of Justice
810 Seventh St. NW
Washington, DC 20531
(202) 307-0765
E-mail: askbjs@usdoj.gov
URL: http://www.ojp.usdoj.gov/bjs

Center on Wrongful Convictions
Northwestern University
School of Law
375 E. Chicago Ave.
Chicago, IL 60611
(312) 503-2391
E-mail: cwc@law.northwestern.edu
URL: http://www.law.northwestern.edu/cwc/

Criminal Justice Legal
Foundation
PO Box 1199
Sacramento, CA 95812
(916) 446-0345
URL: http://www.cjlf.org/

Death Penalty Information Center
1015 18th St. NW, Ste. 704
Washington, DC 20036
(202) 289-2275
FAX: (202) 289-7336
URL: http://www.deathpenaltyinfo.org/

Federal Bureau of Investigation
J. Edgar Hoover Bldg.
935 Pennsylvania Ave. NW
Washington, DC 20535-0001
(202) 324-3000
URL: http://www.fbi.gov/

Federal Bureau of Prisons
320 First St. NW
Washington, DC 20534
(202) 307-3198
E-mail: info@bop.gov
URL: http://www.bop.gov/

Innocence Project
100 Fifth Ave., Third Fl.
New York, NY 10011
(212) 364-5340
E-mail: info@innocenceproject.org
URL: http://www.innocenceproject.org/

JURIST
c/o Professor Bernard Hibbitts
University of Pittsburgh School
of Law
Pittsburgh, PA 15260
(412) 648-1400
E-mail: JURIST@pitt.edu
URL: http://jurist.law.pitt.edu/

Justice for All
(713) 935-9300
E-mail: info@jfa.net
URL: http://www.jfa.net/

Justice Research and Statistics
Association
777 N. Capitol St. NE, Ste. 801
Washington, DC 20002

(202) 842-9330
FAX: (202) 842-9329
E-mail: cjinfo@jrsa.org
URL: http://www.jrsa.org/

Moratorium Campaign
586 Harding Blvd.
Baton Rouge, LA 70807
URL: http://www.moratoriumcampaign.org/

Murder Victims' Families for
Reconciliation
2100 M St. NW, Ste. 170-296
Washington, DC 20037
(877) 896-4702
E-mail: lpost@mvfr.org
URL: http://www.mvfr.org/

NAACP Legal Defense and Educational
Fund
99 Hudson St., Ste. 1600
New York, NY 10013
(212) 965-2200
URL: http://www.naacpldf.org/

National Association of Criminal
Defense Lawyers
1660 L St. NW, 12th Fl.
Washington, DC 20036
(202) 872-8600
FAX: (202) 872-8690
E-mail: assist@nacdl.com
URL: http://www.nacdl.org/

National Center for Victims of Crime
2000 M St. NW, Ste. 480
Washington, DC 20036
(202) 467-8700
FAX: (202) 467-8701
URL: http://www.ncvc.org/

National Coalition to Abolish
the Death Penalty
1705 DeSales St. NW, Fifth Fl.
Washington, DC 20036
(202) 331-4090

E-mail: info@ncadp.org
URL: http://www.ncadp.org/

**National Criminal Justice Reference
Service**
PO Box 6000
Rockville, MD 20849-6000
(301) 519-5500
1-800-851-3420
FAX: (301) 519-5212
URL: http://www.ncjrs.org/

**National District Attorneys
Association**
44 Canal Center Plaza, Ste. 110
Alexandria, VA 22314
(703) 549-9222
FAX: (703) 836-3195
URL: http://www.ndaa.org/

**Office of the United Nations High
Commissioner for Human Rights**
Palais des Nations, CH-1211
Geneva 10 Switzerland
+41 22 917 9000
E-mail: InfoDesk@ohchr.org
URL: http://www.ohchr.org/

Sentencing Project
514 Tenth St. NW, Ste. 1000
Washington, DC 20004

(202) 628-0871
FAX: (202) 628-1091
E-mail: staff@sentencingproject.org
URL: http://www.sentencingproject.org/

U.S. Commission on Civil Rights
624 Ninth St. NW, Ste. 500
Washington, DC 20425
(202) 376-7533
URL: http://www.usccr.gov/

U.S. Department of Justice
950 Pennsylvania Ave. NW
Washington, DC 20530-0001
(202) 514-2000
E-mail: askdoj@usdoj.gov
URL: http://www.usdoj.gov/

**U.S. Government Accountability
Office**
441 G St. NW
Washington, DC 20548
(202) 512-3000
E-mail: contact@gao.gov
URL: http://www.gao.gov/

**U.S. House Committee on
the Judiciary**
2138 Rayburn House Office Bldg.
Washington, DC 20515

(202) 225-3951
URL: http://judiciary.house.gov/

U.S. Senate Committee on the Judiciary
224 Dirksen Senate Office Bldg.
Washington, DC 20510
(202) 224-7703
FAX: (202) 224-9516
URL: http://judiciary.senate.gov/

**U.S. Sentencing Commission
Office of Public Affairs**
1 Columbus Circle NE
Washington, DC 20002-8002
(202) 502-4500
E-mail: pubaffairs@ussc.gov
URL: http://www.ussc.gov/

U.S. Supreme Court
1 First St. NE
Washington, DC 20543
(202) 479-3211
URL: http://www.supremecourtus.gov/

**World Coalition against the Death
Penalty**
3, rue Paul Vaillant-Couturier
Châtillon 92320 France
+33 1 57 63 09 37
FAX: +33 1 57 63 89 25
URL: http://www.worldcoalition.org/

RESOURCES

The U.S. Department of Justice (DOJ) collects statistics on death row inmates as part of its National Prisoner Statistics (NPS) program. Based on voluntary reporting, the NPS program collects and interprets data on state and federal prisoners. Founded by the U.S. Census Bureau in 1926, the program was transferred to the Federal Bureau of Prisons in 1950, to the now-defunct Law Enforcement Assistance Administration (LEAA), and then to the Bureau of Justice Statistics (BJS) in 1979.

Since 1972 the Census Bureau, as the collecting agent for the LEAA and the BJS, has been responsible for compiling the relevant data. Since 1993 the BJS has annually prepared the bulletin *Capital Punishment*, which provides an overview of capital punishment in the United States. Bulletins published through 2006 include much historical data. The BJS also maintains the Web site Capital Punishment Facts at a Glance that includes some historical data on the death penalty and the nation's death rows. The Federal Bureau of Investigation (FBI) collects and publishes crime data through its annual *Uniform Crime Report* and *Crime in the United States*.

The DOJ released *Homicide Trends in the United States* (July 2007), *The Federal Death Penalty System: A Statistical Survey (1988–2000)* (September 2000), and *The Federal Death Penalty System: Supplementary Data, Analysis, and Revised Protocols for Capital Case Review* (June 2001). The National Institute of Justice issued the helpful *Report to the Attorney General on Delays in Forensic DNA Analysis* (March 2003).

The NAACP Legal Defense and Educational Fund (LDF) maintains statistics on capital punishment and is strongly opposed to the death penalty. Despite its name, the LDF is not part of the National Association for the Advancement of Colored People, even though it was founded by that organization. Since 1957 the LDF has had a separate board of directors, program, staff, office, and budget. The LDF publishes *Death Row U.S.A.*, a periodic compilation of capital punishment statistics and information, including the names, gender, and race of all those who have been executed or are currently on death row. Gender and racial information on the victims of those executed is also provided. Data from this publication were helpful in preparing this book.

The Death Penalty Information Center (DPIC) is a nonprofit organization that provides the media and the general public with information and analysis regarding capital punishment. The DPIC, which is against the death penalty, serves as a resource for those working on this issue. Its reports and charts on capital punishment were used in preparing this book. The National Coalition against the Death Penalty maintains an up-to-date list of news stories from the media regarding the death penalty.

Amnesty International is the Nobel Prize–winning human rights organization headquartered in London, England, and is strongly opposed to the death penalty. Amnesty International maintains information on the death penalty and torture throughout the world and periodically publishes its findings. Its publication *Abolitionist and Retentionist Countries* (2009) provided data on the status of capital punishment worldwide.

Charts and data from *The Juvenile Death Penalty Today: Death Sentences and Executions for Juvenile Crimes, January 1, 1973–December 31, 2004* (2005) by Victor L. Streib of Ohio Northern University were used in the preparation of this book. *JURIST* is an online database of legal news and research maintained by the University of Pittsburgh, School of Law. It was an invaluable resource.

Other studies used in this book include the *California Commission on the Fair Administration of Justice: Final Report* (July 2008); the Urban Institute's *Cost of the Death Penalty in Maryland* (March 2008); the *New Jersey Death Penalty Study Commission Report* (January 2007); *Performance Audit Report: Costs Incurred for Death Penalty Cases* (December 2003) by the state of Kansas; *Study Pursuant to*

Public Act No. 01-151 of the Imposition of the Death Penalty in Connecticut (January 2003) by the Commission on the Death Penalty in Connecticut; *Critique of DPIC List ("Innocence: Freed from Death Row")* (2002) by Ward A. Campbell; *Case Histories: A Review of 24 Individuals Released from Death Row* (September 2002) by the Florida Commission on Capital Cases; *Race and the Death Penalty in North Carolina, an Empirical Analysis: 1993–1997* (April 2001) by Isaac Unah and John Charles Boger; *The Disposition of Nebraska Capital and Non-capital Homicide Cases (1973–1999): A Legal and Empirical Analysis* (July 2001) by David C. Baldus et al.; *The Fair Defense Report: Analysis of Indigent Defense Practices in Texas* (December 2000) by Texas Appleseed; and *A Broken System: Error Rates in Capital Cases, 1973–1995* (June 2000) by James S. Liebman, Jeffrey Fagan, and Valerie West.

Important studies published in journals include "Capital Appeals Revisited" (*Judicature*, vol. 84, no. 2, September–October 2000) by Barry Latzer and James N. G. Cauthen; "Capital Punishment Proves to Be Expensive" (*New York Law Journal*, April 30, 2002) by Daniel Wise; and "Explaining Death Row's Population and Racial Composition" (*Journal of Empirical Legal Studies*, vol. 1, no. 1, March 2004) by John Blume, Theodore Eisenberg, and Martin T. Wells.

David G. Chardavoyne's *A Hanging in Detroit: Stephen Gifford Simmons and the Last Execution under Michigan Law* (2003) provided, among other things, information on the rituals of public executions. *Executions in the United States, 1608–2002: The ESPY File* (2005) by M. Watt Espy and John Ortiz Smykla lists every known execution to have occurred in the North American British colonies and the United States from 1608 to 2002.

Media sources consulted for this book include ABC News, CBS News, CNN, Fox News, NBC News, the *Atlanta Journal and Constitution*, *Austin Chronicle*, *Chicago Tribune*, *New York Times*, *Wall Street Journal*, and *Washington Post*. Polls taken by the Associated Press and Ipsos Public Affairs, Gallup Organization, Harris Interactive, Higher Education Research Institute, Opinion Research Corporation/CNN, Pew Research Center, Quinnipiac University Polling Institute, and University of California at Santa Cruz were also used in preparing this book.

INDEX

Page references in italics refer to photographs. References with the letter t following them indicate the presence of a table. The letter f indicates a figure. If more than one table or figure appears on a particular page, the exact item number for the table or figure being referenced is provided.

A

ABA. *See* American Bar Association

Abell Foundation of Baltimore, Maryland, 74

Abolition
death penalty debate, 4
of death penalty in New Jersey, 131
movement, 3
UN call for, 116

"Abolitionist and Retentionist Countries" (Amnesty International), 11

Abolitionist countries
abolitionism in practice, 119
countries that are abolitionist for all crimes, 120t–121t
countries that are abolitionist for ordinary crimes only, 121(t10.6)
countries that are abolitionist in practice, 120(t10.4)
countries that have abolished death penalty, 122t
list of, 119–120

ACLU. *See* American Civil Liberties Union

Actual Innocence (Scheck), 127

Addison, Michael, 100

Addresses/names, 135–136

"The Adequacy of Representation in Capital Cases" (U.S. Senate Committee on the Judiciary, Subcommittee on the Constitution hearing), 130–131

Administrative Office of the United States Court, 59

AEDPA. *See* Antiterrorism and Effective Death Penalty Act

African-Americans
argument against death penalty, 132–133
criminal history profile of prisoners under sentence of death, by race/ethnicity, 69(t6.9)
death row, length of time on, 68
death row inmates, number of, 66
death row inmates, race of, 67, 70–71
defendant/victim racial combinations in execution cases, 85(t7.4)
execution of women, 80
executions by race/ethnicity, 80
executions/other dispositions of inmates sentenced to death by race/ethnicity, 85(t7.3)
number of persons executed, by race/ethnicity, method, 81(t6.19)
public opinion on death penalty/innocence, 113
race and homicide statistics, 85–86
race issue in capital cases, 48–51
race of executed prisoners, 83–84
race of persons executed, 80f
race of victim in death penalty cases, 85f
race of victims of executed prisoners, 84–85
racial bias in death penalty, 86–88, 89–90
racial makeup of death row, 83
support for death penalty by, 110

Age
death penalty for minors and, 39–42
at time of arrest, 69
at time of arrest for capital offense, age of prisoners under sentence of death, 69(t6.9)

Aggravating factors
add responsibility to crime, 39
for death sentence, 4, 19–20
double jeopardy and, 21, 22, 23
error in capital cases and, 130
judge sentencing and, 18

in North Carolina study, 88
overview of, 4–5
state death penalty laws and, 53

AI. *See* Amnesty International

Ake, Glen Burton, 43–44

Ake v. Oklahoma, 44

Alabama
death row inmates in, 66
DPMIP report on, 105–106
execution of woman in, 80
judge sentencing in, 19, 21
legal representation in, 132

Alabama, Beck v., 16

Alabama, Harris v., 19

Alabama, Rudolph v., 4

Alabama, Swain v., 50–51

Albania, as abolitionist country, 120

Aldridge, Joyce, 9

Alfred P. Murrah Federal Building, 59

Allen, Kathleen, 93–94

Allen, Nancy, 40

Allen, Wanda Jean, 80

Alston, Odel, Jr., 123–124

AMA (American Medical Association), 102

American Association on Mental Retardation, 46

American Bar Association (ABA)
contact information, 135
on Florida death penalty assessment, 21
on ineffective counsel, 91
nationwide moratorium, support for, 105–107

American Civil Liberties Union (ACLU)
contact information, 135
on racial bias in death penalty, 88

The American Freshman: Forty Year Trends (Higher Education Research Institute Poll), 111–112

American League to Abolish Capital Punishment, 4

American Medical Association (AMA), 102

Poverty
    due process guarantee and, 44
    legal representation, quality of, 90, 91
Powell, Lewis F., Jr.
    on *Furman v. Georgia*, 13–14
    on race issue in capital cases, 49, 50
    on victim impact statements, 48
Prejudice
    discriminatory application of death
      penalty, 130
    issue of race in capital cases, 48–51
    See also Race/ethnicity; Racial bias in
      death penalty
Presumption of malice, 30–31
Prisoners
    on death row after end of moratorium,
      5–6
    death row inmates, total number of, as
      reported by NAACP, 71*t*
    executed, 6*t*
    psychiatric exam, rights during, 43
    sentence of death, number of inmates
      received under, 70(*t*6.11)
    See also Death row
Prisons, 3
Proffitt v. Florida, 14, 15
Prohibition Era, 4
Prosecutor
    cases involving error by, 29–31
    peremptory challenges of, 125–126
    racial bias in death penalty, 87, 88, 89
    racial bias in jury selection, 50–51, 86
*Prosecutors' Perspective on California's
    Death Penalty* (Criminal Justice Legal
    Foundation & California District
    Attorneys Association), 90
Prothero, Rick, 123–124
Provenzano, Thomas, 36
Provenzano v. Moore, 36
Psychiatrists
    execution of insane and, 44, 45
    execution of mentally retarded people
      and, 45, 46
    prisoner rights during psychiatric exam,
      43
    to prove insanity, 43–44
    validity of psychiatrist's testimony, 42–43
Public executions, 2, 3
Public opinion
    on death penalty, 1, 2, 2*f*
    on death penalty, appropriate use of,
      113*t*
    on death penalty, fairness of, 113, 113*f*
    on death penalty as deterrent to murder,
      112*t*
    on death penalty frequency, 113
    on death penalty support, by political
      party, 111(*f*9.2)
    on death penalty vs. life imprisonment
      with absolutely no possibility of parole,
      111*t*

on death penalty/innocence, 113–114
on execution of mentally retarded
    people, 46
on innocence of executed, 114*t*
international, on death penalty, 120–121
on morality of capital punishment, 109,
    110*t*
support for death penalty, 9–10,
    109–113, 111(*f*9.1)
Puerto Rico, federal death penalty cases in,
    62
Pulanski, Charles A., Jr., 49–50, 86
Pulley v. Harris, 22

Q

Quakers, 1
Quijano, Walter, 51
Quinn, Cynthia, 101
Quinnipiac University Polling Institute, 112
Quinones, United States v., 126

R

*Race and the Death Penalty in North
    Carolina, an Empirical Analysis:
    1993–1997* (Unah & Boger), 88
Race/ethnicity
    argument against death penalty, 132–133
    death row, length of time on, 68
    of death row inmates, 66, 67, 70–71
    execution, number of persons executed
      by, method, 81(*t*6.19)
    execution, race of persons executed, 80*f*
    executions by, 80
    exonerations by, 95*t*
    LDF reports, 65
    minorities on death row, 100
    of prisoners on military death row, 63
    prisoners under sentence of death, by
      region, state, race, 67(*t*6.3)
    prisoners under sentence of death,
      criminal history profile of, by race/
      ethnicity, 69(*t*6.10)
    prisoners under sentence of death, sex,
      race/ethnicity of, 67(*t*6.4)
    prisoners under sentence of death by,
      66(*t*6.2)
    public opinion on death penalty/
      innocence, 113
    support for death penalty and, 109–110
    Supreme Court rulings on issue of race
      in capital cases, 48–51
    women under sentence of death, by race/
      jurisdiction, 72*t*
Racial bias in death penalty
    argument against death penalty, 132–133
    Baldus study, 86
    California study, 89
    death penalty advocates on, 90
    death penalty opponents/proponents and,
      127

execution cases, defendant/victim racial
    combinations in, 85(*t*7.4)
executions, by race, 84(*t*7.2)
executions/other dispositions of inmates
    sentenced to death, by race/ethnicity,
    85(*t*7.3)
homicide statistics, 85–86
jury selection, 86
Maryland study, 89
national study, 89–90
North Carolina study, 88–89
Ohio study, 90
plea bargaining, 87
prisoners on death row, by region, state,
    race, 84(*t*7.1)
race of executed prisoners, 83–84
race of victim in death penalty cases, 85*f*
race of victims of executed prisoners,
    84–85
racial makeup of death row, 83
risk of, 130
U.S. Department of Justice studies,
    87–88
U.S. GAO study, 86–87
*Racial Disagreement over Death Penalty
    Has Varied Historically* (Saad), 109–110
"Racial Discrimination and the Death
    Penalty in the Post-*Furman* Era: An
    Empirical and Legal Analysis with
    Recent Findings from Philadelphia"
    (Baldus et al.), 86
Radelet, Michael, 89
Randa, Laura E., 1
Rape
    DNA testing and, 9, 98
    House, Paul, 32
    Penry, Johnny Paul, 45, 46
    state death penalty laws, 53
    Supreme Court on rape of women/
      children, 25–26
    Williams, Michael Wayne, 34
Rebuilding Together program, 134
"Recent Legislative Activity" (DPIC), 37
Recession, economic, 10
Reckless indifference, 27–28
Recommendations to Governor Rick Perry
    (Criminal Justice Advisory Council), 105
"Reducing the Risk of Executing the
    Innocent: The Report of the Illinois
    Governor's Commission on Capital
    Punishment" (U.S. Senate Committee on
    the Judiciary), 96
Reed, Jonathan, 86
Rees, Baze v., 37, 101, 125–126, 129–130
Reforms, death penalty law
    in Maryland, 103–104
    in Nebraska, 104
    North Carolina, Innocence Inquiry
      Commission, 104
    Ohio, new injection protocols of, 104
    in Texas, 105